the female
grotesque

risk, excess and modernity

mary russo

routledge • new york london

Published in 1994 by
Routledge
29 West 35th Street
New York, NY 10001

Published in Great Britain by
Routledge
11 New Fetter Lane
London EC4P 4EE

Library of Congress Cataloging-in-Publication Data

Russo, Mary J.
    The female grotesque : risk, excess, and modernity / Mary Russo.
      p. cm.
    Includes bibliographical references and index.
    ISBN 0-415-90164-2 (hb) : ISBN 0-415-90165-0 (pb) :
      1. Grotesque in literature.   2. Women in literature.   3. Body, Human,
in literature.   4. Literature, Modern —History and criticism.
I. Title.
RN56.G7R87   1995
809'.9352042—dc20   94-26631
                                                      CIP

British Library Cataloging in Publication Data also is available.

Contents

Preface

FEMINISM IN THE 1990S HAS STOOD INCREASINGLY for and with the normal. I mean this in two senses. It is identified with the norm as a prescription of correct, conventional, or moralizing behavior or identity, and with the normal as it is commonly misapprehended as the familiar. What I would characterize as the normalization of feminism is, no doubt, a function of contradictory impulses and forces within and without its discursive and institutional borders. Whatever its sources, it has led to a cultural and political disarticulation of feminism from the strange, the risky, the minoritarian, the excessive, the outlawed, and the alien. To some extent, this is a question of appearances. The concern that feminism appear normal, for instance, can be traced to dominant media images or to long-standing accusations that feminism cannot appeal to the mainstream. What is often forgotten in these strategies of reassurance is that the normal is not the same as the ordinary. The norm signifies nothing more or less than the prevailing standard.

This project was inspired by earlier feminist writing and art which honored the ordinary, the everyday life in the public and private sphere. An ordinary feminism (as opposed to the standard or normal variety) would be heterogeneous, strange, polychromatic, ragged, conflictual, incomplete, in motion, and at risk. As a body politic, it would not be so easily recognized or so easily disavowed. In 1980, the artist May Stevens gathered a series of paintings and drawings, juxtaposing images of Rosa Luxemburg, the socialist leader, and Alice Stevens, a working-class woman whose historically uneventful life ended in hospitals and nursing homes. She called this series *Ordinary/Extraordinary* to mark the uneasy, but to her necessary, connection between visible and invisible lives. I would locate my own interest in the grotesque as a bodily category at that same anxious and hopeful point in between.

Although it departs from previous studies of the grotesque in various ways, this work draws upon their strengths in ways which I acknowledge throughout my text. One distinct feature of my study is that I invert the usual vertical scheme which associates the grotesque with the "low" to revisit the "high" registers of modernism, the sublime, and discourses of liberation. The postmodernist fiction of Angela Carter discussed in the concluding chapter has functioned for me as a theoretical fable, in its juxtaposition of nineteenth and twentieth-century versions of the *"fin-de-siecle"* in relation to the grotesque female within a culturally imperialist geneaology. Of course, there are other tales of the grotesque to be told, drawing on other historical and geographical contexts.

Many social and intellectual encounters informed this project. Teresa de Lauretis invited me to give a paper at the 1985 conference on the topic "Feminist Studies: Reconstituting Knowledge" at the Center for Twentieth Century Studies of the University of Wisconsin-Milwaukee. That paper, entitled "Female Grotesques: Carnival and Theory," put me in dialogue with work in many fields. Because it has been reprinted and cited widely, I have chosen to alter it only slightly in the version which appears as Chapter Two. My thanks to Indiana University for permission to reprint it. I am grateful to Teresa not only for the opportunity to participate in a very lively conference, but for her much cherished support and especially for her own daring and committed scholarship. Kathleen Woodward, the Director of the Center, facilitated that conference with her usual grace and intelligence. Her important work on aging impressed me with the complexity and significance of that category in relation to the grotesque.

This book began to to take shape during my tenure as a Fellow at the Mary Ingraham Bunting Institute at Radcliffe College in 1988–1989. In the precious and unforgettable ten months I spent in the company of gifted scholars, artists, activists, and scientists, I somewhat uncharacteristically indulged a fierce optimism in regard to the future of feminism. This optimism (to use the metaphor which opens my first chapter and closes the last) "flew in the face" of much evidence to the contrary. Perhaps it is only in such extraordinary and provisional spaces that some of us can imagine deep social transformation. On the other hand, Mamphele Rampele, the South African writer, physician and activist who was also in residence at the Bunting that year, spoke often and movingly of the necessity of modelling new social relations, including gender relations, in spaces open and constrained, before what seemed to her to be the inevitable end of Apartheid. Her language of defiant anticipation in describing the role of those seemingly untimely and unrepresentative figures whom she referred to as "models of deviance" stayed with me as I attempted to rethink the category of the grotesque in relation to deviance, temporality, and liberation in a different context.

From my Bunting days, I wish to thank Ann Bookman, Jane Cooper, May Stevens, and Abha Sur—activist, poet, painter, and scientist respectively—for continuing inspiration. I wish I could recall the name of the person at the Institute who suggested that I contact the retired Professor Mary Anne Ferguson for a room of my own. Mary Anne provided me with shelter and incomparable intellectual companionship for almost a year. She also tracked down an obscure reference in *Trilby* for me in no time flat.

Although I have presented material from this book at several universities and colleges, I want to acknowledge one other occasion which seemed vital to its completion. Susan Foster invited me to the Center for Advanced Study in the Humanities at the University of California at Irvine where I met with theorists and historians of of Dance and Performance last year as I was preparing the final draft. I wish all of academic life could be as high-spirited and interesting as the afternoon and evening I spent with that talented and generous group.

Although I mention their work on the grotesque in the book, two partners-in-crime have helped make this a particularly exciting caper.

Peter Stallybrass has the intellectual equivalent of nerves of steel and if I'm occasionally out there without a net, his friendly example is one of the reasons. His book with the late Allon White set a high standard, and I refer to it often. Patsy Yaeger shares the same philobatic propensities in her work on the Southern grotesque and feminist theory.

Eve Kosofsky Sedgwick, Nancy Fitch, and Michael Wilson almost ruined this project by moving away from Amherst. They appear in scholarly vignettes within the text but I wish they were here constantly and in person.

My colleagues in Literature and Cultural Studies at Hampshire College deserve enormous raises for their dedication, talent, and ability to cope with hard times. Thanks, instead, for their general support to Jay Garfield, Norman Holland, David Kerr, Joan Landes, Sura Levine, and Jeff Wallen, to Deans David Smith and Judith Mann, and especially Linda McDaniel. Richard Burt, Catherine Portuges, Susan Jahoda, and Robert Schwartzwald of the University of Massachusetts gave tips and encouragement all the way along.

Several of my colleagues contributed specifically to this project. Joan Braderman, Jacqueline Hayden, Stash Kybartus, and Sherry Millner have all explored different versions of high-risk body politics in their image making and I am grateful to have their work and conversation nearby. Susan Douglas has been prolific in her own writing on women and the media, running circles around me while I moved slowly towards completion of this project. Still, in anxious phone call after phone call, she made it seem as if we were crossing the finish line together. Meredith Michaels read over several sections of the manuscript, offering very astute suggestions. Co-teaching feminist theory with her provided me with a challenging interlocutor and a fast friend.

Kaja Silverman suggested that I consider Ulrike Ottinger's film *Freak Orlando*, the centerpiece of the fourth chapter. She facilitated my viewing of that film and assisted me in obtaining the film stills from Germany. As a stunning practitioner of philosophy on the telephone, Kaja continues to influence my thinking in all critical areas.

I am most indebted to the three readers who carefully reviewed the draft of the entire manuscript: Ann Rosalind Jones, Andrew Parker, and Michael Silverman. My respect and affection for each of these individuals is boundless.

Finally, thanks to Bill Germano of Routledge for his patience and to Sean Holland and Erica Moody for research assistance in gathering images, and to Alex Russo for help in preparing the manuscript. This book has been dedicated for a long time to my parents and extended family, including and especially to Dan Warner who made it possible.

Introduction

Anyone who does not grasp the close juxtaposition of the vulgar
and the scholarly has either too refined or too compartmentalized a
view of life. Abstract and visceral fascination are equally valid and
not so far apart.

> —Stephen Jay Gould
> "Living with Connections:
> Are Siamese Twins One Person or Two?"[1]

TO LIVE WITH THE GROTESQUE AS I HAVE DONE for an extended
period can be a claustrophobic experience. The word itself, as almost
every writer on the topic feels obliged to mention sooner or later,
evokes the cave—the grotto-esque. Low, hidden, earthly, dark, material, immanent, visceral. As bodily metaphor, the grotesque cave
tends to look like (and in the most gross metaphorical sense be
identified with) the cavernous anatomical female body. These associations of the female with the earthly, material, and the archaic
grotesque have suggested a positive and powerful figuration of culture and womanhood to many male and female writers and artists. I
refer here not only to the influential work of Mikhail Bakhtin whose
image of the "senile, pregnant hag" as the strongest expression of the
grotesque provoked my early, critical article on the topic, "Female
Grotesques: Carnival and Theory,"[2] but also to a certain archetypal
view of these materials which is still prevalent in a vein of nonacade-
mic, "cultural feminism." This view valorizes traditional images of
the earth mother, the crone, the witch, and the vampire and posits a
natural connection between the female body (itself naturalized) and
the "primal" elements, especially the earth.

Fig. 1   Medusa. Corfu, Temple of Artemis, pediment: ca. 600–580 B.C. Courtesy
of Hillyer Art Library, Smith College.

It is an easy and perilous slide from these archaic tropes to the
misogyny which identifies this hidden inner space with the visceral.
Blood, tears, vomit, excrement—all the detritus of the body that is
separated out and placed with terror and revulsion (predominantly,
though not exclusively) on the side of the feminine—are down there
in that cave of abjection. And just as feelings of abjection are open to
men, so, as Laura Mulvey points out in her commentary on Cindy
Sherman's "bulimic" photographs, "the female psyche may well identify with misogynistic revulsion against the female body and attempt
to erase signs that mark her physically as feminine."[3] As Mulvey suggests, Cindy Sherman's literalization of the metaphoric relationship
between the female and bodily abjection in the photographs of decay-
ing matter and vomit makes explicit what is merely implied in
Sherman's earlier fashion photographs, film stills, and historical mas-
querades: the uncanny, nonidentical resemblance between female and
grotesque. For the viewers of Sherman's photographs who have become accustomed to reading her self-portraits only in relation to

postmodern parody, these later grotesque photographs may seem to have nothing to do with masquerade, glamour, identity, or gender. Read instead as necessary oppositions inherent in the structure of fetishism, the playful images of the female "model" or the film star can be seen as literally "played out" in the expulsion of the body from its earlier representation.[4]

The regression signified by this literalization of the female body as grotesque should not obscure or reduce the complex figurations of the these terms to one model.[5] Likewise, the literalization of the grotesque as grotto-esque should not naturalize that category either: Strictly speaking, the cave or grotto-esque referred to etymologically was not a natural or elemental phenomenon at all, but an historic, cultural event —an ex-cavation in fifteenth-century Rome of Nero's Domus Aurea or Golden Palace across from the Coliseum.[6] This excavation represented one of the most significant and controversial retrievals of Roman culture in the Italian Renaissance because what was found there was nearly unrecognizable: a series of strange and mysterious drawings, combining vegetation and animal and human body parts in intricate, intermingled, and fantastical designs.

This singular event cannot, however, be taken as the discovery, much less the origin, of the grotesque; art historians have identified many examples of drawings and objects in the grotto-esque style which predate both classical and renaissance Rome. The category of the grotesque, as such, emerged only later in the renewed interest in aesthetic treatises such as Vetruvius' *De Architectura* (ca. 27 B.C.), which linked the classical style with the natural order and, in contrast, pointed to the grotesque as a repository of unnatural, frivolous, and irrational connections between things which nature and classical art kept scrupulously apart. It emerged, in other words, only in relation to the norms which it exceeded. The well-known juxtaposition of these "grottesche" with Christian art in the Vatican Loggias designed by Raphael and executed by Giovanni da Udine at once incorporated these hybrid creatures of the "pagan" imagination and marginalized them as mere fanciful decoration without moral import. As Geoffrey

Fig. 2   Cindy Sherman, "Untitled Film Still, 1978 (MP #7)." Sunglasses link this early glamor shot with her later "bulimic" images of vomit and decay, suggesting an uncanny connection between masquerade and bodily abjection.

Fig. 3   Cindy Sherman, "Untitled, 1987 (MP #175)." Copyright Cindy Sherman.
Courtesy of Metro Pictures.

Galt Harpham and others have pointed out, it was the combination of
the fantastic with the Renaissance artist's technique in rendering real-
istic detail, which so astounded and even infuriated critics like John
Ruskin who condemned Raphael's grotesqueries as "the fruit of great
minds degraded to base objects," "a tissue of nonsense" and "an
unnatural and monstrous abortion": "If we can draw the human head
perfectly, and are masters of its expression and its beauty, we have
no business to cut it off, and hang it up by the hair at the end of a
garland. If we can draw the human body in the perfection of its grace
and movement, we have no business to take away its limbs, and termi-
nate it with a bunch of flowers."[7] Trivialized and debased by critics
throughout the late Renaissance and with Ruskin's famous diatribe
into the nineteenth century, these grotesqueries were nonetheless enormously popular as design elements around and to the side of more
serious art work.

     This positioning of the grotesque—as superficial and to the mar-
gins—is suggestive of a certain construction of the feminine, as it is

often described by poststructuralist and feminist critics as bodily surface and detail. Naomi Schor's important study *Reading in Detail:
Aesthetics and the Feminine* traces the association of misogyny and aesthetics from the mid-eighteenth century, emphasizing the links
between the feminine and the particular in normative treatises. The
metaphorics of the particular, as she shows, tend to give way to the
strange, the peculiar, the monstrous.[8] Feminist readings of Nietzsche
are quick to note the identification of woman with mere appearances,
fashion, and ornamental detail.[9] For the modern spectator/interpreter,
woman as the object of critical scrutiny has no longer anything to hide
or to reveal. In Nietzsche, woman is literalized in the manner of the
famous grotesque alphabets, to be cruelly observed in intricate detail
but never allowed to make words. Significantly, Nietzsche's image for
this hermeneutical impasse is the grotesque figure of Baubô, the
obscene crone impudently displaying her genitals like an ironic smile.[10]

This mode of the grotesque is in seeming opposition to the depth
model of the cavernous female "insides" described above, but as I will
argue throughout the book, particularly in chapters three and four in
relation to the films of Ulrike Ottinger and David Cronenberg, the late
Renaissance and baroque combinations of depth and surface models of
the body resurface in the twentieth century to produce the spectacular
category of female grotesque which Cronenberg and Ottinger name
respectively "mutant woman" and "freak." Before venturing further
out into what will be the project of this entire book, an investigation
and reworking of the association of these two terms in relation to the
spatial and temporal dimensions of modern spectacle, I would like to
briefly characterize the two currents of contemporary critical discourse
on the grotesque which intersect in this project. Between Vetruvius and
Ruskin, there are many interesting commentators on the grotesque,
and there are several excellent accounts of the tortuous path of the concept of the grotesque through European and Anglo-American writing
and art work. Although many of these works are cited in specific contexts in the book, there are two discursive formations which dominate
contemporary discussion, organized around the theory of carnival on
the one hand and the concept of the uncanny on the other.[11]

Two Kinds of Grotesque:
Carnival and the Uncanny

By the end of the nineteenth century, the concept of the grotesque had wandered far from art history and aesthetics. In 1892, for instance, in the context of one of Arthur Conan Doyle's last adventures of Sherlock Holmes, the detective receives a perplexing telegram, citing the sender's "most incredible and *grotesque experience*" (emphasis mine).[12] The shift of reference from discernible grotesque figures or style to the rather vague and mysterious adjectival category of "experience" marks the modern turn towards a more active consideration of the grotesque as an interior event and as a potentially adventurous one. The dangers of a "grotesque experience" are deduced by the detective, after Dr. Watson (here described as "a man of letters") fails to define the grotesque as anything beyond the "strange" or the "remarkable."

> There is surely something more than that . . . some underlying suggestion of the tragic and terrible. If you cast your mind back to some of those narratives with which you have afflicted a long-suffering public, you will recognize how often the grotesque has deepened into the criminal.

Strange, remarkable, tragic, terrible, criminal, grotesque: strong and close associations at the end of the nineteenth century, particularly if we add the word "*uncanny.*" This postRomantic sequence by no means exhausts the historical associations of the grotesque, of course, since it has strong ties as well to the outrageous, the hilarious, and the comic. The comic grotesque has come to be associated above all with the writings of Mikhail Bakhtin on carnival in *Rabelais and His World*,[13] while the grotesque as strange and uncanny is associated with Wolfgang Kayser's *The Grotesque in Art and Literature*,[14] with the horror genre, and with Freud's essay "On the Uncanny."[15]

The discursive formation identified with the carnivalesque is understood as historical and locatable, that is, within a certain nexus of space and time, marked by dates, material events, and exteriority. It has been used, prominently by Bakhtin, to conceptualize social formations, social conflict, and the realm of the political. In the language of classical political theory, it is a virile category associated with the active, civic world of the public. In contrast, the grotesque as uncanny moves inward towards an individualized, interiorized space of fantasy and introspection, with the attendant risk of social inertia. Emerging with the concept of the Romantic sublime, the category of the uncanny grotesque is associated with the life of the psyche, and with the particular "experience" of the "strange" and "criminal" variety described by Sherlock Holmes and Dr. Watson.

Each of these categories relies heavily on the trope of the body. In the first case, the grotesque body is conceived of first and foremost as a social body. "The material bodily principle," writes Bakhtin, "is contained not in the biological individual, not in the bourgeois ego, but in the people, a people who are continually growing and renewed" (*RW*, 19). The grotesque body is not separated from the rest of the world; "it is blended with the world, with animals, with objects" (*RW*, 27). Most of all, it is identified with the "lower bodily stratum" (*RW*, 20) and its associations with degradation, filth, death, and rebirth. The images of the grotesque body are precisely those which are abjected from the bodily canons of classical aesthetics. The classical body is transcendent and monumental, closed, static, self-contained, symmetrical, and sleek; it is identified with the "high" or official culture of the Renaissance and later, with the rationalism, individualism, and normalizing aspirations of the bourgeoisie. The grotesque body is open, protruding, irregular, secreting, multiple, and changing; it is identified with non-official "low" culture or the carnivalesque, and with social transformation.

The most interesting application of carnival and the grotesque in relation to class formation is contained in Peter Stallybrass and Allon White's *The Politics and Poetics of Transgression.*[16] In their chapter on the nineteenth century and bourgeois culture, they argue that the grotesque returns as the repressed of the political unconscious, as those hidden culture contents which by their abjection had consolidated the cultural identity of the bourgeoisie.

In the second case, the grotesque is related most strongly to the psychic register and to the bodily as cultural projection of an inner state. The image of the uncanny, grotesque body as doubled, monstrous, deformed, excessive, and abject is not identified with materiality as such, but assumes a division or distance between the discursive fictions of the biological body and the Law. The strange image of the body which emerges in this formulation is never entirely locatable in or apart from the psyche which depends upon the body image as a "prop."[17] Subjectivity as it has been understood in the West requires the image of the grotesque body. The Freudian canon, with its "creature features" as case studies, is filled with horrific dismemberments, distortions, hybridities, apparitions, prostheses, and, of course, uncanny doubles. The figure of the female hysteric, ungrounded and out of bounds, enacting her pantomime of anguish and rebellion, is as foundational to psychoanalysis as the image of the "senile, pregnant hags" is to the Bakhtinian model of grotesque realism (*RW*, 25). Of course, this image of the hysteric is contrasted to the bodily canons of the bourgeoisie of Vienna, when Freud turns to the "normal-looking" citizens of his city as his true patients and to the investigation of neurosis rather than hysteria. Need I mention that the uncanny body in culture predates Freud, who draws upon the fiction of E. T. A. Hoffmann and others in his papers? Wolfgang Kayser, in his study of nineteenth and twentieth century European literature and art, refers prominently to Hoffmann and the German Romantics, and expands the sense of uncanniness into a generalized *alienation* from the-world-which-has-become-strange. Emphasizing the *reception* of the grotesque as an alien experience, Kayser's study is more psychological and finally less bodily than Freud's writings. Nonetheless, like many other studies of the grotesque which work outside the strict confines of psychoanalysis, Kayser's work is dependent, indeed unthinkable, without the concept of the unconscious. Julia Kristeva, in the early *Révolution du langage poétique* and

the more recent study, *The Powers of Horror*, effects a compelling syn-
thesis of Bakhtin's carnivalesque and Jacques Lacan's theory of subjectivity in her account of transgression and abjection.[18] In figures like
Céline, Baudelaire, Lautréamont, and Bataille, she rediscovers the carnivalesque in the radical negativity of the literary *avant-garde*. In
assuming an identification between the social and political potential of
transgression and the linguistic transgressions of the norms, codes, and
structures of language, she makes a case for the literary and psychoanalytical fascinations of extremity, derangement of identity, and abjection—horror—as an "ultimate coding of our crises."[19] The privileged
site of transgression for Kristeva, the horror zone par excellence, is the
archaic, maternal version of the female grotesque. I will return several
times to the issue of transgression in Kristeva, as well as in Stallybrass
and White. I cite these examples here, mainly to emphasize that the two
types of grotesque which I have roughly outlined above are not mani-
fest poles facing off against one another. To locate one significant convergence, I would point out that the grotesque in each case is only
recognizable in relation to a norm and that exceeding the norm
involves serious risk.

Norms, Risks, and "Errors"

As Michel Foucault has argued so forcefully, normalization is one of
the great instruments of power in the modern age, supplementing if
not replacing other signs of status and rank. "In a sense," he writes,
"the power of normalization imposes homogeneity; but it individual-
izes by making it possible to measure gaps, to determine levels, to fix
specialties and to render the differences useful by fitting them into one
another."[20] The careful scrutiny and segmentation of female body
types, and the measures, cataloguing and segmentation of different
"models" for different consumption, separate out individual bodies as
exceptions that prove the rule.

True heterogeneity is a much riskier business, but as I argue in the
first chapter, risk is not a bad thing to be avoided, but rather, a condi-

tion of possibility produced, in effect, by the normalization of the body across disciplines in the modern era. Risk belongs properly to the discourse of probability and "error." As Foucault remarks in his introduction to *On the Normal and the Pathological*, the influential work of the French historian of science, Georges Canguilhem, at the most general level, error makes thought and history:

> For at life's most basic level, the play of code and decoding leaves room for chance, which, before being disease,deficit, or monstrosity, is something like the perturbation in the information system, something like a "mistake." In the extreme, life is what is capable of error.[21]

The discourse of risk taking which occupies the first chapter is intended to introduce the grotesque into this space which "leaves room for chance." Unlike the models of progress, rationality, and liberation which disassociate themselves from their "mistakes"—noise, dissonance, or monstrosity—this "room for chance" emerges within the very constrained spaces of normalization. It is not, in other words, that limitless, incommensurable, and transcendent space associated with the Kantian sublime.

The role of the sublime in this study is highly qualified by "aerial"—a term I use to designate a zone which is at once historical and imaginary. As historical, it belongs to the late-nineteenth and twentieth century preoccupation with modernity and the specific technological contents of those Futurist aspirations for progress, associated with spectacle. As imaginative, "the aerial sublime" posits a realm of freedom within the everyday. For latecomers to the scene of political identity, freedom as expressed in boundless flight is still an almost irresistible image. In women's writing, for instance, it appears again and again. As I argue, however, "women's liberation" as so imaged, is imbricated with the history and ideology of bourgeois exceptionalism which marks off categories of irregular bodies to leave behind.

As I have indicated, the grotesque, particularly as a bodily category, emerges as a deviation from the norm. Normalization as it is enforced

in what Teresa de Lauretis has referred to as the "technologies of gender" has been harsh and effective in its highly calibrated differentiation of female bodies in the service of a homogeneity called gender
difference—that is, the (same) difference of women from men.[22] It
might follow that the expression "female grotesque" threatens to
become a tautology, since the female is always defined against the male
norm. Indeed, in many instances, these terms seem to collapse into
one another in very powerful representations of the female body as
grotesque. The frequency, intensity and salience of the association of
these terms suggests a mutually constituted genealogy, but this is not
to posit an exclusive or essential relationship between the terms.
While acknowledging the mimetic quality of these terms, it is their
long-standing and historically irreversible *connection* that is at issue
for me. The figure of the Siamese twin in the first and third chapters
stands for this state of intimacy without oneness.

As a model of sociality, the configuration of the Siamese twin suggests to me the possibility of an odd sisterhood worth considering in
place of the failed, unitary model of female solidarity which spent so
much time defending its normalcy. At least in the United States, con-
siderable effort has been put into reassurances that feminists are "normal women" and that our political aspirations are "mainstream."
With the best intentions (which include prominently the wish to be
maximally inclusive) this normalizing strategy cannot conceal its class
bias and attachment to an "upward mobility" which depends upon
leaving others behind. Furthermore, it concedes much to the misogyny which permeates the fear of "losing one's femininity," "making
a spectacle of oneself," "alienating men" (meaning powerful men) or
otherwise making "errors." Most importantly, it leaves uninterrogated
the very terms and processes of normalcy. I begin this study on the
side of the freak and the uncanny.

In the context of this study, the term "female grotesque" does not
guarantee the presence of women or exclude male bodies or male sub-
jectivities. The category of the female grotesque is crucial to identity-
formation for both men and women as a space of risk and abjection.

What might be called "male grotesques" are featured in this book, but I will argue their identities as such are produced through an association with the feminine as the body marked by difference. The male twins in David Cronenberg's *Dead Ringers* (1990) discussed in chapter three, and the infamous Svengali in Georges du Maurier's *Trilby* discussed in chapter five, are all set apart as heterogeneous *particular* men rather than the generic or normal men who stand in for mankind. In these cases, male homosexuality and marked ethnicity interact with the iconography and aesthetics of the grotesque. The relationship between the grotesque as feminism's "odd sisterhood" of mixed social ensembles and ethnic studies and queer theory, remain to be articulated more fully, but I believe the connections are there.

"A Cunning Array of Stunts"

In this book, I assemble a series of theoretical, historical, autobiographical, literary, and visual texts—somewhat in the mode of the sexual anagram above. Because the practice of risk, as I develop it, points more to possibility than to sustained progress, this book is filled with images of female performers who are, one way or another, in error. Each of these agents is marked by specificities of age, body shape, class, ethnicity, and sexuality; each performs with irony and courage in the face of danger, ridicule, disbelief, injury, or even death. These avowedly personal and somewhat idiosyncratic examples have provided me with much more than a content for my discussion; they have suggested to me that the very structure for rethinking the grand abstraction of "liberation" for women depends upon the flexibility and force of juxtaposition—the communal repetitions and differences much multiplied which characterize, for instance, the cinema of Ulrike Ottinger's *Freak Orlando* and Angela Carter's fiction, especially her penultimate work, *Nights at the Circus.* It goes without saying that my examples are, like Dr. Watson's definition of the grotesque, bound to ring false in other contexts and to be necessarily incomplete. The fantasies, dreams, and visions of liberation are very different in contexts other than one I am describing as problematical in relation to the discourses of modernity in the West. Nonetheless, the impetus of this project, if not its destination, lies in the direction of a reconfigured body politic which recognizes similarity and coincidence, not as the basis of a new universalism, but as an uncanny connection characteristic of discourses of the grotesque.

Finally, it may be useful to my readers to restate what this book does not set out to do. Most prominently, it does not attempt to catalogue the varieties of grotesque figures coded as female. Neither does it assiduously seek out and identify an essential or paradigmatic grotesque female. The examples in this book are not carefully chosen in that sense. Rather, they are encountered in the highly contingent style of critical practice which I describe in the first chapter as "stunting."

Often, however, I have recourse to stereotypical grotesques. Despite its obvious drawbacks, there is a crucial advantage in describing social types or a certain female iconography. Naming represents a particularly vivid way of recalling the persistence of those constrained codings of the body in Western culture which are associated with the grotesque: the Medusa, the Crone, the Bearded Woman, the Fat Lady, the Tattooed Woman, the Unruly Woman, the Hottentot Venus, the Starving Woman, the Hysteric, the Vampire, the Female Impersonator, the Siamese Twin, the Dwarf.[23] Worth recalling is the historical association of the grotesque with women's social movements from the "shrieking sisterhood" of the suffragettes to the "bra-burners" and harridans of the second wave.[24] And we may begin a long list which would add to these curiosities and freaks those conditions and attributes which link these types with contemporary social and sexual deviances, and more seemingly ordinary female trouble with processes and body parts: illness, aging, reproduction, nonreproduction, secretions, lumps, bloating, wigs, scars, make-up, and prostheses. Contemporary performance artists, visual artists, and filmmakers have encoded these potentially grotesque qualities across gender, in relation to both the female-coded and male-coded body.[25] Going on, the list would extend to increasingly artifactual postmodernist bodily modalities, the heretofore "interior" spaces of the body unbound and dispersed in surface fields and semiotic networks—reorganized, as Donna Haraway has noted, around new technologies and biomedical practices. These "odd boundary creatures" ("simians, cyborgs, women") move "tactically" and ergonomically outward and are capable of extensive reconfiguration, replication, and monstrous metamorphoses.[26] Like earlier manifestations of the grotesque, these "promising and non-innocent monsters . . . may be signs of possible worlds—and they are surely signs of worlds for which we are responsible".[27]

It has never been my purpose or interest to develop a comparative typology of female bodies or the grotesque. The examples of bodies above, and all others in the book, could be substituted by many others, but they are not meant to represent a mere multiplicity. They have been taken up, instead, like the "cunning *array*" of the adolescent joke, for their doubleness and generativity.

The book is arranged in interrelated chapters. The first chapter, "Up There, Out There: Aerialism, The Grotesque, and Critical Practice," inverts the usual vertical scheme which associated the grotesque with the "low," setting out instead in the "high" registers of modernism and symbolic topography. It emphasizes the crucial connections between the sleek, transcendent, spectacularized bodies that modelled the ideals of progress and liberation, and the grotesque. It includes a critical discussion of Bakhtin, Freud, and Michael Balint's *Thrills and Regressions*. The second chapter, "Female Grotesques: Carnival and Theory," is an updated version of my earlier essay on the grotesque and feminism which appeared in *Feminist Studies/Critical Studies* edited by Teresa de Lauretis. Chapter three, "Freaks, Freak Orlando, and Orlando," considers the "freak body" as a radical model of sociality which exceeds the Bakhtinian grotesque, making connections between and within genders, subcultures, architectures, and temporalities. The fourth chapter, on David Cronenberg's *Dead Ringers*, focuses on the relationship between the irregular male body and the "mutant woman," speculating on the limits of surgical reconfigurations of gender in the production of "possible bodies." The fifth chapter attempts to rethink the social production of class, nationality, and ethnicity in relation to the spectacle of female performance. In considering the visually and acoustically excessive body of Georges du Maurier's extremely popular heroine, Trilby, this chapter also reiterates the strong connection between the grotesque, fashion, and models of the body. Chapter six, "Revamping Spectacle: Angela Carter's *Nights at the Circus*," recapitulates many of the major themes of the project. Within the expanded spatial dimensions of late twentieth-century spectacle, the female spectacle which emerges as a de-formation of the normal suggests new political aggregates—provisional, uncomfortable, even conflictual coalitions of bodies which both respect the concept of situated knowledges and refuse to keep every body in its place.

Up There, Out There:
Aerialism, the Grotesque,
and Critical Practice

> "Of course, stunting may be an art if perfected and practiced by those who have the talent. It is popular for exhibitions where crowds like to see airplanes doing spectacular loops or dives or flying upside down. It should be understood that this precision flying is like tight rope walking—it only looks easy."
> —Amelia Earhart

> "Godard once said, 'Technique is the sister of Art.' Would you agree with his attribution of gender?"
>
> "Art has many Siamese twins."
> —Interview with Ulrike Ottinger[1]

WELL INTO HER MIDDLE AGE, MYRTLE BUTLER, *my aunt and my mother's identical twin, was asked to perform a stunt for the United States Air Force. A licensed pilot herself, she was given the opportunity to take over the controls of a jet fighter from her son, a test pilot—the first grandmother to do so. The irony of the "flying grandmother" depends, I suppose, upon the body marked by gravity defying gravity. Asked to comment on her experience while being photographed in full flight gear in the cockpit with her son (looking at the faded newspaper clipping depicting the event, I imagine her hesitant and straining to rise to the spectacular occasion), she replied grandly but with some imprecision: "The future for women . . . is in the air!"*

The child of an identical twin is already produced within the marvelous confines of a reproductive stunt. For such a child, born into the world of the split-sign, knowledge of the mother's body is posed as an uncanny question of difference within the same, requiring an acute sensitivity to bodily accoutrement, make-up, dress, scars, hair, perfume, and performance style. The high-flying young grandmother with lacquered nails and auburn hair was not the meticulously unadorned woman in white who left silently for work each morning; that was another woman, but one who in my mind was never entirely alone or self-same. The attachment of similarity could grow or diminish through time; but like the shared flesh of the Siamese twin, the psychic "extra" produced by the maternal doubling made the space in between bodies an uncomfortable, even frightening, but nonetheless attractive site of speculation; a place to look but never to find or "figure out" the body in that monstrous calculus feminist psychoanalytic critics have adduced, where the numbers never add up: "For the/a woman, two does not divide into ones."[2]

Twin mothers are literally extraordinary in the sense that they confound familiar notions of origin and selfhood with the prospects of an extraneous self. These, in turn, produce the further possibility of the kinds of divisions and replications which Freud identifies in his well-known discussion of the double in relation to the notion of the *unheimlich,* or uncanny. The redoubled and ghostly body takes up residence at the site of the maternal, threatening always to monstrously reproduce: "In other words," writes Freud, "there is a doubling, dividing, and interchanging of the self. And finally there is the constant recurrence of the same thing—the repetition of the same features or character traits or vicissitudes, of the same crimes, even the same names through several consecutive generations."[3] What possible good could come from such grotesque repetition?

But let me begin again. After all, critical practice has more to do with ordinary ways of doing things than is generally allowed. This is particularly true of beginnings.

Amelia Earhart, for instance, in her role as everyday theorist of flying practice (as opposed to modernist, feminist icon), describes her initiation into flying, as a convergence of many apparently unrelated and often commonplace experiences.[4] Her belief in the power of everyday randomness and felicitous conjunction is confidently expressed in her choice of chapter headings for her memoir, *The Fun of It: Random Notes of My Own Flying and of Woman in Aviation*: "Growing Up Here and There," "Aviation and I Get Together," "Joy Hopping and Other Things;"[5] preparation for life or for flying (and the two were inseparable in her case) involved a drift from one site of knowledge to another, sometimes literally a transfer from university to university or from one course of study to another. More often she simply travelled and took up whatever seemed promising. Flying lessons, like everything else in her life, were a question of mastering lateral movement. Everyday considerations of what to wear, how to move, and how to wear her hair ("But you don't look like an aviatrix. You have long hair") all contribute to her approach to flying and to flying lessons (Earhart, 26).

Yet, her approach was not entirely idiosyncratic. In general, the content and arrangement of flying lessons was much less hierarchized in the early days of aviation than was the case later, once the protocols of aeronautical professionalism were regulated. In Earhart's day, the distinction between serious pilot training and learning stunts was only gradually put in place until eventually the stunt was defined by the Department of Commerce as *"any manoeuver not necessary for normal flight"* (Earhart, 35). Though constitutive of early flying practice (what one did to *become* a pilot), stunting became the abnormal and increasingly liminal activity with regard to official flying. Its liminality is underlined in Earhart's account by the association of stunt flying with tightrope walking. This association is by no means original, since many popular histories of women and aeronautics begin similarly with an account of early aerial entertainers from the eighteenth and nineteenth centuries—aerialists, balloonists, and parachutists.

The stunt bears a special relationship to groups who are exceptional or abnormal in relation to the "normal activity." As Earhart notes, a

woman in aviation was (and to some extent still is) considered a novelty. Nonetheless, female stunt pilots were quite common. The element of spectacle which Earhart alludes to is what distinguishes the
stunt from "normal flying" or practice figures. In discussing women
pilots, Earhart mentions Laura Ingalls, who was initially discouraged
by her instructors, but through her perseverance became an "aerial
acrobat" of some note. She held a "feminine record" for nine hundred
and eighty consecutive loops (at a dollar a loop, a good wage for a
woman in those days), and eventually held the record for both sexes in
barrel rolls (Earhart, 179). Of course, such feats were disparaged
despite their popularity because, although they contributed to the
growing definitions of professionalism within aviation, they were
increasingly the sign of the counterfeit, exhibitionistic, unprofessional
pilot. Women in this category were doubly suspect, even as they were
intriguing to audiences.

Earhart, however, defends stunting and women as stunt pilots:

> Some critics protest against such exhibitions. I myself cannot see
> what harm they do. Certainly their execution requires sturdy
> equipment and skill and determination on the part of the pilot.
> *They may not point the way to progress in aviation but they demon-*
> *strate its possibilities.* As for a woman's doing them, that probably
> will be necessary for some time—for contrary to legal precedent,
> they (women) are considered guilty of incompetence until proved
> otherwise (emphasis mine) (Earhart, 179).

Earhart is cognizant of the dangers and difficulties of those women
who are "already guilty" and marked as novelties within stunt flying:
stunts within stunts. Their status as "already guilty" consigns them to
the very activities which further their marginalization and eventual
abjection from "normal" flying. In fact, normal flying comes to be defined in relation to "abnormal" moves and vice-versa. Significantly, the
relationship between the two does not depend upon the prior status of
one or the other; rather they are mutually involved and constitutive.

My interest here is with the status of the stunt and of the stunters or
stunted poised in relation to risk and blame. Stunt flying and similar

Fig. 4   "The Goddess of Flight," 1921. A commercial image of the sleek, aerodynamic woman on top of the world. Amelia Earhart was the historical
embodiment of this modernist myth of woman/airplane. Courtesy of The
Library of Congress.

activities, which I will characterize as "grotesque performances," are risky activities. On the one hand, they perpetuate the blaming, stigmatization, and marginalizing of groups and persons who occupy this self-perpetuating loop and are seen as "high-risk" groups; on the other hand, they elicit "risk-control" tactics which characterize risk as almost entirely negative, seeking to out-regulate (or make invisible) those performances and groups which enact or embody such double riskiness. In our day, this is perhaps most vividly present in the moralizing of the risk of AIDS; indeed, the term "high-risk" is by now laminated to the designations "gay men" and "intravenous drug users," as if these categories and activities were naturally bonded.[6]

A stunt may be thought of more theoretically as a tactic for groups or individuals in a certain risky situation in which a strategy is not possible. Strategies depend upon a proper place, a place of one's own, from which a certain "calculus of force" can be organized and projected outward. By contrast, in *The Practice of Everyday Life*, Michel de Certeau defines the "tactic" as a "logic of action" for the displaced. In spatial terms, "the place of the tactic belongs to the other. A tactic insinuates itself into the other's place, fragmentarily, without taking it over . . . without being able to keep it at a distance. Because it does not have a place, a tactic depends on time, it is always on the watch for opportunities, that must be seized on the wing."[7] As a temporal category, the tactic, or in Earhart's terms, the practice of stunting, belongs to the improvisational, to the realm of what is possible in the moment.

I offer Earhart's critical anecdotes and an opening biographeme, if you will, as *stunted* versions of the theoretical modelling of the grotesque as female bodily performance which I will be advancing in the course of this book.[8] The double meaning of the word "stunt" bifurcates the notion of the extraordinary into 1) a model of female exceptionalism (stunting) described by Amelia Earhart as comparable to tightrope walking and elaborated in her memoirs as metonymically related to female flying, and 2) the doubled, dwarfed, distorted (stunted) creatures of the sideshow which stand in as the representatives of a well-known cultural presentation of the female body as

Fig. 5   Anne Noggle, "Myself as a Pilot, 1982." Anne Noggle refigures the
female pilot, restoring the material dimensions of the body and space. The
continuum of body, plane, face, and landscape refuses to separate or transcend these phenomenal zones. By permission of the artist.

monstrous and lacking (one has height, the other does not). These
distinct spectacles of female stunting in the active and passive modes
may be thought of in terms of the careful calibration of anatomical
differences and body types which characterize disciplines of bodily
production in consumer society; in terms, that is, of the continuing
market segmentation which requires different models for different
markets and accordingly sorts and measures one female body or body
part from and against another.

One might choose any number of categories to illustrate this comparative process of bodily distribution and valuation. Fatness, for
instance, functions as an extremely significant differential in separating off women of different classes and ethnicities, placing them in
different fields or markets of representation. As Maud Ellmann forcefully asserts in her study of disembodiment, *The Hunger Artists*, "fat
. . . has come to represent the very hallmark of modernity":

The fat woman, particularly if she is nonwhite and working-class, has come to embody everything the prosperous must disavow: imperialism, exploitation, surplus value, maternity, mortality, abjection, and unloveliness. Heavier with projections than with flesh, she siphons off this guilt, desire, and denial, leaving her idealized counterpart behind: the kind of woman one sees on billboards, sleek and streamlined like the cars that she is often used to advertise, bathed in the radiance of the commodity.[9]

The figure of the fat woman works to literally "abject," by way of her abjected body, those disavowed aspects of production and "dangers of overproduction." This abjection constitutes a hard and hidden work —a work that is easily misrecognized as the very overconsumption it is designed to hide. This labor of the fleshly sign is the semiotic "work-in" of female bodies marked by class and race which subsidizes the "work-out" of their more mobile (exercised) and affluent neighbors.[10]

Like other categories of abjection which have historically been related to the grotesque, fatness and bodily excess of various kinds are most often thought of in passive, individual, or merely descriptive terms and, indeed, as Ellmann shows, fat women in the United States particularly, are repositories of shame and repressed desire.[11] But fatness in her analysis has both a constitutive and a performative aspect: it contributes to definitions of femaleness and to class, although it is not essentially or exclusively class or gender-bound. In other historical periods and in other countries and representational domains, fatness may be a quite different social sign.[12] As a certain kind of bodily enactment, the Fat Woman has been an important figure of spectacularized womanhood in the West since the nineteenth century. In our own day, feminist performance artists have played upon the variations of fleshly display and exaggeration associated with femaleness as a tactic of counter-pornography.[13]

Though it may seem intuitively more evident why one might describe an excessive body or psyche as grotesque (which is not to say that there is an essential quality which makes this the case), it may be less clear why the high-flying female body in space is not simply a thrilling and emancipatory icon, an instance of the gendered sublime, of progress, of modernity, and freedom.[14] The image of Amelia Earhart—tall, slim, and aerodynamic like the planes beside which she modelled—came to stand for all these liberatory aspirations for individual women in the United States in the 1920s and 1930s.[15] The image has survived into the 1990s as the emblem conflating liberal feminism and consumer progress in the Virgina Slims ("you've come a long way, baby") advertisements. Earhart's image, while representing the advancement of women in the postsuffrage era, simultaneously came to represent an unloading of the female body as identified with weightiness—the "unbearable weight" which Susan Bordo has identified as part of "the gendered nature of mind/body dualism."[16] Earhart's body, unlike my aunt's, was unencumbered. It left behind the marks of the old models of womanhood and of course, all signs of non–Anglo-Saxon ethnicity. She and her lookalike, Charles Lindbergh, were said to be attractively "boyish" in a distinctively "American" way.

Earhart's "boyishness" and the symbolic virility of flight as active and dangerous opened the way for interpretations of her activities as trangressive, making her a somewhat more ambivalent figure than might first appear. Furthermore, this vastly overproduced Modernist image of women's liberation is deliberately compromised in positing a link between freedom and the construction of femaleness as a stunt. As her own writings indicate, Earhart was acutely aware of the need to negotiate this association carefully, and by the end of her short career was increasingly accused of commercializing aeronautical culture—as if this had ever been absent from its history. Had she survived into the second phase of aeronautical history, with the normalization of flight and aeriality in the military/industrial sphere, her reputation might have merged with that of the many women pilots who contributed quietly to the war effort. Like the liberal feminism she came to represent, she might have "settled down." But then, in a final and much criticized attempt at "long-distance stunt flying," she disappeared.[17]

Flight and No-Flight

> Sky being meeting of sky and no-sky
>
> . . .
>
> Flight, thus, is meeting of flight and no-flight.
> —Muriel Rukeyser, *Theory of Flight*[18]

Reclaiming space has been a central metaphorical concern of modernism and liberation discourse, including women's liberation where
it is often understood as a freedom from oppressive bodily containment. I have tried to suggest, thus far, that there may be affirmative
models of risk and deviance in the high registers of modernism, and
ways in which the image of freedom as limitless space, transcendence,
individualism, and upward mobility of various kinds may be embodied and diverted, giving way to a model of feminist practice.[19] The
imaginary geometry of this spatial trope, however, requires careful
examination. The identification of "inner space" with the feminine in
the work of Eric Erikson, for instance, reinforces a view of women as
receptacles, "the receptive and passive half of a phallic dual unity."
"Viewed in this way," as Jessica Benjamin writes, "reclaiming inner
space becomes uncomfortably close to accepting anatomical destiny.
If feminists are not to ignore the importance of the body in shaping
our mental representations, they must read such metaphors differently."[20] Such rereadings must involve a reshaping of the entire woman/
space configuration away from the inner/outer dichotomies of bodily
and spatial representation. For just as inner space has been classically
identified with feminine containment, so outer space—foreign, ex-
plorable, empty—has been marked off as feminine.

The mere deconstruction of these categories does not guarantee a
place for female agency, however. As Alice Jardine has pointed out in
Gynesis: Configurations of Woman and Modernity, even those poststructuralist discourses which set about to reconfigure the time/space
relationships within the crisis of modernity in the West, "often turning back upon their own discourse, in an attempt to create a new *space*
or *spacing within themselves* for survivals (of different kinds)," identify

the Other space as female: "This other-than-themselves is almost
always a 'space' of some kind (over which the narrative has lost control), and this space is coded *feminine*, as *woman*."[21] There is a vexing
coincidence here which feminist critiques of deconstruction and poststructuralism have noted: While the "crisis of modernity" has been
articulated as a crisis of sexual difference which threatens to undo the
phallocentric logic of the same, folding the bodily envelope into itself
in a feminization of philosophy, there remains, in Rosi Braidotti's
term, a critical "dissonance" which is both historical and theoretical in
nature between a philosophical surrender of old binarisms and feminism as philosophy and politics. In *Patterns of Dissonance*, Braidotti
argues for a "fundamental asymmetry between the mainstream and
the feminist readings of the crisis of modernity."[22] (276). Of course, as
she points out, this asymmetry begins with the fact that feminist
philosophers and theorists are rarely read, much less read seriously, by
those poststructuralist writers whose work they have so seriously
engaged. More importantly, however, the crisis of modernity is not a
sad story for groups who see it as marking an "opening-out of unex-
plored possibilities" rather than as a historical loss of faith in reason
and (male) identity.[23]

The discourse of postmodernism which arises contemporaneously
with poststructuralism and feminism offers it own "spatial turn"[24] to
distinguish itself from modernism.[25] The displacement of depth models of epistemology, architecture, and the body by the play of surfaces
offers interesting possibilities for reconfiguring cultural identity
and, for some postmodernist feminists, a way out of essentialist models of woman-as-body or woman-as-space.[26] For others, like Celeste
Olaquiaga for instance, the emphasis on spatiality, bodies, and the
translocation of cultural objects has been an opportunity to resituate
postmodernist discourse as a part of the metropolitan "latinization"
of culture which anticipated it.[27] In relation to gender, the politics of
surface can be another opportunity to scapegoat the feminine. David
Harvey's influential *The Condition of Postmodernity*, for example, produces an association of postmodernism with "surface glitter," "dis-

play," and "ephemerality"—attributes of the feminine which are illustrated by the nude female bodies which accompany his text.[28] The
inference is that we must somehow get beyond the politics of "jouis-
sance" which Harvey derides,[29] and back to the truths of a more virile
and substantial model of the political. This nostalgia, which is often
camouflaged in postmodernist texts themselves, is on the surface of
his critique of postmodernism.[30]

If Harvey exemplifies a desire to both return to and get beyond the
female body *in depth,* what are we to make of the aspirations of writers like Jean-François Lyotard and Slavoj Žižek to find a new transcendence in the female body as sublime and material?[31] When Lyotard
describes "transcendence in immanence" as the negative answer to
the question "Can Thought Go on Without A Body?" he seems com-
pelled to return to the gendered body ("She" in the essay) as the place
of lack. Tania Modleski, in a very cogent critique of Lyotard's essay,
identifies this "transcendence in immanence" with the figure of the
trapeze artist in Wim Wenders film, *Wings of Desire.* In this film,
Damiel, an angel, falls in love with a young trapeze artist and chooses
at the conclusion of the film to become a man and to accept mortality.
Writes Modleski:

> As a figure of contradiction, the trapeze artist is emblematic of this
> film's desire to have it both ways: while purporting to be undertak-
> ing the painful work of remembering the horrors of the past, revis-
> ing concepts of masculinity and femininity, coming to terms with
> the body and its mortality, and holding out an ideal of freedom and
> hence of responsibility . . . it consoles itself with nostalgia—for
> simple stories and mother's womb—and a hackneyed notion of
> "destiny" embedded in the "happily ever after," greatest-story-ever-
> told narrative of a man and a woman.[32]

Modleski's incisive reading of this film as an instance of the "male
desire to escape the human limits of the body" is reinforced by bell
hooks' comments on the same film in terms of race and male privi-
lege. While I am in general agreement with their ideological assess-

ments of the film, I would be in bad faith (and transparently so, since this book is filled with aerialists and off-beat angels) if I did not admit to my own desire to have it both ways on the transcendence/immanence issue, and to share the dual purposes which Modleski identifies as "coming to terms with the body and its mortality, and holding out an ideal of freedom and hence, responsibility." I mark this dual aspiration in my own work as the "aerial sublime." The "aerial sublime"—precisely like the trapeze artist Modleski describes as a "figure of contradiction"—is an embodiment of possibility and of error. In my view, it is not the failed attempt to have it both ways that is problematic for feminism, but rather the normalization of the trapeze artist (a daring and ambivalent figure who reappears throughout this book) as a safe woman.

Beginning this book on the female grotesque "up there" and "out there" represents an attempt to acknowledge the historical chasm between the twentieth century versions of this category which necessarily involve a consideration of the technologies of spectacle as multi-vectored, in contrast to an earlier identification of the grotesque with the symbolically "low." The emphasis on aeriality (rather than loftiness) is meant to introduce a principle of turbulence into the configuration female/grotesque. Mikhail Bakhtin's model of the bodily grotesque is initially useful here because, as I elaborate in the second chapter, it presupposes the body as *process and semiosis*—a grotesque that moves—but as I have indicated, his emphasis on the production of a *general grotesque* leaves a static and universalistic notion of the feminine securely in place. In theories of the grotesque, the etymological starting point that links the grotesque with the grotto-esque, or cave, proceeds quite swiftly to the further identification of the grotto with the womb, and with woman-as-mother. This move—which I have argued previously, in relation to Bakhtin's dramatic use of the image of the "female, pregnant hag" as the deepest expression of the grotesque—is certainly regressive in both the psychic and the political register.[33]

I am also attempting to dislodge the connections between woman, space, and progress, to pull them out of sync through the use of the grotesque as a valuable category for rethinking temporality. Earhart's model of stunt flying as pointing to inherent possibility rather than future progress moves in this direction. In the following section of this chapter, I follow up her insight in brief comparative discussions of three theorists who consider temporality in relation to spectacle and/ or the grotesque.

Finally, as models of deviance, I revisit some familiar performances of women "in the air." These instances of aerial leaps and falls may suggest an alternative to the notion of liberation as upward mobility and flight forward, but I warn the reader that they end badly. Future examples are less death-driven. These "repeat performances" raise the dilemma of repetition and difference: What are the possibilities of reinhabiting the old in a way that will alter it? Can one predict which performances, mimetic acts, or re-presentations will do so? Can one promise, in the words of Myrtle Butler, a "future for women . . . in the air" which allows women to beg off the burdensome duty to forever represent the new?

Sublime Thrills and Regressions: Freud and Bakhtin

In his paper, "On the Uncanny," Freud identifies the uncanny double with two different psychic moments: 1) the primary narcissism characteristic of childhood; 2) the development of the conscience in later life.[34] The relationship between these two psychic formations is presented as a kind of temporal layering which permits the "conscience" (later, as Strachey points out in his note, developed into the concepts of the superego and the ego-Ideal) to look critically at the "old surmounted narcissism of earlier times." The shame associated with this self-observation does not however, in Freud's view, incorporate all the aspects of the double. There is a particularly interesting temporal remainder in his formulation, which suggests that not only shame, but

regret and hopefulness reside in this recollection of *"unfulfilled but pos-*
sible futures to which we still like to cling in phantasy:"

> The fact that an agency of this kind exists, which is able to treat the
> rest of the ego like an object—the fact that is that man is capable of
> self-observation—renders it possible to invest the old idea of a
> "double" with a new meaning and to ascribe a number of things to
> it—above all, those things which seem to self-criticism to belong
> to the old surmounted narcissism of earlier times. But it is not only
> this latter material, offensive as it is to the criticism of the ego,
> which may be incorporated in the idea of a double. There are also
> all the unfulfilled but possible futures to which we still like to cling
> in phantasy, all the strivings of the ego which adverse circum-
> stances have crushed, and all our suppressed acts of volition which
> nourish us in the illusion of Free Will.[35]

Freud's identification of this temporal dimension, suggesting a kind
of nostalgia for the future in the effects of the uncanny, suggests both
the limits and the possibilities of an ethical appropriation of the
grotesque, an already "surmounted" if not perjured category like the
sublime, one of its many Siamese twins. In 1976, Thomas Weiskel, in
his powerful study of the Romantic sublime, emphatically stated that
the move from the aesthetic of the sublime to an ethics of the sublime
was "risky business" and that it was therefore no accident that it would
be missing from the aesthetics of activists and idealists.[36] In fact, the
attraction towards the sublime and the ideology of the sublime has only
increased since the mid-seventies; indeed, idealists and cultural "activists" have incorporated its structure and psychology, as outlined by
Weiskel himself, in many discourses.[37] Patricia Yaeger's influential
essay, "Towards A Female Sublime," begins with Weiskel's negation of a
contemporary sublime, emphasizing how his negation only increases a
desire for those impossibilities which he so compellingly suggested.[38]
   Weiskel's description of the sublime as a "moribund aesthetic"
(Weiskel, 6) in an age when transcendence and expansionism were no
longer thinkable, is related to the Freudian moment cited above, when
the yearnings and imaginings of the adult are exposed—most interest-

ingly for our purposes here, when they are degraded and turned towards the grotesque which epitomizes its curtailment. Writes Weiskel:

> Freud was definitely and remarkably immune to the sublime mo-
> ment, whose "oceanic" and demonic guises he brilliantly exposed.
> To please us, the sublime must now be abridged, reduced, and par-
> odied as the grotesque, somehow hedged with irony to assure us we
> are not imaginative adolescents (Weiskel, 6).

Is the grotesque, then, just one more version (turning) of the sublime? Are they the same, except in degree, as lessenings or heightenings of identical apprehensions? Or may the qualitative differences suggested in at least the Kantian sublime set it off and up away from the standards, the finitude, the commensurability associated with the grotesque? To reverse Weiskel's priorities, can the Romantic sublime be read as an historical version of the grotesque, as it turns inward and back in the regressive and privatized moments described by Freud?[39] In fact, this structure is strongly implied in historical accounts of the grotesque.

The massive disappointment and mood of shameful abjection which overtakes the narcissistic scene (in the passage quoted above, a function of the "return of the repressed," and later in the essay a function of castration) is evocative of the anxieties, sarcasms, and embarrassments of the grotesque in its postRomantic or modernist guises. The interiority and bitterly derisive quality of the Romantic grotesque, as described by both Wolfgang Kayser and Mikhail Bakhtin, sets it apart from earlier comic and public manifestations.

Bakhtin, whose model of grotesque realism in *Rabelais and His World* has been the preeminent influence in recent studies of the grotesque and cultural politics, looked to carnival in early modern Europe for that form of the grotesque which embodied material and social transformation, and indeed celebrated it in all its cultural aspects. In contrast, he viewed with great skepticism the "private and egotistic form" of the body and the grotesque expressed in the Romantic and Modernist canons and genres, where "the carnival

spirit was transposed into a subjective, idealistic philosophy."[40] With
Romanticism, "laughter was cut down to cold humor, irony, sarcasm"
(RW, 38). For Bakhtin as for Kayser, whom he criticizes for seeing the
grotesque only in relation to this benighting moment, the grotesque
turns inward and the familiar becomes the alien and the uncanny:

> All that is ordinary, commonplace, belonging to everyday life, and
> recognized by all suddenly becomes meaningless, dubious and hos-
> tile. Our own world becomes an alien world. Something frighten-
> ing is revealed in that which was habitual and secure. Such are the
> tendencies of the Romantic grotesque in its extreme expression
> (RW, 38–39).

In this account, the grotesque goes underground in the course of the
nineteenth century, becoming increasingly hidden and dispersed—a
private and "nocturnal" category, to be retrieved by Freud as *socially
disembodied* in the theory of the unconscious.[41]

It should be added that even Bakhtin, in his admittedly limited and
polemical treatment of the Romantic and postRomantic grotesque,
acknowledged the positive significance of the "discovery" of "the interior infinite" which, he asserts, was made possible by the use of the
grotesque in "its power to liberate from dogmatism, completion, and
limitation. The *interior infinite* could not have been found in a closed
finished world" (RW, 44). The grotesque, then, is a constitutive aspect
of what is elsewhere called the sublime. Even in its most withholding,
secretive, and anorexic forms, the grotesque retains for Bakhtin its
association with the carnivalesque view of the body and the world as
regenerative and incomplete projects, implying those "unfulfilled but
possible futures" which Freud identifies as an important aspect of the
uncanny double. In Freud's view, of course, "all the strivings of the
ego which adverse circumstances have crushed" and "all our suppressed acts of volition" represent a clinging to phantasy and to the
illusion of free will.[42]

This is not to say that Freud and Bakhtin are in any fundamental
agreement on the nature or function of the self or the relationship

between the constitution of the self and possible (real) worlds. They are not. As Bakhtin's commentators rightly point out, Bakhtin and his circle were highly critical of the classical psychoanalytical model of identity formation and its relationship to the social. Katerina Clark and Michael Holquist place Bakhtin's model as the "polar opposite" of Freud's: "In Freud, self is suppressed in the service of the social; in Bahktin, self is precisely a function of the social. In Freud, the more of the other, the less of the self; in Bakhtin, the more of the other, the more of the self."[43] In the following chapter on the grotesque and gender, I will return to an elaboration and reconsideration of these differences. What I want to suggest here is less a common ground than a certain provisional space, or, to put it in temporal terms, a brief instance, of the anterior past—in Freud, the "future of an illusion" long suppressed, and in Bakhtin, the nostalgic yearning for the bright promise of that early and lost carnival which is locked away in the "chamber" of bourgeois privatism.

Michael Balint:
Aerialism and The Philobatic Imagination

In a short and provocative study published in 1959, entitled *Thrills and Regressions,* the object relations psychoanalyst Michael Balint coined the term "philobatism" for the field of activities and sensations organized around the thrills of seeing, feeling, or imagining the self-supported human body in space.[44] The thrill-seeking individual who habitually leans out into dangerous and "friendly" expanses away from the zone of security (home base and its familiar objects) he calls a philobat. The philobat risks external danger with a mixture of pleasure, fear, and confidence that the universe will hold her up.

The term "philobat" is modelled on the Greek "acrobat," the performer of antiquity who literally goes up on her toes to spring away from the earth. As Balint notes, the acrobat survives as a cultural figure represented in Greek and Roman representations of the street performer, and in carnivals and circuses as contemporary versions of the

Fig. 6   Lillian Leitzel, ca. 1930. The aerialist in the city. Courtesy of Circus
World Museum, Baraboo, Wisconsin.

trapeze act. In the late nineteenth and early twentieth century, the
figure of the acrobat becomes the privileged subject of representation
by writers and artists, often, in fact, the figure of the male artist himself. At this historical juncture, the acrobat belongs to a class of pro-
fessionals who are "paid for their skill which causes thrills to the
spectators and possibly also to themselves" (Balint, 24). The philobat,
in contrast, is an amateur, a lover and seeker of such experiences in the
external world and in the workings of the imagination. The tenuous
distinctions between the professional and the amateur, and between
enacting and experiencing the thrills of philobatism, are even more
fragile, as we will see, when gender difference is taken into account.

Because Balint's primary interest is in the psychology of such thrills,
he sees in adult philobats or in philobatic activities residual, primitive
reenactments of early sensations, phantasms, and psychic scenes.

Without observing a strict chronology, he locates and describes, in general terms, a source in the recall of a free-floating, maternal environment, similar to that theorized by Julia Kristeva as the semiotic chora, an unsignified free space, anterior to language and culture, but nonetheless powerfully remaindered within symbolization as an ambivalent (safe and dangerous) Otherness.[45] Ultimately unrecuperable, this "space" is unlocatable except in relation to the Oedipal markers which point "elsewhere." The similarities in these two conceptualizations of an archaic spaciousness which is both thrilling and regressive continue in their use of carnival to describe the symbolic register of philobatism, formed in Kristeva's terms through "an homology between the body, dream, linguistic structure, and structures of desire."[46] Kristeva's evocation of the carnivalesque in many of her early essays is directly inspired by Bakhtin, although her trajectory through the discourse of carnival in Western literature radicalizes it in the service of an exclusive, literary *avant-gardism*.[47] Balint's descriptions of carnival and circus activities seems to have been based primarily on his own observations of twentieth century amusement parks, or "funfairs" as they were called in England.

Theoretically, *Thrills and Regressions* is heavily influenced by his colleague Sandor Ferenczi's *Thalassa,* which argues that adult genital sexuality is driven by the impulse to regress to the intrauterine or "thalassal" environment.[48] Balint tends to identify both the "friendly spaces" between objects and the safety zone or "home base" of philobatic activities with the mother's body, but at different stages or layers of the experience of spatiality. In other words, the philobatic imagination operates, at different stages, both *within and away from* the maternal body. Despite Balint's uncertainty about the relative chronology of philobatic behavior in relation to the clinging behavior which he calls "ocnophilic," the philobat pushes off in a stance of independence and autonomy, suggesting to Balint a more advanced stage of development related to symbolization in general, and a symbolic identification of philobatism with genitality and the phallus. The body walking away from the mother in an erect posture, the transitional objects of young children (toys, blankets, etc.), and the batons, tightrope walkers' pole, sticks, guns, pens, and other accoutrements which accompany sport and artistic activity, suggest to Balint that philobatism is "symbolically related to erection and potency, although it is difficult to decide whether the philobatism should be considered as an early, primitive stage of genitality or, the other way round, as a retrospective, secondary genitalisation in adult age of an originally non-genital function" (Balint, 29). Leaving the origins of philobatism uncertain, he moves his investigation into the symbolic realm of adult myth-making and culture, where typology, symbols, architectures, rituals, and language link psychoanalytic theory with history.[49]

What emerges from Balint's descriptive account is the historically vivid instance of the repressive effects of gender formation within the "strange carnivalesque diaspora" of the twentieth century.[50] Given the convincing feminist critiques of the Kristevan model of the carnival which privileges the pre-Oedipal and the Imaginary as a negative, unavailable, and unrepresentable space, there would seem to be very little here to negotiate. As Juliet Mitchell has put it most starkly: "You cannot choose the imaginary, the semiotic, the carnival as an alternative to the law. It is set up by the law precisely in its own ludic space, its area of imaginary alternative, but not as a symbolic alternative."[51] My own position in relation to the constraints and possibilities of carnival as a liminal space is staked out in the following chapter, "Female Grotesques: Carnival and Theory." It is much closer to that of Laura Mulvey, who in her writing and in her filmmaking with Peter Wollen (here, I am thinking particularly of the deliberately awkward acrobatic sequence in *Riddles of the Sphinx* and the aviatrix film, *Amy*) attempts a feminist philobatics.[52] As she has written, the possibilities of carnival and the carnivalesque are not those of a symbolic alternative nor of a Kristevan Imaginary, "but rather an intermediate that hovers on the threshold ... the terrain in which desire nearly finds expression, in which stuff (magra) is repressed by the dominant political culture, and in which the psycho-analytical structures of society erupt into gesture" (Mulvey, 28).

Returning to Balint's own reflections on these materials, he singles
out acrobatics as a primary example of philobatic activity as spectacle
that "symbolically represent[s] the primal scene ... the specific
difference between shows in general and philobatic shows and feats is
the presence of *real external danger*" (Balint, 30). For the spectator at
circuses, theater, and sideshow exhibitions, the philobatic performance is marked by a powerful ambivalence which combines admira-
tion, envy, and awe. Balint's own concerns are not historical, but he
offers a suggestion as to a significant cultural shift in the nineteenth
century from spectatorial thrills to a more active philobatism:

> The dynamic reason for this ambivalent respect is that acrobats and
> actors are allowed and dare to perform publicly philobatic acts
> symbolizing primal scenes. The community, however, is allowed to
> participate in the form of passive spectators only, thrilled by
> identification.
>
> The question of what happened, mainly during the nineteenth
> century, that turned the spectators into actors is an interesting
> problem ... *It is possible that this change is only one symptom of a
> general tendency of that epoch, perhaps best expressed by Nietzsche,"to
> live dangerously"* (emphasis mine) (Balint, 31).

Balint's evocation of Nietzsche in relation to the shift in roles
between performers and spectators in the carnival scene effectively
modernizes the discourse of carnival. For Bakhtin, spectacle was the
antithesis of the carnivalesque. Spectacle assumed a partitioning of
space and a creation of discrete sightlines. It broke down the reciprocal roles played by performers and spectators in carnival, as actors
became passive spectators or contemplatives involved in increasingly
interiorized monodramas. What Balint is evoking under the sign of
Nietzsche is, in effect, a new extroversion of the spectator-performer
relationship as the passive spectator leaps, imaginatively at least, out
of his seat and into the "spectacle without a stage," thus creating a new
and split subject of spectacle and a new sociality.[53] In Nietzschean
terms, however, it is not only the spectacle participant who is divided
in the thrilling identification described by Balint, for there is also the

collective category of the crowd. (The antagonism between "the crowd" and the subject who has elected to live dangerously, is played out paradigmatically in the Prologue of Zarathustra, in the descriptions of the aerialist, Zarathustra's rope-dancer).[54]

Balint's accounts of these modern carnivalesque spectacles are very gender and role-specific. For instance, in reading the so-called primal scene as philobatic, he showcases the male circus performer:

> . . . We may say that the philobatic thrills represent in a way the primal scene in symbolic form. A powerful and highly skilled man produces on his own a powerful erection, lifting him far away from security, performing in his lofty state incredible feats of valour and daring, after which, in spite of untold dangers, he returns unhurt to the safe mother earth. In this connection the earth has a double aspect corresponding to the ambivalent situation; she is dangerous because of her irresistible attraction which, if unconditionally surrendered to, may cause mortal damage; but at the same time she is loving and forgiving, offering her embracing safety to the defiant hero on his skillful return. It is traditional in the circus for the hero-acrobat while performing high-up in the air to be assisted, admired, and finally received back to the ground by an attractive young girl. Acrobatics, therefore, are one special form of shows all of which symbolically represent the primal scene (Balint, 29–30).

Although Balint does not limit the philobatic experience or tendency to men, his cultural model is clearly the "Batman." In his remarks on the circus act and funfairs, however, he includes female figures in the aerial act or in the "primitive" sideshows as essential "showpieces":

> One type of showpiece is either beautiful, attractive women, or frightening, odd, and strange females; the other type is powerful, boasting, challenging men. Simplified to bare essentials, practically all stage plays or novels, however highbrow, are still concerned with these three kinds of human ingredients (Balint, 30).

His shifting syntax here suggests that both the "beautiful, attractive" and the "odd and strange" female finally belongs to the same

"type." But are there two types or are there three, since they separate
out into "three kinds of human ingredients? Here, indeed, is the sex
that is not one! In that part of the twin category of the female/women
that includes the "frightening, odd, and strange *females*," one assumes
the presence of freaks and other grotesque curiosities who produce in
the viewer a certain state of ambivalent *dis*traction which is somehow
involved or transformed in the attraction of the other *"women"*
(emphases mine).[55] The proximity of female grotesques to their
attractive counterparts has a long history in the typology of Western
art and theater, especially comedy, in which the whorish matron, the
crone, the ugly stepsisters, and the nurse are brought onstage for comparison and then dismissed.

Conceptually, the disjuncture between the relationship of the two
(male and female) and the three (male and two female) categories provides a space of differentiation between women which is covered over
in the dominant fictions of gender and heterosexuality. Teresa de
Lauretis has written eloquently of the "in-difference" of much contemporary critical discourse, including feminist criticism, to those sexual
differences which cannot be contained within or placed definitively
outside the heterosexually presumed oppositional difference of male to
female.[56] These "eccentric subjects" occupy a position in what she designates, following film theory, as a "space-off," the "space not visible in
the frame but inferable from what the frame makes visible." De
Lauretis sees this as an existing "else-where" produced by and in representational practices and by what they leave out or cannot represent;
she also sees it as "a theoretical condition of possibility"[57] for feminism, defined as a heterogeneous and contradictory process, rather
than (as its critics and some of its friends would have it) a finished
product built along an untroubled axis of gender[58] (perhaps this "finished feminism" is somewhere so simple, but nowhere I have been).[59]

Something like this theoretical "space-off" is certainly necessary if
feminism is to even posit a "nonrepressive narcissism."[60] The possibilities of an expanded, in Sandra Bartky's term, "revolutionary aesthetic
of the body" (Bartky, 43) would depend certainly on the radical alter-

nation of sightlines and internalized witnesses to the performing scene.[61] The collective witness which she imagines will itself be differentiated and "while not requiring body display, will not make it taboo either" (Bartky, 43).

The nonrequirement of visibility in her formulation seems to me as important as the opportunity to show off in a new way. Although the grotesque is a category traditionally identified with expression and hypervisibility, the surrender of visibility and the acknowledgement of somatic lack so that "missing" body parts and missing bodies (virtual, unrepresented, unrepresentable, disappearing, or dead) would surely have to be part of this new scene of narcissistic performance. Of course, as Peggy Phelan has written, "performance is the art form which most fully understands the generative possibilities of disappearance."[62] Female performance has been a privileged site of enacting disappearance from Camille to Amelia Earhart; feminism, understandably, has turned away from these images as ideologically dangerous. But even the Romantic figure of the dying woman, as I argue in chapter five, can be read or performed differently.[63] In the modernist canon, the obsession with Earhart's last flight and her repeated "sightings" years afterwards may stand for this invisible potential.

The Female Philobat: Flying and Falling as Allegories of Femininity

Although Balint keeps them analytically apart, his two or three essential types are very susceptible to transmigratory codings, particularly in the simultaneity of carnival and circus activities. The philobatman shows through in the unexpected virility of the female acrobat in, for instance, the striking figure of Miss Urania in J. K. Huysmans's *A Rebours* (Against the Grain).[64] Miss Urania of the magnificent, steely physique—"arms of iron"—is, finally, a great disappointment to the novel's hero, Des Esseintes, since her virility, it turns out, is only muscle deep; she fails to provide him with the inverted "sex-change"

Fig. 7   Nancy Spero, "Sheela and the Dildo Dancer," 1987. Handprinting and
collage on paper and on wall.

which he imagined, preferring to keep for herself the passive ("feminine") sex role which he had coveted.

Of course, the male gaze can be read much more complexly in relation to sexuality and the trapeze. In the 1920s, Jean Cocteau described
a music hall act performed by a trapeze artist and female impersonator called Barbette.[65] Barbette's only props were a divan and a
trapeze. The vertical schema of high-low replaced the axis of gender in
his act so that his "femininity" was enacted on the divan to throw
"dust into the audiences eyes" (Franko, 596); his virile performance
up on the trapeze would (along with his feminine costume) persuade
the audience of his femininity.[66] In Djuna Barnes' *Nightwood*, Frau
Mann, an androgynous trapeze artist whom I discuss in chapter six,
uses her virility in performance and her costume to foreclose heterosexuality so that it is clear she is "the property of no man."[67]

Miss Urania, Barbette and Frau Mann are precursors of the fabulous Fevvers, the heroine of Angela Carter's postmodernist novel,
Nights at the Circus, discussed in the concluding chapter of this book.

Fig. 8   Nancy Spero, "The Acrobat," 1990. Handprinting and collage on paper.
Courtesy of the Artist and Josh Baer Gallery.

A suggestion of the transgressive potential of the female usurpation of
the phallic function of the philobat is hilariously present, as well, in
the procession of archaic female forms in the scroll work of the artist
Nancy Spero, where female acrobats and "Dildo-dancers" wield huge
batons, not, as Balint would assume, for balance and security, but
rather as symbols of disequilibrium and release.

   With the advent of mass culture, as Jean Starobinski notes, the powerful ambivalence in the male viewing of these female icons is associated with the scandal of the female body exposed and provocative,
offering itself as simultaneously accessible and unattainable within the
performance because of the very intensity of light and spaciousness,
which provide a separation and a distance between flier and watcher.[68]
The spectator pays his money for this withholding, as well as for the
temporary capture of the girl on the wing (Starobinski, 65–66). For the
modernist mythologists, the figure of the performer signified ironic
detachment both from the heaviness of the flesh and from the class of
paying spectators; the female performer as muse was lifted off the clas-

sical pedestal to fly or at least dangle in the heavens. Femininity air-
borne and in motion figured as the highest expression of the lightness
of being. The intensification of commercial spectacle within the new,
gaslit venues of art and artistic performance, mixing high and low culture to build a new spectatorship with monetary exchange at its center,
figured the woman in the air as the very "élan hyperbolique" of the
New Age (Starobinski, 33).

Some Leaps and Falls

"A girl jumps differently . . .
—Søren Kierkegaard[69]

This description of the structure of desire and exchange in female
spectacle calls for analysis according to the theories of spectatorship
developed so intensively in feminist film theory under the rubric of
the gaze. What makes these female figures in the air so compelling and
dangerous for men is not just their similarity to other women, but
rather their dissimilarity from themselves. As Starobinski points out,
this female performer is not so different from other women, but
"different from her own femininity" (Starobinski, 52). The representation of femininity as an effortless mobility implies enormous control, changeability, and strength. "She possesses an immense power of
metamorphosis associated with her mobility . . . in the suppleness of
this body is hidden, in fact, an aggressive and dangerous virility"
(Starobinski, 52). She is, in other words, "an idol of perversity."[70] For
the artist who both identifies with and desires the female acrobat, several fantasies converge: the fantasy of a controlling spectatorship, the
fantasy of artistic transcendence and freedom signified by the flight
upwards and the defiance of gravity, and the fantasy of a femininity
which defies the limits of the body, especially the female body.

The risk of such leaps and flights lies in the danger of the fatal fall.
The impasse of this modernist symbolization for the entity marked
"Woman" is that there is only one way out: death, whatever its repre-

sentation—hysterical breakdown, unconsciousness, loss of visibility, or more literally loss of life. The endlessly repeated accounts of the disappearance of Amelia Earhart in the Pacific may stand provisionally for this critical crux (The Lady Vanishes). Slavoj Žižek sums up the situation in baldly Lacanian terms: "The elevation of an ordinary, earthly woman to the sublime object always entails mortal danger for the miserable creature charged with embodying the Thing, since 'Woman does not Exist.'"[71]

As brief cinematic examples, two spectacular high-altitude falls immediately come to mind: Dorothy Arzner's *Christopher Strong* (1933) and Max Ophuls' *Lola Montes* (1955). Both of these films have been written about extensively as paradigmatic of the construction of femininity in dominant cinema. In *Christopher Strong,* Cynthia Darrington (Katharine Hepburn) is a famous "girl flier" who falls in love with the very monogamous, married Christopher Strong. Both characters are significantly introduced into the film as "Exhibit A and Exhibit B," the discoveries of a high society treasure hunt for a faithful husband and a girl over twenty who hasn't had an affair; both are shown as deviates, if only because of their radical heterosexual conventionality. As Judith Mayne has argued, "Cynthia's 'virginity' becomes a euphemistic catchall for a variety of margins in which she is situated."[72] Like her putative virginity, her costumes tend to exceed the norms of work, gender, and heterosexuality which they would seem to model, placing her increasingly "out there." During the affair with Strong, she suspends her flying activities to become, in his eyes, something attractive, new, and strange. In an earlier scene, masquerading in evening dress and hat, she becomes, for him, "something exquisite, a moth perhaps" who, he fears, "might fly out the window and disappear forever." Later, when she has taken up flying again, a close-up of her face through the plane's window, masked behind her leather helmet and goggles, her eyes wet with tears, underlines her metamorphic identity as woman-becoming-moth in the film's final sequence. At 33,000 feet, in the midst of setting a new altitude record, she begins to disintegrate. The generous pieties of Strong's good wife ringing in her ears, she removes her oxygen mask and loses control of the plane; ambiguously clutching the mask (suicide or an accident?), her rocking side to side and downward suggests an hysterical fit. In contrast, the plane's descent is shot at a distance to show off what might have been hers but for love; an aeronautical virtuosity and absolute control. The plane expertly spirals down and inward in a magnificent looping stunt maneuver until, in another shot, it crashes.

When Lola Montes takes a dive from a platform under the big top, she elects to do it without the net. A former "dancer," social climber, and emancipated woman whose fatal charms have captivated artists, royalty, and revolutionaries, she appears in the film first and last, as the centerpiece of a circus act constructed around elaborately costumed and orchestrated episodes in her life. Flashbacks suggest another version of her life in forward motion, when she was in diegetic control. But, reduced to a main attraction at the circus, she is almost entirely immobile. The camera moves around her in swirling, wide shots while the ringmaster snaps his whip and narrates her life as a series of commands and announcements. Her life risks are enacted as acrobatic acts or on the trapeze. Her incredible rise, "higher and higher, to the height of her career," is mimicked in her rise to the upper regions of the circus tent, where she readies herself for the inevitable descent.

Poised to jump, she sways back and forth while the dizzying camera movement (part of the act?) suggests illness, fear, and hesitation, until suddenly she seems to faint into the downward spaces which unfold before the viewer's eyes as if they too were plunging to oblivion. Blackout. Lola then is seen for the last time as a sideshow, behind bars, in the menagerie with the animal acts, extending her "extraordinary and piquant favors" to the masses of men willing to buy cheap tickets. Her identity is reduced to precisely what earlier as an "attractive woman" she denied: "I am not a fairground freak."

The excess of both examples lies in the double loss of balance within the fall. The heroines both faint/feint *and* fall, and the two moments are not identical, or at least the relationship between the faint/feint is not certain (out of sync). Does Lola collapse and (tumble) inadvertently downward, landing miraculously? Does Lady Cynthia pass out or is she committing suicide? Furthermore, the falls in both cases are radically denaturalized, in *Christopher Strong* by the expert stunt flying which guides the plane downward, and in *Lola Montes* by the virtuosic camera work which shows Lola's fall as if she were operating the camera herself, eyes wide open and in perfect control until the blackout. Both of these women are, to use Balint's terms, "attractive" but also "odd, frightening, and strange."

This supplemental distortion and disintegration of the female subject presents an additional threat to the male viewer for whom the female hurdling in space is "the symptom of Man." Žižek's reading of such ontologically destabilizing moments in which, "through hysterical breakdown," the woman "*assumes* her nonexistence" and "constitutes herself as 'subject,'" depends on a shift from the model of desiring woman to a transgendered identification with her (Žižek, 65). Describing this transversion in *film noir,* he writes:

> What is so menacing about the femme fatale is not the boundless enjoyment that overwhelms the man and makes him woman's plaything or slave. It is not Woman as object of fascination that causes us to lose our sense of judgment and moral attitude but, on the contrary, that which remains hidden beneath this fascinating mask and which appears once the masks fall off: the dimension of the pure subject fully assuming the death drive. To use Kantian terminology, woman is not a threat to man insofar as she embodies pathological enjoyment, insofar as she enters the frame of a particular fantasy. The real dimension of the threat is revealed when we "traverse" the fantasy, when the coordinates of the fantasy space are lost via hysterical breakdown (Žižek, 66).

Žižek's insistence on the authenticity of the hysterical leap as an *assumption* of nonexistence in which the female figure is constituted as a subject (as opposed to the masquerade which hides her nothing-

ness) is a dangerous and regressive dare, if thought of only from the
sightlines of the crowds of male spectators shouting upwards, "Jump!
Jump!" As I have written elsewhere, the pitfalls of a cultural politics
based on a voluntaristic female hysteria seem evident. But the
assumption of death, risk, and invisibility may be the price of moving
beyond a narrow politics of identity and place. Žižek's description of
the male traversing of fantasy space, and the resulting loss of sightlines and coordinates in that moment when the heroine of these hysterical spectacles is "assuming *her own* fate," (Žižek, 66) not only
suggests a radical "male subjectivity at the margins,"[73] but also suggests, in the terms elaborated by Judith Butler, an understanding of
performativity as a compulsory practice but not one that forecloses
agency.[74] To "assume one's own fate" in this instance is not a deliberate, willful choice made by an already existing (female) subject.
Identity is "assumed" within the compulsory enactment of falling, a
reversal of the usual metaphors of coming into visibility as the model
of empowerment and liberation.

The cinematic examples offered above have been surpassed implic-
itly in contemporary feminist performance which assumes an "*active
vanishing*" which Peggy Phelan descibes as "a conscious refusal to take
the payoff of visibility."[75] In experimental critical writing, the unusual
tactic of spectacularizing the nonvisible has been extremely effective
in thematizing the absent subject. A striking example is contained in
Sue-Ellen Case's witty evocation of the impatient "lesbian vampire" as
a ghostly double waiting representationally offstage.[76]

Eve Kosofsky Sedgwick, who frequently uses the image of her body
to suggest the complexities and tensions of identity politics, describes
another kind of active vanishing. Here again is the fallen woman, but
this time not one who has plunged or tumbled from a great height,
but one who under the multiple influences of heat, excitement, and
the residual effects of surgery and chemotherapy simply sits down in a
faint. She is marching at a public demonstration in the Summer of
1991 in North Carolina, protesting the the local PBS station's censor-
ship of *Tongues Untied,* a film by Marlon Riggs which presents images

of Black gay men in the U.S. A large, pale, white woman, dressed in a
black ACT-UP tee-shirt with the SILENCE=DEATH graphic across her
chest, she is standing (up) for the "apparently unrepresentably dangerous and endangered conjunction, *queer* and *black*," and she is,
however inadvertantly, about to stand down, resign from, be cut out
of this political frame of reference:

> After awhile I could tell I was feeling tired and dizzy; sensibly I sat
> down. There was something so absorbing and so radically hetero-
> geneous about this space of protest that when, next thing I knew,
> the urgent sound of my name and a slowly-dawning sense of dis-
> orientation suggested that I seemed very oddly to be stretched out
> in the dirt—coming to—surfacing violently from the deep pit of
> another world—with a state trooper taking my pulse and an ambu-
> lance already on the way—the gaping unbridgeable hole left in my
> own consciousness felt like a mis-en-abîme image of the whole
> afternoon; not least because the image, a compelling one on which
> both TV cameras were sightlines ("Now *that's* censorship," the TV
> people rumbled, with some justice)—that image, of a mountain-
> ous figure, supine, black-clad, paper-white, weirdly bald (since my
> nice African hat had pitched to a distance), SILENCE=DEATH
> emblazoned, motionless, apparently female, uncannily gravid with
> meaning, but with what possible meaning? what usable meaning?,
> was available to everybody there except herself.[77]

Both Case and Sedgwick have produced excessive bodies, and each
in a different way has suggested the cruel protocols of exclusion and
invisibility which govern contemporary political spectacle. The compulsory demand to "produce the body" as the *sine qua non* of identity—to prove that a person or a group is "represented" in the political
and technological sense—is answered uncannily with images that are
in and out of sight simultaneously. Sedgwick's image points, as well, to
the narrative inadvertencies which produce images of the self that
unpredictably and unconsciously stand *as* and *for* others. What new
model of sociality could accomodate these improvisatory ensembles
of accidental bodies?

A Final Stunt and an Animal Act

In the modernist conflation of a certain female iconography with bourgeois ideology, freedom is often uncritically conceived as limitless space, transcendence, newness, individualism, and upward mobility of various kinds. Contemporary theories of spatiality and power have suggested, on the contrary, that space is socially and materially saturated whatever its dimensionality. No space is too small to replicate, or, to begin to overthrow structures of power, no space is too large (here read the United States as offering itself to the world as the model of freedom) to dissolve constraints effortlessly. What might substitute for this expansionist model? Can one locate the philobatic imagination within the confines of the grotesque?

In *Kafka, or Minor Literature*, Gilles Deleuze and Felix Guattari suggest a more limited and ironic concept of the "line of escape" or "way out" as a reformulation of freedom.[78] They refer to Kafka's short story, "A Report to an Academy," in which a "former ape" who has been forced into captivity describes the very grotesque absurdity of the trapeze act as uncanny, mimetic performance:

> I fear that perhaps you do not quite understand what I mean by "way out." I use the expression in its fullest and most popular sense. I deliberately do not use the word "freedom." I do not mean the spacious feeling of freedom on all sides. As an ape, perhaps, I knew that, and I have met men who yearn for it. But for my part I desired such freedom neither then nor now. In passing: may I say that all too often men are betrayed by the word freedom. And as freedom is counted among the most sublime feelings, so the corresponding disillusionment can be also sublime. In variety theaters I have often watched, before my turn came on, a couple of acrobats performing on trapezes high in the roof. They swung themselves, they rocked to and fro, they sprang into the air, they floated into each other's arms, one hung by the hair from the teeth of the other. "And that too is human freedom" I thought, "self-controlled movement." What a mockery of holy Mother Nature! Were the apes to see such a spectacle, no theater walls could stand the shock of their laughter.

No, freedom was not what I wanted. Only a way out; right or left, or in any direction; I made no other demand; even should the way out prove to be an illusion; the demand was a small one, the disappointment could be no bigger. To get out! Only not to stay motionless with raised arms, crushed against a wooden wall.[79]

What the ape sees in the circus act (retrospectively, since he has gone some way in becoming human through careful imitation) is the ludicrousness of the humanistic ideal of freedom as "self-controlled motion." From his perspective, the "positive biological discontinuity" which holds spectators in awe looks like a hilarious parody, an awkward imitation of animal grace and exuberance. Human freedom looks like the adaptive, mimetic behavior of trained animals—a form of self-defense which is finally less vital than entropic. The much sought after differentiation of the species—freedom as that which makes "us" human—turns out to be another version of imprisonment: the animal act is always dangerously contiguous to the trapeze, the clown is always around somewhere taking his pratfalls, the "odd, frightening women" are stashed somewhere in the sideshow. These grotesque and "inhuman" exhibitions are never left entirely behind by the enactments of freedom in the air because the very idea of freedom as a flight from the bodily takes wing, so to speak, from the very shapes and movements it would leave behind.

2

Female Grotesques

Carnival and Theory

Pretext

There is a phrase that still resonates from childhood. Who says it? The mother's voice—not my own mother's, perhaps, but the voice of an aunt, an older sister, or the mother of a friend. It is a harsh, matronizing phrase, directed towards the behavior of other women:

"She" [the other woman] is making a spectacle out of herself.

Making a spectacle out of oneself seemed a specifically feminine danger. The danger was of an exposure. Men, I learned somewhat later in life, "exposed themselves," but that operation was quite deliberate and circumscribed. For a woman, making a spectacle out of herself had more to do with a kind of inadvertency and loss of boundaries: the possessors of large, aging, and dimpled thighs displayed at the public beach, of overly rouged cheeks, of a voice shrill in laughter, or of a sliding bra strap—a loose dingy bra strap especially—were at once caught out by fate and blameworthy. It was my impression that these women had done something wrong, had stepped, as it were, into the limelight out of turn—too young or too old, too early or too late—and yet anyone, any *woman,* could make a spectacle out of herself if she was not careful. It is a feature of my own history and education that in contemplating these dangers, I grew to admire both the extreme strategies of the cool, silent, and cloistered St. Clare (enclosed, with a room of her own) and the lewd, exuberantly parodistic Mae West.

Although the models, of course, change, there is a way in which radical negation, silence, withdrawal, and invisibility, and the bold affirmations of feminine performance, imposture, and masquerade (purity and danger) have suggested cultural politics for women.

Theory of Carnival
and the Carnival of Theory

The above extremes are not mutually exclusive, and in various and interesting ways they have figured around each other. Feminist theory, and cultural production more generally, have most recently brought together these strategies in approaching the questions of difference and the reconstruction or counterproduction of knowledge. In particular, the impressive amount of work across the discourse of carnival, or, more properly, the carnivalesque—much of it in relation to the work of Bakhtin[1]—has translocated the issues of bodily exposure and containment, disguise and gender masquerade, abjection and marginality, parody and excess, to the field of the social constituted as a symbolic system. Seen as a productive category, affirmative and celebratory (a Nietzschean gay science), the discourse of carnival moves away from modes of critique from some Archimedean point of authority without, to models of transformation and counterproduction situated within the social system and symbolically at its margins.[2]

The reintroduction of the body and categories of the body (in the case of carnival, the "grotesque body") into the realm of what is called the "political" has been a central concern of feminism. What is of great interest at this critical conjuncture is the assessment of how materials on carnival as historical performance may be configured with materials on carnival as semiotic performance; in other words, how the relation between the symbolic and cultural constructs of femininity and Womanness, and the experience of *women* (as variously identified and subject to multiple determinations), might be brought together towards a dynamic model of a new social subjectivity. The early work of Julia Kristeva on semiotics, subjectivity, and textual rev-

Fig. 9 Jacqueline Hayden, "Figure Model Series" 1991–92. Aging and excess as female performance. By permission of the artist.

Fig. 10   Jacqueline Hayden, "Figure Model Series" 1991–92. By permission of
the artist.

olution, and the more recent contributions of Teresa de Lauretis in
mapping the terrain of a genuinely sociological and feminist semiotics, are crucial to this undertaking.[3] This project is the grand one.
More modestly, an examination of the materials on carnival can also
recall limitations, defeats, and indifferences generated by carnival's
complicitous place in dominant culture. There are especial dangers
for women and other excluded or marginalized groups within carnival, though even the double jeopardy that I will describe may suggest
an ambivalent redeployment of taboos around the female body as
grotesque (the pregnant body, the aging body, the irregular body),
and as unruly when set loose in the public sphere.

Not at all surprisingly, much of the early work on carnival in
anthropology and social history dates from the late sixties, when
enactments of popular protest, counterculture, experimental theater,
and multimedia art were all together suggestive of the energies and
possibilities of unlimited cultural and social transformation. In many
ways, this chapter is generated from the cultural surplus of that era.
The work of Mary Douglas and Victor Turner—which was as influen-

Fig. 11   Jacqueline Hayden, "Figure Model Series" 1991–92. By permission of
the artist.

tial in social history as, more recently, the work of Clifford Geertz—
saw in the human body the prototype of society, the nation-state, and
the city, and in the social dramas of transition and "rituals of status
reversal" evidence of the reinforcement of social structure, hierarchy,
and order through inversion.[4] In liminal states, thus, temporary loss
of boundaries tends to redefine social frames, and such topsy-turvy
or time out is inevitably set back on course. This structural view of
carnival as essentially conservative is both strengthened and enlarged
by historical analysis, which tends, of course, to be the political
history of domination. The extreme difficulty of producing lasting
social change does not diminish the usefulness of these symbolic
models of transgression, and the histories of subaltern and counter-
productive cultural activity are never as neatly closed as structural
models might suggest.

Natalie Davis, in what remains the most interesting piece on carnival and gender, "Women on Top," argues dialectically that in early
modern Europe, carnival and the image of carnivalesque woman
"undermined as well as reinforced" the renewal of existing social
structure:

> The image of the disorderly woman did not always function to keep
> women in their place. On the contrary, it was a multivalent image
> that could operate, first, to widen behavioral options for women
> within and even outside marriage, and second, to sanction riot and
> political disobedience for both men and women in a society that
> allowed the lower orders few formal means of protest. Play with an
> unruly woman is partly a chance for temporary release from the tra-
> ditional and stable hierarchy; but it is also part of the conflict over
> efforts to change the basic distribution of power within society.[5]

Among Davis' very interesting examples of the second possibility—
that is, the image of the unruly or carnivalesque woman actually
working to incite and embody popular uprisings—are the Wiltshire
enclosure riots of 1641, where rioting men were led by male cross-
dressers who called themselves "Lady Skimmington" (a skimmington
was a ride through the streets mocking a henpecked husband, the

name probably referring to the big skimming ladle that could be used for husband beatings).[6] The projection of the image of the fierce virago onto popular movements, especially a movement such as this one, involving the transgression of boundaries, is suggestive from the point of view of social transformation. What may it tell us about the construction of the female subject in history within this political symbology? Merely to sketch out the obvious problems in working toward an answer to this question, one might begin with the assumption that the history of the enclosure riots and the image of the unruly woman are not direct reflections of one another; both contain ambiguities and gender asymmetries that require historical and textual readings.

These readings are difficult in both areas. First, the history of popular movements has been largely the history of men; a stronger history of women in mixed and autonomous uprisings is needed to assess the place of women as historical subjects in relation to such uprisings.[7] Second, as a form of representation, masquerade of the feminine (what psychoanalytic theory will insist is femininity par excellence) has its distinct problems. The carnivalized woman such as Lady Skimmington, whose comic female masquerade of those "feminine" qualities of strident wifely aggression, behind whose skirts men are protected and provoked to action, is an image that, however counterproduced, perpetuates the dominant (and, in this case, misogynistic) representation of women by men. In the popular tradition of this particular example, Lady Skimmington is mocked alongside her henpecked husband, for she embodies the despised aspects of "strong" femininity, and her subordinate position in society is, in part, underlined in this enactment of power reversal.

Furthermore, although the origins of this image in male-dominated culture may be displaced, there remain questions of enactment and gender-layering. Are women who have taken on this role (as opposed to men cross-dressing) as effective as male cross-dressers? Or is it, like the contemporary "straight" drag of college boys in the amateur theatricals of elite universities, a clear case of sanctioned play for men, always risking self-contempt for women to put on "the feminine?"[8] In

addition, one must ask of any representation other questions—questions of style, genre, and contextuality which may cut across the issue
of gender. Is the parodistic and hyperbolic style of Lady Skimmington
as a leader of men a sign of insurgency and lower-class solidarity for
women and men? Does this comic female style work to free women
from a more confining aesthetic? Or are women again so identified
with style itself that they are as estranged from its liberatory and
transgressive effects as they are from their own bodies as signs in culture generally? In what sense can women really produce or make spectacles of themselves?

Historical inquiry may yield instances of performance (symbolic
and political) that may bypass the pessimism of psychoanalytically
oriented answers to this last question, but only if that history begins to
understand the complexity of treating signifying systems and "events"
together.[9] In this regard, even the work on female political iconography and social movements by very distinguished social historians,
such as Maurice Agulhon and Eric Hobsbawm, remains problematic.[10] This methodological difficulty does not prevent historians from
becoming increasingly aware of gender differences in relation to the
carnivalesque. Other social historians have documented the insight of
the anthropologist Victor Turner, that the marginal position of
women and others in the "indicative" world makes their presence in
the "subjunctive" or possible world of the topsy-turvy carnival "quin-
tessentially" dangerous; in fact, as Emmanuel Le Roy Ladurie shows in
Carnival at Romans, Jews were stoned, and there is evidence that
women were raped during carnival festivities.[11] In other words, in the
everyday indicative world, women and their bodies, certain bodies, in
certain public framings, in certain public spaces, are always already
transgressive—dangerous, and in danger.

With these complexities no doubt in mind, Davis concluded her
brilliant article with the hope that "the woman on top might even facilitate innovation in historical theory and political behavior" (Davis,
131). Since the writing of her article, the conjuncture of a powerful
women's movement and feminist scholarship has facilitated further

interrogation of the relationship between symbology and social change. The figure of the female transgressor as public spectacle is still powerfully resonant, and the possibilities of redeploying this representation as a demystifying or utopian model have not been exhausted.

The Carnivalesque Body

Investigation of linguistic and culture contexts in relation to categories of carnival and the body have been inspired recently by a new reception in English-speaking countries of the work of Bakhtin. Like the work of Davis and Le Roy Ladurie, Bakhtin's work on carnival is at one level an historical description of carnival in early modern Europe. It offers, as well, a prescriptive model of a socialist collectivity.

In the introduction to his study of Rabelais, Bakhtin enumerates three forms of carnival folk culture: ritual spectacles (which include feasts, pageants, and marketplace festivals of all kinds); comic verbal compositions, including parodies both oral and written; and various genres of billingsgate (curses, oaths, profanations, marketplace speech). The laughter of carnival associated with these spectacles and unconstrained speech in the Middle Ages was, for Bakhtin, entirely positive. The Romantic period, in contrast, saw laughter "cut down to cold humor, irony, sarcasm" (*RW*, 37–38). The privatism and individualism of this later humor made it unregenerative and lacking in communal hilarity. Without pretense to historical neutrality, Bakhtin's focus on carnival in early modern Europe contains a critique of modernity and its stylistic effects as a radical diminishment of the possibilities of human freedom and cultural production. He considers the culture of modernity to be as austere and bitterly isolating as the official religious culture of the Middle Ages, which he contrasts with the joy and heterogeneity of carnival and the carnivalesque style and spirit. Bakhtin's view of Rabelais and carnival is, in some ways, nostalgic for a socially diffuse oppositional context which has been lost, but which is perhaps more importantly suggestive of a future social horizon that may release new possibilities of speech and social perform-

Fig. 12   May Stevens, "Go Gentle," 1983 (Detail). A painting of the artist's
mother from the Ordinary/Extraordinary series. The painful and defiant
gestures of the institutionalized Alice Stevens seem to interrupt the narrative spaces of her "ordinary" life. By permission of the artist.

ance. The categories of carnivalesque speech and spectacle are heterogeneous, in that they contain the protocols and styles of high culture
in and from a position of debasement. The masks and voices of carnival resist, exaggerate, and destabilize the distinctions and boundaries
that mark and maintain high culture and organized society. It is as if
the carnivalesque body politic had ingested the entire corpus of high
culture and, in its bloated and irrepressible state, released it in fits and
starts in all manner of recombination, inversion, mockery, and degradation. The political implications of this heterogeneity are obvious: it
sets carnival apart from the merely oppositional and reactive. Carnival
and the carnivalesque suggest a redeployment or counterproduction
of culture, knowledge, and pleasure. In its multivalent oppositional
play, carnival refuses to surrender the critical and cultural tools of the
dominant class, and in this sense, carnival can be seen, above all, as a
site of insurgency, and not merely withdrawal.

   The central category around which Bakhtin organizes his reading of
Rabelais as a carnivalesque text is "grotesque realism," with particular
emphasis on the grotesque body. The grotesque body is the open, protruding, extended, secreting body, the body of becoming, process, and

change. The grotesque body is opposed to the Classical body which is
monumental, static, closed, and sleek, corresponding to the aspirations of bourgeois individualism; the grotesque body is connected to
the rest of the world. Bakhtin finds his concept of the grotesque embodied in the Kerch terracotta figurines of senile, pregnant hags. Here
is Bakhtin describing the figurines:

> This is typical and very strongly expressed grotesque. It is ambiva-
> lent. It is pregnant death, a death that gives birth. There is nothing
> completed, nothing calm and stable in the bodies of these old hags.
> They combine senile, decaying, and deformed flesh with the flesh
> of new life, conceived but as yet unformed . . . Moreover, the old
> hags are laughing (*RW*, 25–26).

Homologously, the grotesque body is the figure of the socialist state
to come, a state unfinished, which, as it "outgrows itself, transgresses
its own limits" (*RW*, 26). For Bakhtin, this body is, as well, a model for
carnival language; a culturally productive linguistic body in constant
semiosis. But, for the feminist reader, this image of the pregnant hag is
more than ambivalent. It is loaded with all of the connotations of fear
and loathing around the biological processes of reproduction and of
aging. Bakhtin, like many other social theorists of the nineteenth and
twentieth centuries, fails to acknowledge or incorporate the social
relations of gender in his semiotic model of the body politic, and thus
his notion of the Female Grotesque remains in all directions repressed
and undeveloped.

Yet, Bakhtin's description of these ancient crones is at least exuber-
ant. Almost to prove his point about the impossibility of collective
mirth over such images in the period of late capitalism here, in contrast, the voice of Paul Céline: "Women you know, they wane by candlelight, they spoil, melt, twist, ooze! [. . . The end of tapers is a
horrible sight, the end of ladies too . . .]"[12] Quoted and glossed by
Julia Kristeva as a portrait of "a muse in the true tradition of the lowly
genres—apocalyptic, Menippean, and carnavalesque," this passage
suggests the dark festival of transgression which she charts in *Powers*

of Horror (Kristeva, 169). This book—which contrasts with her indispensable application of Bakhtin in, for instance, "Word, Dialogue,
and the Novel" and *Polylogue*—draws on Mary Douglas' categories of
purity and defilement to arrive, through the analytical processes of
transference, at the brink of abjection.

Through the convolutions of Céline's relentlessly misogynist and
anti-Semitic writing, Kristeva as author and problematized subject has
projected herself towards the grotesque, which she sees as the "undoer
of narcissism and of all imaginary identity as well" (Kristeva, 208). As
Kristeva focuses on Céline, her own text increasingly takes on his
rhetoric of abjection, which interestingly comes to rest in the category
of the maternal. Kristeva writes: "Abject . . . the jettisoned object is radically excluded and draws me toward the place where meaning col-
lapses . . . on the edge of non-existence and hallucination" (Kristeva,
2). And elsewhere: "Something maternal . . . bears upon the uncertainty of what I call abjection" (Kristeva, 208). The fascination with the
maternal body in childbirth, the fear of and repulsion from it throughout the chosen texts of Céline, constitutes it here again as a privileged
site of liminality and defilement. Kristeva writes:

> When Céline locates the ultimate of abjection—and thus the
> supreme and sole interest of literature—in the birth-giving scene,
> he makes amply clear which fantasy is involved: something *horrible
> to see* at the impossible doors of the invisible—the mother's body.
> The scene of scenes is here not the so-called primal scene but the
> one of giving birth, incest turned inside out, flayed identity. Giving
> birth: the height of bloodshed and life, scorching moment of hesi-
> tation (between inside and outside, ego and other, life and death),
> horror and beauty, sexuality and the blunt negation of the sexual
> . . . At the doors of the feminine, at the doors of abjection, as I
> defined the term earlier, we are also, with Céline, given the most
> daring X-ray of the "drive foundations" of fascism (Kristeva,
> 155–156).[13]

While there are many general reasons for questioning the use of
the maternal in recent French criticism, here I think the point may be

that the accumulated horror and contempt these descriptions of
the maternal body suggest generate a subliminal defense of the maternal, which then reemerges in Kristeva as an idealized category far
from the realities of motherhood as a construction or as a lived experience. Jews, unlike mothers, would seem to merely drop out of the
field of abjection, as the anti-Semitism of Céline becomes for Kristeva
a problem of maintaining the categorical imperatives of identity and
the political.[14]

The book ends on a note of mystical subjectivity: near "the quiet
shore of contemplation," far from the polis (Kristeva, 210). On the
verge, at the limit of this avant-garde frontier, there remains only
writing.[15] Peter Stallybrass and Allon White, in their book on the politics and poetics of transgression, have called the exclusion of the
already marginalized in moves such as these "displaced abjection."[16]
As I have argued, both in the history of carnival and in its theory, the
category of the female body as grotesque (in, for instance, pregnancy
or aging) brings to light just such displacements. How this category
might be used affirmatively to destabilize the idealizations of female
beauty, or to realign the mechanism of desire, is discussed elsewhere
in this book.[17]

Carnival of Theory

There has been, as well, a carnival of theory at the discursive level, in
the poetics of postmodernist criticism and feminist writing. This has
included all manner of textual travesty, "mimetic rivalry," semiotic
delinquency, parody, teasing, posing, flirting, masquerade, seduction,
counter-seduction, tightrope walking, and verbal aerialisms of all
kinds. Performances of displacement, double displacements, and more
have permeated much feminist writing in our attempts to muscle in on
the discourses of Lacanian psychoanalysis, deconstruction, and avant-
garde writing and postmodernist visual art. It could even be said, with
reservation, that in relation to academic institutions, what has come to
be called "theory" has constituted a kind of carnival space. The practice

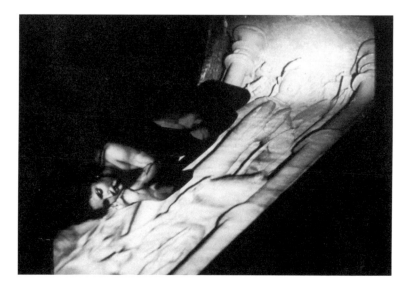

Fig. 13   Sutapa Biswas, "Synapse Series," 1992. In an intercultural palimpsest, the artist projects Indian temple images (which Hegel identified with the grotesque) with images of her own body as layered narratives of memory and displacement. By permission of the artist.

of criticism informed by this theory has taken great license stylistically, and in its posing posed a threat of sorts.

It is interesting to consider the discourse of carnival and poststructuralism together. In 1980, Michèle Richman, in her essay, "Sex and Signs: Language of French Feminist Criticism," saw in the proliferation of literature on festival in France a reaction primarily to structuralism and to the structuralist economy of exchange within which, as Lévi-Strauss described it, women circulate as signs but are not theorized as sign producers.[18] The festival or carnival discourse drew upon the work of Marcel Mauss (and, as importantly, on the writing of Georges Bataille) on the gift, or *dépense,* as that which exceeds this linguistically modelled economy. As Richman indicates, the discussion of *dépense* was relocated within a more general libidinal economy of desire. The generosity of femininity and feminine writing (*écriture féminine*) is privileged over male *dépense,* which is understood as being simultaneously a demand. The female body is the site of this desirous excess.

In terms strikingly similar to Bakhtin's formulation of the grotesque body as continuous process, Hélène Cixous calls it "the body without beginning and without end."[19] Female sexuality and especially the mother's body, as it figures simultaneously demarcation and dissolution of identity, serve this cultural project of disrupting the political economy of the sign as it is produced in dominant discourse. This écriture féminine, which has been admirably discussed elsewhere by U.S. feminists, can be and has been done by men (in fact, modernist writers such as Joyce are often mentioned as models); how the male-authored or travestied "feminine" is different, and how the inscription of the female body in the texts produced by women may be usefully contextualized elsewhere, are still important and unanswered questions, although the critiques of this feminization of writing as essentialist must be taken into account in reconsiderations of these topics.[20] Beyond essentialism there are, as I have indicated earlier, other historical and anthropological warnings to heed. Even within France, there have been critiques of the feminine textual festival. Annie Leclerc has chided the "delirious adulators of the festival," and Hélène Cixous and Catherine Clément in The Newly Born Woman parallel the carnivalesque with hysterical crisis. In terms similar to earlier critiques of carnival, they see the cultural category of hysteria

> as the only form of contestation possible in certain types of social organization, within the context of the village community; it is also a safety valve. This language not yet at the point of verbal expression, restrained within the bond of the body . . . remains convulsive. Men look but they do not hear.[21]

Historically, Cixous and Clément are right: Hysterics and madwomen generally have ended up in the attic or in the asylum, their gestures of pain and defiance having served only to put them out of circulation. As a figure of representation, however, hysteria may be less recuperable.

The famous photographs commissioned by Charcot, which chart the various stages in the patients of Salpêtrière, fix in attitude and gesture, in grimaces and leaps, a model of performance not unlike the fashionable histrionics of the great Romantic actresses and circus artists of the late nineteenth century. These paid performers were, like women hysterics, "seen but not heard," in one sense, since the scene of their livelihood, their context, it can be argued, was arranged by and for the male viewer. Nonetheless, they used their bodies in public, in extravagant ways that could have only provoked wonder and ambivalence in the female viewer, as such latitude of movement and attitude was not permitted most women without negative consequences.

This hyperbolic style, this "overacting," like the staged photographs of Salpêtrière (whatever Charcot's claims were to scientific documentation), can be read as double representations: as mimicries of the somatizations of the women patients whose historical performances were lost to themselves and recuperated into the medical science and medical discourse which maintain their oppressive hold on women. The photographs of Salpêtrière especially strike us as uncanny because of the repetitiveness of the hysterical performance. It is not only the content of the hysterical behavior that strikes us as grotesque, but its representation: if hysteria is a dis-play, these photographs display the display. If hysteria is understood as feminine in its image, accoutrements, and stage business (rather than its physiology), then it may be used to rig us up (for lack of the phallic term) into discourse. The possibility, indeed the necessity, of using the female body in this sense allows for the distance necessary for articulation. Luce Irigaray describes this provisional strategy as follows:

> To play with mimesis is thus, for a women, to try to recover the place of her exploitation by discourse, without allowing herself simply to be reduced to it. It means to resubmit herself—inasmuch as she is on the side of "perceptible," of "matter"—to "ideas," in particular to ideas about herself, that are elaborated in/by masculine logic, but so as to make "visible," by an effect of playful repeti-

tion, what was supposed to remain invisible: the cover-up of a possible operation of the feminine in language. It also means to "unveil" the fact that, if women are such good mimics, it is because they are not simply reabsorbed into this function.[22]

What is called mimesis here is elsewhere, with various modifications, called masquerade (Irigaray herself reserves the latter term to refer negatively to the false position of women experiencing desire only as male desire for them). Female sexuality as masquerade is a well-noted psychoanalytic category. Jacques Lacan, a great *poseur* himself, has written of female sexuality as masking a lack, pretending to hide what is, in fact, not there:

> Paradoxical as this formulation might seem, I would say that it is in order to be the phallus, that is to say, the signifier of desire of the Other, that the woman will reject an essential part of her femininity, notably all its attributes through masquerade. It is for what she is not that she expects to be desired as well as loved.[23]

The mask here is seen as feminine (for men and women), rather than something that hides a stable feminine identity. Femininity is a mask which masks nonidentity. According to Lacan, that produces an unexpected side effect for the man anxious to appear manly:

> The fact that femininity takes refuge in this mask, because of the *Verdrangung* inherent to the phallic mark of desire, has the strange consequence that, in the human being, virile display itself appears as feminine (Lacan, 85).

In film theory Mary Anne Doane has problematized the female spectator, using the essay of Joan Riviere on "Womanliness and Masquerade."[24] Her argument is that masquerade can "manufacture a distance from the image, to generate a problematic within which the image is manipulable, producible, and readable by women."[25] It is, in other words, a way around the theorization of the spectator only in

terms of the male gaze, and the male categories of voyeurism and
fetishistic pleasure. More generally, Doane's discussion of Riviere is
extremely useful in explaining the asymmetries of transvestism,
which, for a woman, has always been necessary, in some sense, in
order for her to take part in a man's world. For a woman to dress, act,
or position herself in discourse as a man is easily understandable and
culturally compelling. To "act like a woman" beyond narcissism and
masochism is, for psychoanalytic theory, trickier. That is the critical
and hopeful power of masquerade. Deliberately assumed and foregrounded, femininity as a mask, for a man, is a take-it-or-leave-it
proposition; for a woman, a similar flaunting of the feminine is a take-
it-*and*-leave-it *possibility*. To put on femininity with a vengeance suggests the power of taking it off.

These considerations account for some of the interest in masquerade for those contemporary artists and critics whose work on imposture and dissimulation tends to stress the constructed, invented, and
(to use Gayatri Spivak's wonderful phrase) the "scrupulously fake."[26]
Spivak reads Nietzsche's characterization of female sexual pleasure as
masquerade ("They 'give themselves,' even when they—give themselves. The female is so artistic") as an originary displacement, oc-
cluding "an unacknowledged envy: a man cannot fake an orgasm"
(Spivak, 170).[27] Reading Derrida, she sees the figure of woman displaced twice over. "Double displacement," she suggests, might be
undone in carefully fabricated "useful and scrupulously fake readings
in place of the passively active fake orgasm." Such readings may suggest new ways of making new spectacles of oneself.

Other work on masquerade has a more explicitly sociopolitical
dimension, which greatly enriches psychoanalytic and deconstructive
approaches to the material (I am thinking, for instance, of Dick
Hebdige's work on subculture and Homi Bhabha's work on mimicry
and the colonial subject).[28] For feminist theory, particularly, a more
specifically historical and social use of masquerade may be needed,
perhaps in the context of larger discussions of social groups and categories of the feminine mask in colonized and subcultural contexts, or

in relation to other guises of the carnivalesque body. Nonetheless, the hyperboles of masquerade and carnival suggest, at least, some preliminary "acting out" of the dilemmas of femininity.

General Laughter and the Laughter of Carnival

Feminist theory itself has been travestied, hidden and unacknowledged in many discussions of subjectivity and gender. It is part of what Elaine Showalter has called "critical cross-dressing."[29] The fathers of French theory alluded to here are, in fact, all masters of *mise-en-scène*. Even Derrida, whose persona has been more diffidently drawn in his writings, has been recently showcased as a carnival master.

The interview with Derrida published in *Critical Exchange*, in which he speaks of women and feminism, is quite as interesting for what he says about feminists as for the *mise-en-scène*.[30] Derrida restates his reservations about feminism as a form of phallogocentrism (fair enough). Later, he says that feminism is tantamount to phallogocentrism (not so fair).[31] James Creech, who edited and translated the interview, states that he attempted "to reproduce its conversational tone, with interruptions, ellipses, suspensions and laughter that marked a very cordial and freeform discussion. Essentially nothing has been edited out, and the reader can follow the subtext of associations which lead from one moment of discussion to another." (Creech, et. al, 30) The transcription is punctuated by parenthetical laughter and occasionally in bold face "General Laughter." For instance:

> . . . certain feminists, certain women struggling in the name of feminism—may see in deconstruction only what will not allow itself to be feminist. That's why they try to constitute a sort of target, a silhouette, a shooting gallery almost, where they spot phallocentrism and beat up on it [*tappent dessus*]. Just as Said and others constitute an enemy in the image [LAUGHTER] of that against which they have ready arms, in the same way, I think certain feminists as they begin to read certain texts, focus on particular themes out of haste

and say, "Well, there you have it . . ." (I don't know exactly who one
could think of in this regard, but I know it goes on.) In France I
recall a very violent reaction from a feminist who upon reading
Spurs and seeing the multiplication of phallic images—spurs,
umbrellas, etc.—said, "So, it's a phallocentric text," and started
kicking up a violent fuss, charging about like a bull perhaps . . .
    [GENERAL LAUGHTER] (*Critical Exchange*, 30)

This is a startling scene—the feminist as raging bull: ("I don't know
exactly who one can think of in this regard, but I know it goes on").
The bull in the shooting gallery, spotting and targeting, "kicking up a
violent fuss, charging about." Is this textual spotting and targeting a
reverse image? Is phallogocentrism really tantamount to feminism
here? Is this a male dressed as a female dressing as a male? What kind
of drag is this? Who is waving the red flag? And, who must join this
"general laughter"? The laughter of carnival is communal and sponta-
neous, but general laughter in this context is coercive, and like much
comedy, participated in by the marginalized only in an effort to pass.
But it can be heard from another position.

A counter scene is offered in the films of Yvonne Rainer, whose past
as a performance artist puts her in a particularly good position to stage
theory and intellectual comedy. In her 1985 film *The Man Who Envied
Women* ("I don't know exactly who one can think of in this regard, but
I know it goes on"), the man stands behind a female student, his hands
gripping her shoulders as she asks the difference between the subject-
in-process and the everyday individual with choices and identifications
to make. He replies (paraphrasing Foucault): in the very enactment of
the power relations which are being almost simultaneously affirmed
and denied.

In another Rainer film, *Journeys from Berlin/1971* (1980), the joke is
Jean-Paul Sartre's in another interview. Reference is made to Sartre's
trip to West Germany to visit the imprisoned terrorists awaiting trial.
When asked why he only visited the cell of Andreas Baader and not
that of his accomplice Ulrike Meinhoff, he replies, "The gang is called
Baader-Meinhoff not Meinhoff-Baader, isn't it?" In the voice over, two

people laugh, the man because he is pleased with the old intellectual's intellectual prowess, the woman because she hears the joke as on Sartre himself in decadence.

What Rainer stages is a dialogical laughter, the laughter of intertext and multiple identifications. It is the conflictual laughter of social subjects in a classist, racist, ageist, sexist society. It is the laughter we have now: other laughter for other times. Carnival and carnival laughter remain on the horizon with a new social subjectivity.

For now, right now, as I acknowledge the work of feminists in reconstituting knowledge, I imagine us going forward, growing old (I hope), or being grotesque in other ways. I see us viewed by ourselves and others, in our bodies and in our work, in ways that are continuously shifting the terms of viewing, so that looking at us, there will be a new question, the question that never occurred to Bakhtin in front of the Kerch terracotta figurines—Why *are* these old hags laughing?

Freaks,
Freak Orlando,
Orlando

3

The freak leaves us   bereft, forcing a little
Mutilation somewhere   to set things right
To wreak   penance
To set   the freak flags flying.
—Cynthia Macdonald, "Celebrating the Freak"[1]

But I'm going to wave my freak flag high, high.
—Jimi Hendrix, "If 6 Was 9"[2]

WHAT IS NOW CALLED "IDENTITY POLITICS" may be traced to the 1960's identification of and with the "freak." Radically democratic and open to the most individualistic self-appropriations of class, race, ethnicity, gender, and sexuality, "freakiness" is a distinctly U.S. style of dissent. Although the tradition of the freak as monster—literally, the de-*monstrater* of the marvelous power of the divine—has a long history in European culture, the demonstrations of the sixties in the United States were characterized by a new articulation of heterogeneous social groups, and by a mixing of external and internal demands for dramatic visibility. Being a freak was, and remains, an individual choice for some and an oppressive assignment for others, as in Jimi Hendrix's famous "If 6 Was 9": the "white plastic finger" pointed at Black men like Hendrix, but other, self-designated freaks, pointed at themselves. Strikingly, no particular quality seemed to exclude one definitively from the imaginary community of freaks. For even the "white-collared conservative flashing down the street" or his suburban wife could, and did, "freak out," and the narratives of their rage and mental illnesses were often allegories of conversion to new, better families or communities. The freak ethos required an identification with otherness within the secret self. It also demanded a certain openness to recruits and volunteers. Anyone could march in some guise under the freak flag.

The appropriation of the term "freak" in the 1960s in rock music and street culture as a marker of life-style and identity parallels the powerful, historic detours of words like "black," or more recently "queer," away from their stigmatizing function in the hands of dominant culture, a trajectory that is often described as moving from shame to pride. Only the smallest space is left in these "meaning maps" for ambivalence. "Real Freaks" or "freaks of nature," as the sideshow "curiosities" (Barnum's term) were called, had alternately rejected the term in reaction to the intense ostracism and display of human anomalies as scientific spectacle, and reclaimed it as properly theirs in the face of market extinction as the popular entertainment venues which had featured their bodies as exhibitions began to die out.[3] Threatened with invisibility, the professional freak would often prefer the risk and blame associated with an intensely marked body and identity to the disregard and neglect which had always characterized one particularly hypocritical aspect of bourgeois Anglo-American culture which admonished its children, "Don't stare." In Stalinist Russia and in Nazi Germany, freak shows were banned by the state, displacing the containment of the freak within fairs and circuses to encampments for socially designated anomalies. In the United States, an individualistic culture tended increasingly to ignore "real freaks" and to steal the magic of their spectacularity.

There are many fictional and historical anecdotes which figure freaks as either resisting or taking up the names and stereotypes of dominant culture. In "La patente" (The License), a short story by Luigi Pirandello typifying the Sicilian grotesque, a hunchback with the "evil eye" demands a license to certify his status as a dangerous presence so that he can be paid for avoiding certain public and commercial areas in the village. More recently, in Katherine Dunn's novel, *Geek Love,* a woman who has begun her career as a geek biting off the heads of chickens (though she had a secret wish to be in an aerial act) is persuaded to breed freak children through the ingestion of drugs and insecticides in order to save the family carnival.[4] In other contexts, lines were drawn by communities and subcultures reclaiming the representations of their bodily identities as their own. Towards the end of her life, Diane Arbus, whose photographs of freaks and urban subculture made her a cult figure in her own right, was devastated to receive a letter from the organizers of a convention of midgets in Florida who wrote: "We have our own little person to photograph us."[5]

Leslie Fiedler wrote his important work on this topic, *Freaks: Myths and Images of the Secret Self*, in the wake of the counterculture in 1978.[6] At once a deeply personal and expansive study of freaks and freak culture, Fiedler's chronicle narrates the popular history of freaks from carnivals, circuses and fairs into science fiction and film. Fiedler dedicates his book to "my brother who has no brother" and to "all my brothers who have no brothers," suggesting the alienation and community (or at least fraternity) of freakdom for him. He also acknowledges, preliminarily, that the adoption of the word "freak" by technical non-freaks and the injunction to "Join the United Mutations" (Mothers of Invention) implies "as radical an alteration of consciousness as underlies the politics of black power or neofeminism or gay liberation" (Fiedler, 14–15). Fiedler, in other words, acknowledges here and sporadically throughout his book the shadow presence of those social movements whose programs included a politics of style and counterproduction.

Fiedler's book was written as a "belated tribute" to the director Tod Browning whose film, *Freaks* (1932) was almost as inspirational as Frank Zappa and the Mothers of Invention in advancing the mythology of contemporary freaks. Arbus' biographer, Patricia Bosworth, for instance, reports that the photographer attended repeated showings of the film, often stoned, and "was enthralled because the freaks in the film were not imaginary monsters, but *real*" (Bosworth, 189). Like Arbus and many others who flocked to the revival of the cult which had been banned and then ignored in its own time, Fiedler found the film most remarkable in its use of well-known sideshow performers like Harry Earles and his sister Daisy, who play the dwarfs whose romance is ruined by a "normal" female aerial performer called Cleopatra, and Daisy and Violet Hilton, famous Siamese twins who were making their film debut after a legal fight to win their freedom from the family that bought them as infants. There are very different levels of performance in the film. As Fiedler notes, Harry Earles had other roles in cinema, and here plays a melodramatic role as a rich and betrayed husband. Other performers like Joseph/Josephine (the Half-Man, Half-Woman), Slitzie (the Pin-Head), and Olga Roderick (the Bearded Lady) seemed indistinguishable in their film roles from their "real" parts in sideshows. This documentary aspect of Browning's project has been seen variously as daring, exploitative, and authentic. The conflation of the authentic with the unconventional in the bodies of the freaks in a prevalent (and in my view greatly romanticized) reception of the film tends to ignore the meaning of the film's most spectacularized image: the apparently mutilated body of the "normal woman," Cleopatra, after she has been literally cut down to size for violating the code of the freaks.

Before elaborating on this point, some clarification of the relation-ship between the freak and the grotesque is necessary. If we follow Bakhtin on this point, the distinction is clear. The grotesque body of carnival festivity was not distanced or objectified in relation to an audience. Audiences and performers were the interchangeable parts of an incomplete but imaginable wholeness. The grotesque body was exuberantly and democratically open and inclusive of all possibilities. Boundaries between individuals and society, between genders, be-tween species, and between classes were blurred or brought into crisis in the inversions and hyperbole of carnivalesque representation. Grotesque realism presented a dynamic, materialist, and unflinching view of human bodies in all stages and contours of growth, degenera-tion, anomaly, excess, loss, and prosthesis. The grotesque body had nothing to do with "modern canons" of the body, drawn from science, bourgeois psychology, or nineteenth and twentieth century fictional realism: "The fact is that the new concept of realism has a different way of drawing the boundaries between bodies and objects."[7]

> The new bodily canon, in all its historic variations and different genres, presents an entirely finished, completed, strictly limited body, which is shown from the outside as something individual. That which protrudes, bulges, sprouts, or branches off (when a body transgresses its limits and a new one begins) is eliminated, hidden or moderated. All orifices of the body are closed. The basis of the image is the individual, strictly limited mass, the impenetrable facade (*RW,* 320).

For Bahktin, the new bodily canon extends to codes of speech: "There is a sharp line of division between familiar speech and 'correct' language" (*RW,* 320).

The freak and the grotesque overlap as bodily categories. Susan Stewart, in her wonderful study of culture and scale, has pointed out that "the physiological freak represents the problems of the boundary between self and other (Siamese twins), between male and female (the hermaphrodite), between the body and the world outside the body (the *monstre* par excès), and between the animal and the human (feral and wild men)." Of course, the "physiological freak," like the grotesque, is produced through discursive formations including, but not restricted to, empiricism. "Often referred to as a 'freak of nature,' the freak, it must be emphasized, is a freak of culture."[8] As a cultural representation in the late nineteenth century, the freak belongs to the increasingly codified world of spectacle, appearing in culturally varied venues. Within the confines of spectacle, the freak appears only as a particular image which may appear, reproduce, or simulate the earlier carnivalesque body described and idealized by Bakhtin, but also and more importantly as a bodily construct produced within different social relations. More than merely an image or collection of images, the spectacle is a way of looking, "a world vision which has become objectified."[9]

A spectacle, by definition, requires sight lines and distance. Audiences do not meet up face to face or mask to mask with the spectacle of freaks. Freaks are, by definition, apart, as beings to be viewed. In the traditional sideshow, they are often caged and most often they are silent while a barker narrates their exotic lives. Also, given the history of freaks in the nineteenth and twentieth century (as medical discoveries and exhibitions defined the limits of the normal), it must be remembered that it was the discourse of biology which constituted their status as performers of the objective bodily "truth." Modern biology and empirical social science constituted them as "real." This biological "realness," of course, separates the freak from an earlier, archaic history which viewed them as divine monsters who mediated the natural and cosmic world. This is not to say that freaks are born freaks, only that they are made to seem like "real, living breathing monsters" in the intersection between their presentation in freak shows, photography, cinema, the discourses of biology, and, increasingly, eugenics, all of which supported this illusionism.

Stewart makes an important historical distinction between the grotesque body in earlier times as described by Bakhtin and the grotesque spectacle of the freak show in pointing out that the freak is doubly marked as object and other within the world of spectacle:

> We find the freak inextricably tied to the cultural other—the Little Black Man, the Turkish horse, the Siamese twins (Chang and Eng were, however, the children of Chinese parents living in Siam), the Irish giants . . . The body of the cultural other is by means of this metaphor both naturalized and domesticated in a process we might consider to be characteristic of colonization in general. For all colonization involves the taming of the beast by bestial methods and hence the conversion and projection of the animal and human, difference and identity. On display, the freak represents the naming of the frontier and the assurance that the wilderness, the outside, is now territory (Stewart, 109–110).

Produced historically in the same field of vision, freaks shared the same distancing, scrutiny, classification and exchange value as other colonial and domestic booty as the discourses of medicine, criminology, tourism, advertising, and entertainment converged. In the twentieth century, the discourses of medicine (particularly eugenics)

Fig. 14   Millie and Christine, Siamese Twins. Born into slavery in 1851, the
North Carolina twins were taken to England where they were displayed
as the United African Twins. Courtesy of The Sophia Smith Collection,
Smith College.

contributed increasingly to the ways in which freaks were presented.
Robert Bogdan, in a study of the social history of freak shows, distinguishes between the "exotic" and the "aggrandizing" modes of presenting freaks, the difference, in his example, between presenting the same
giant as a Zulu and as a military figure.[10] The most famous instance of

Fig. 15   Chang and Eng, the original Siamese Twins. Courtesy of the Circus
World Museum, Baraboo, Wisconsin.

the aggrandized model was the aristocratic General Tom Thumb, born Charles Stratton. In Bogdan's chronology of freak shows, he charts an increasing tendency to medicalize the freak so that "by the early twentieth century the audience was learning to view freaks as people who were sick—who had various genetic and endocrine disorders—and the exotic hype lost its appeal."[11] As his own study indicates, however, the hype around freaks never entirely lost its appeal, and exoticism exists in even in the continuing lore of "aliens" and extraterrestrials as monsters to be conquered or adopted.[12] The freak show has always been something of a hybrid production, existing in proximity to other acts in carnival and circus contexts, and within various visual media.

Outside "show business," the role of the freak converged with the social roles available to the racially marked and underclasses—despite the aristocratic and exotic pretensions of their acts. Sometimes the freak was literally a slave. The "North Carolina Twins," Millie and Christine, were born into slavery in 1851, kidnapped, and taken to England where they became "The United African Twins," visiting and delighting, as did so many freaks of the period, Queen Victoria. Later, they returned to the United States through the efforts of their original owner, who reunited them with their family. Eng and Chang, the original Siamese twins, were "discovered" by a Scottish merchant and brought to America by his trading partner. Chang and Eng enjoyed relative prosperity and supported twenty-two children when they retired to the rural South. In an unusual turn, the Siamese twins, like other North Carolina farmers, were said to rely on slave labor themselves.

Violet and Daisy Hilton, who appear in Browning's film, while not literally slaves, were sold by their mother to Mary Hilton, whose family and associates exploited them until they obtained legal representation at twenty-three years of age. Like Millie and Christine, they were multitalented performers and worked in various entertainment venues, joining the ranks of not quite respectable popular performers who lived very modest, if not impoverished, lives after they dropped out of sight.

Although Bakhtin's model of carnival was surely nostalgic and utopian in its portrayal of the social relations of carnival, it more

importantly did not consider the complexities of twentieth century
popular entertainments, advertising, and media. He provides, as
Stewart shows, a very useful model of contrast for considering freaks
in the nineteenth and twentieth century as grotesque spectacles. The
question is not whether or not these modern grotesques are produced
in very different conditions of visibility, but whether, on the one hand,
there is still a model of community available to them which internally
produced that "reciprocal democracy" imagined by Bakhtin, or, on the
other hand, whether that spectacularity embodied by the freak can be
reworked or counterproduced as distinctly twentieth century grotesque
representations, available not only as the post-Freudian "creature features" of the individual psyche gone underground, but as a means of
connection to existing social groups and to new socialities.

Any critical viewer of these materials intent upon keeping things in
their place might simply see the freak as "ruined" by spectacle and
commodification. Fiedler, writing in the seventies, saw in the new
reception of the movie *Freaks* a latter-day tribute, if not worship, of lost
"sacred" monsters by the enchanted youth of the counterculture.
Comparing his own generation with theirs, he writes:

> We all firmly believed in those days that "science" which had failed
> to deliver us from poverty but was already providing us with
> weapons for the next Great War, had desacralized human monsters
> forever. Three decades later, however, Browning's *Freaks* was to be
> revived for a new audience capable of recognizing in the Bearded
> Lady, the Human Caterpillar, and the Dancing Pinhead, Slitzie, the
> last creatures capable of providing the thrill our forebears felt in the
> presence of an equivocal and sacred unity we have since learned to
> secularize and divide (Fiedler, 19).

Fieldler's comment here, and his book generally, is as nostalgic and
idealizing in its way as are aspects of Bakhtin's writings on carnival in
early modern Europe, although it reads much more autobiographi-
cally. The sense of a Romantic belatedness and lost unity in relation to
the sacred world of earlier monsters is prefaced by Fieldler's recollec-
tions of his lost youth: ". . . his movie has played and replayed in my

troubled head so often that merely recalling it, I call up again not only its images, but the response of my then fifteen-year-old self" (Fiedler, 18–19). The thrills and wonderment of seeing "actual" freaks, or imagining oneself as, or in solidarity with, the freaks, is a function, in part, of the recollection of the fantasies of youth. It is an instance, if you will, of the Freudian sublime in renewed proximity to the primitive and the archaic as stand-ins for "the presence of an equivocal and sacred unity we have since learned to secularize and divide."

It could be said that the countercultural production of the freak to which Fiedler refers was an unanticipated expression of the carnivalesque as an historic and imaginative possibility, what Wini Breines has called a "prefigurative politics."[13] In my view, however, this attitude can only be understood in relation to grotesque spectacle, not as the ruination of a lost, truer, or more complete world, but in full acknowledgement of the extent to which spectacle, the body, and politics are by now inseparable as distorted and hyperbolized aspects of media culture, which is to say the world we have now. Freak bodies appear not as collections of weird images assembled somewhere else, but as events and experiences, as is said of news events, "blown out of proportion." The freak embodies the most capacious aspects of media culture, taking in and consolidating otherwise lost or fragile identities. The freak can be read as a trope not only of the "secret self," but of the most externalized, "out there," hypervisible, and exposed aspects of contemporary culture and of the phantasmatic experience of that culture by social subjects.

Social movements in the United States in the last thirty years have all been acutely aware of the importance of producing and controlling images. Sheila Rowbotham has described what has become the dominant allegory of political progress as a coming into visibility in the midst of false images:

> The vast majority of human beings have always been mainly invisible to themselves while a tiny minority have exhausted themselves in the isolation of observing their own reflections. Every mass political movement of the oppressed necessarily brings its own vision of itself

into sight . . . In order to create an alternative an oppressed group must at once shatter the self-reflecting world which encircles it and, at the same time, project its own image onto history.[14]

She compares the media to a "prism which refracts reality" and a "hall of mirrors" which "turns itself into a fun house." Much effort has gone into straightening out the grotesque images of the fun house variety and in establishing "real" histories and normalizing and neutralizing representations of women, sexual and racial minorities, and the disabled (Rowbotham, 29). A riskier gambit by far lies in the strange mimesis of counterproducing such stretched and stunted caricatures, of posing and parading in these fun house mirrors, of surrendering one's identity as no longer possibly correct, recognizable, or selfsame, but inevitably bound to other bodies and strange selves.

Browning's Freaks: Marginalia

Browning's film opens with a fundamental dilemma for film audiences: *"Believe it or Not"* is scrolled onto the screen, followed by a long pseudo-historical and pseudo-scientific preamble calculated to tease the viewer:

> *Believe it or not . . .*
> *Strange as it seems . . .*
> In ancient times, anything that deviated from the normal was considered an omen of ill-luck or representative of Evil. Gods of misfortune and adversity were invariably cast in the form of monstrosities, and deeds of injustice and hardship have been attributed to the many crippled and deformed tyrants of Europe and Asia . . . misshapen misfits who have altered the world's course: Goliath, Caliban, Frankenstein, Gloucester, Tom Thumb, and Kaiser Wilhelm.
>
> For the love of beauty is a deep-seated urge which dates back to the beginning of civilization. The revulsion with which we view the abnormal, the malformed and the mutilated is the result of long conditioning by forefathers.
>
> The majority of freaks . . . are endowed with normal emotions

. . . a code of ethics to protect them from the barbs of normal people. The joy of one is the joy of all, the hurt of one is the hurt of all.

As the text scrolls down, a set of images on the margins depicts a collection of freak performers: a fat lady, a living skeleton, Siamese twins, the Half-Man, Half-woman. This classic positioning of the freak as an illustrative detail and as a pictorial object requiring narration by a barker, or in other contexts, a clinician, eventually gives way to a far more complex view of these performers. This first set of words and images is immediately displaced and exposed as a *trompe l'oeil,* as the screen appears to be torn through and discarded by a "real" barker who in turn leads the spectator into another exhibition: "We told you . . . living, breathing monstrosities, accidents of birth, they did not ask to be born."

The camera leads us, with a crowd of spectators, to the top of a deep pen, and the barker continues: "She was the most beautiful woman in the world." The audience gathers round in anticipation and the camera closes in to reveal: nothing. Cut to a long shot from below of a large, blond woman on a trapeze. A point of view shot then directs our attention to a blond midget (Harry Earles, called "Hans" in the film) in a tuxedo, looking upward. He confides to his fiance Frieda: "She is the most beautiful *big* woman I have ever seen."

This classificatory comment and the camera work emphasize the inversion of visual politics as the scale of the midget body becomes a norm for viewing the "big" woman in space. Temporarily powerful in his gaze upwards at the female body abjected from everyday spatial relations, Hans becomes increasingly impatient and dismissive of Frieda, the "little woman" he has asked to become his wife. Frieda is first portrayed in a tutu as if she were a little girl or doll astride a circus pony; later, she is seen nagging him for smoking big cigars, and at the clothesline, like a petit-bourgeois housewife, complaining to a friend about the aerialist who is taking away her man. As Hans aspires upward, Frieda is symbolically put down. As the movie progresses, and Hans comes into an inheritance and marries Cleopatra, Hans leaves Frieda behind, as an upwardly mobile young man might leave behind a woman associated with his own social class in life or in novels.

Browning's film is very interesting in its representation of class in relation to the body. In literal terms, Hans stands in for the upper classes. He is identified early on as having money, which, of course, is the reason that Cleopatra schemes with her lover Hercules to marry and eventually kill him. Even within the circus he is dressed formally; in the final scene, he is portrayed as a wealthy gentleman in stately retirement in a grand, panelled room with books, fireplace, and other accoutrements of his station, including a servant to keep visitors away. His privacy above all distinguishes him from his community of freaks. In the final scene, it is clear that Hans is personally shocked and devastated by the violent revenge enacted upon Hercules and Cleopatra, who are killed or mutilated by his fellow performers.

The actual mutilations of the "big" people are not shown, but the filming of the chase with the camera at "ground" level, as the freaks advance through the rain and mud, is terrifying and inspired. Each performer, no matter how "handicapped" or reduced in relation to the size and putative completeness of Hercules and Cleopatra, reveals a power and virtuosity unimaginable in their portrayals earlier as children or novelty acts. Most strikingly, the scene suggests a shocking, almost unrepresentable collective violence. Using their mouths, torsos, sizes, and most of all their keen powers of observation to track and overcome the oppressors, the procession of freaks suggests a violent and revolutionary underclass as they move deliberately through the darkness. The film is so dark at certain points that the viewer can barely make out their forms as they emerge from all points and advance together.

The Wedding Feast

Ancient humanity, an essentially public and visual world, unable to conceive of happiness without spectacles and feasts, was full of tender regard for the "spectator." And, as we have said before, punishment too has its festive features.

　　　　　　　　　　　　—Nietzsche, The Genealogy of Morals[15]

Fig. 16   The Wedding Feast from Tod Browning's *Freaks* (1932). Courtesy of
MOMA Film Stills Archive.

This is not the first portrayal of the freak community as grotesque.
A formlessness and heterogeneity also characterized this social body
at the wedding feast for Hans and Cleopatra.

Browning subtitled "the wedding feast" in the film, setting it off as a
freestanding sequence. The performance of the wedding ceremony is
not shown, but the physical asymmetries of the bride and groom, and
the fact that Hercules, Cleopatra's lover, sits on her right, at the head of
the table, indicates that this is not a regular wedding. The presence of
Hercules in the frames of the "couple" emphasizes Hans' diminutive
stature, and the threesome suggests a configuration of child and parents. Neither is this a "Tom Thumb" wedding, that popular miniatur-
ized ceremony Susan Stewart has convincingly described as "an
exaggeration of an ideal of the wedding." The scene seems much closer
to a carnival grotesque exaggeration in the film. Many aspects of the
scene recall the charavari in early modern Europe, which accompanied
the marriages of unsuitable couples.

A noisy impromptu band, featuring the Siamese twins on clarinets, accompanies a "chicken" dancing on the table. Eating and drinking are carried out unconventionally with hands and sometimes feet. The most outrageous ingestive styles are exhibited by the "sword-swallower" and by the "fire-eater" as the feast becomes more hilarious and parodic in its play of equivalences. Substitution of body parts (foot for hand), prosthetic extensions and costumes, laughter, and jokes at the feast bring together the various freak performances which Browning has respectfully gathered as vignettes of everyday life at the carnival. Each performer is given individual space in the film to show how they could smoke or drink without arms, move without legs, or, in the case of Slitzie and the other "pinheads," how a ribbon or the promise of a Parisian hat could extend (and feminize) their characteristic bodily performance as novelty heads. A brilliant touch is the running joke of the stuttering husband who marries Siamese twins: he seems to mimic their bodily redundancies by his own compulsive repetitions. His re-curring line when his wife has to leave with her sister, is that it is her "a-a-a-libi," her other place (her elsewhere/*alius ibi*). As the wedding feast recalls the earlier film segments, a sense of solidarity and community emerges from the participants' collective differences. Even Cleopatra's mocking of her jealous husband as a "little green-eyed monster" might be part of the fun, except that it reveals her contempt for the entire group; Cleopatra's speech suggests literal and secretive meanings far from the extroversions of the group. In fact, she panics at the moment when the freaks approach her with their offer of acceptance.

In the extraordinary sequence which ends the wedding feast, the freak community approaches Cleopatra, chanting: "We accept you, one of us/Gooble, gobble, gooble, gobble/we accept you, one of us." As the chant builds in a crescendo, an oversized loving cup is passed from mouth to mouth, carried by a midget who marches down the table towards the couple. Their noisy, mirthful offer of acceptance is repug-nant and frightening to Cleopatra who screams derisively, "Freaks, Freaks, Freaks . . ." and orders them to get out. She then turns to her new husband and asks, "Are you a man or a baby?"

This question, and the scene which prompts it, reveal two incompatible, internal models of the social body.[16] The first, offered performatively by the freaks on their own behalf, is characterized by a great internal tolerance for extremely differentiated bodily techniques and a corresponding openness to "freaks" from the outside. Admittance to the group is offered on the basis of difference rather than sameness. The heterogeneity of the freaks as a social group corresponds closely to the active image of the freak body in the film.[17] Their speech code within the travelling freak show is similarly multivocal, open to linguistic anomaly and diversions in the form of puns, stutters, jokes, name-calling, and nonsense. The second model, signalled by Cleopatra's refusal to drink and, hence, be contaminated by freak identity, insists on sameness as a basis for exclusion. Within this social group, which is represented in the scene only by Cleopatra and Hercules, there is very little differentiation: only the horizontal axis of gender and the vertical axis of size.[18] The question "are you a man or a baby?" works on *both* axes simultaneously.

Internally, the freak community offers a model of tolerance which viewers of the film are certainly meant to value as good. The freak community is shown, initially at least, as better than the two representatives of the normal. But Browning reminds us in the film titles (directed to an external audience) that, as a group, the freaks have their own code for dealing with hostile outsiders. This identification of the freak body *against* other social bodies is, of course, a function of that play of forces which have constituted the realm of the political: us against them.

The totemic representation of the freaks—the visible, external sign of freakness—is the chicken. Internally, all manner of hybrid identities are suggested in the film, but the speech (gooble, gobble), gestures (chicken dance), and image of the chicken body (chicken woman dancer/Cleopatra as "chick") stands, for the group, as a mediation of the inside/out. The "chicken" represents the boundary condition of the freak. It is not surprising, then, that the violence resulting from the encounter of separate and oppositional bodies would transform

Fig. 17   Cleopatra's mutilated body as a chick-woman on display.

the body of the beautiful aerialist into a baby chick, head and face mutilated and feathered, hands redesigned prosthetically as claws, and finally exhibited as a freak. In the symbolic economy of the narrative, her body, which was first exhibited in the air as an idealization of womanhood, is cut down to size to fit the sacrificial requirements of freak justice—two kinds of abjection.

Her downfall is staged in the same spectatorial terms as her debut in the film: She is a female attraction who becomes a sideshow distraction because of her relationship to men. Looking down at the disfigured exhibit in the crib below, the barker claims that a famous prince shot himself because of her. Hard to believe, but, in the realist terms of the film, it is impossible for her to be read as a carnivalesque or cinematic hoax. This residual piece of flesh is insisted upon *as a real woman*. The bottom line here is that she has—as is said of and to women who undergo mastectomies and are immediately presented with all manner of prosthetic and cosmetic accoutrements—"managed to keep her femininity." Femininity is here inert, hypervisible, and sadistically contained as the greatest horror on earth.[19]

The culminating image of the film remarginalizes the sideshow freaks as commercial oddities who, perhaps, should not be blamed for their inhuman behavior. The freak female trophy completes the normalizing narrative of heterosexual relations which tend to override, in my view, all of the radical and compassionate details of this extraordinary film.

In the most widely circulating cut of the film, there is an epilogue. It shows a reclusive and melancholy Hans (Harry Earles) ensconced in a stately townhouse, dressed to the nines, with a servant. He has come into his patrimony and has definitively distanced himself from the freaks whose violence on his behalf he now claims to abhor. He is the very model of the tragic gentleman. Frieda, the blond midget who resembles him, arrives to offer her comfort. In the vertical logic of things, they are a normal couple—a short, heterosexual dyad. Presumably, this is the prelude to another Tom Thumb wedding, a ritual which idealizes class as well as gender in an adorable miniaturization. Safely domesticated now that the excessive body of Cleopatra as monster of monsters (bad woman and bad freak) is "cut out," the rich Hans finally has room for Frieda, a good (normalized) freak and a good (little) woman.

Freak Orlando:
A Genealogy of the Female Grotesque

Writers on the grotesque often begin by pointing out the difficulties of tracing a history of the concept, since its past is as tortuous and unorthodox as its present meaning and uses. Foucault's notion of a genealogy, with its emphasis on rupture, boundary crises, discontinuities, accretions, distensions, and discursive formations, resembles the shapes of the grotesque. In the first volume of *The History of Sexuality*, Foucault describes the particularly modern forms of power which simultaneously produced sexuality as a discursive field of force and located those sites of sexual production in bodies and tendencies which required special elaboration and surveillance.[20] This intensification of interest and control often operated under the guise of discovery within specific domains of, for example, religion, medical science, the family, criminology, and colonial geography. These discoveries, the designated "freaks" of history, include the pervert, the hysteric, the deformed, the "precociously" sexual child, the criminal, and the mad. The links between these special subjects do not produce a community of shared identity, much less a social totality, but they meet up nonetheless in those "transfer" or "relay" points of the knowledge/ power network. Within the genealogical model, these subjects are imbued with transgressive potential not because they are essential victims (the neoconservative view of which is described as "victimology"), but because they have been produced and positioned as such within the mechanisms of power. Transgression, in this context, refers to specific, insurrectionary encounters with rules and structures in particular domains. In theory, collective transgression could work transversely across networks, but this is precisely a "work" and not a question of natural affiliation between social groups or between relations of sexuality across discontinuous geographies of desire. Transgression takes place differently, for instance, in an aesthetic domain than in a social, political one. As Allon White has written, "there are profoundly complex links between transgressive aesthetics and radical politics, but they are neither essential nor univocal."[21]

What then is the relationship between a court dwarf during the Spanish Inquisition and a midget in a freak show? Which hierarchies are overturned in the marriage of female Siamese twins to a lesbian transsexual? Could a new social justice emerge from a mock "beauty contest" for the "ugly" which inverts its own rules and crowns as the ugliest man and woman on earth a 1950s "normal" playboy Bunny and a travelling pharmaceuticals salesman?

Ulrike Ottinger's *Freak Orlando* (1981) is a genealogy of sexual difference in which such questions of grotesque inversions, intertwinings, and details are raised as no less than the visualizations of the crisis of reason in Western culture.[22] For her, the freak represents the

Fig. 18   Chicken-babies in Ulrike Ottinger's *Freak Orlando* (1981).

disturbance of rationality in the visual field: "If one is working with
visual means, then freaks are there, whether it is invented freaks in
films, or they are really natural phenomena, which also appear in
films, or whether it is a construction of fictitious ones. I think one
should work with all these disturbing possibilities."[23] Ottinger's cinema has strong links to the historical avant-garde in the production of
surreality and in the juxtaposition of everyday freaks with extraordinary, fictitious, and mythological ones.[24] But Tod Browning, in his
modest cult film, had already confounded the category of freaks in
cinema by casting performing freaks who in turn counterproduced
the normal woman as a chicken-woman freak—an image of their
own. As Ottinger has acknowledged, *Freak Orlando* is greatly indebted
to Browning's film, as well as to the "art cinema" tradition. Repeatedly
in this film, the popular and the high cultural grotesque meet. When
two chickens with female doll's heads are dropped into the "Goya"
sequence of her film, Browning's famous image of the woman-becom-
ing-chicken freak is reversed: the chicken freaks are "becoming-

women." And there are more than one of them. The dwarf painter in
this episode is named Galli ("Roosters, Goya, Dali").

The film borrows its protagonist, Orlando (alias Orlando Capricho,
Orlando Zyklopa (Cyclops), Herr Orlando, Frau Orlando, Freak
Orlando) from Virginia Woolf's novel, *Orlando, A Biography*.[25] Inspired by the life and personality of her lover, Vita Sackville-West, the
novel relates the adventures of Orlando, who travels through the centuries as man and as woman, changing gender as lightly as she changes
clothes or pronouns.[26] In the language of high fashion, Woolf declares
"There is much to support the view that it is clothes that wear us and
not we them."[27] Woolf's novel, in fact, supports a view that transvestism and transsexuality are more or less the same: Orlando need
only choose from a closet that is always full, and the sexual plot will
follow. Woolf's upper-class romance promises an expanding, modernist world of social mobility ("a society," as Gilbert and Gubar put it,
"where there need be no uni-forms") through the metaphor of transsexuality (Gilbert and Gubar, 345). Orlando's happy transgressions are
limited only by the admonition that, like Peter Pan, she "never grow
old." The attractions of such a stylish fantasy correspond to what I
have associated earlier with aeriality and the philobatic imagination—
if one has a room of one's own, one doesn't have to stay there.

Feminists in many countries have been inspired by Woolf's
Orlando. The recent and, in my view, much deserved success of Sally
Potter's film adaptation, *Orlando* (1993), makes a brief comparison
necessary. Like *Freak Orlando*, Potter's *Orlando* is concerned with gender, politics, and social transformation. *Freak Orlando* is much closer
to Browning's film than to Potter's adaptation, however, despite the
similarities between Potter and Ottinger as independent, feminist
filmmakers with impressive knowledge and experience of the visual
and performing arts. *Freak Orlando* is a far less conventional film than
Potter's. It is much less centered on the main character (Tilda Swinton
as Potter's Orlando appears in nearly every frame of the sumptuous
film) and on cross-gender identification as such, than on the ensembles of male, female, and male/female freaks who come together and
disperse as couples, troupes, families, employees, workers, patients,

fanatics, male flagellants, skinheads, heretics, vagrants, "ugly" contestants, irate consumers, and carnival performers. And, of course, in the list of bodily ensembles, one would include the two-in-ones and split-selves embodied in the figure of Orlando (again, less the integrated androgyne, more like Tiresias than Swinton's Orlando), and also the Siamese twins, the double-headed woman, the black and white dwarf-mastiff, and many, many more. Only Quentin Crisp playing the old Queen Elizabeth in Potter's film approaches the grotesque bodily representations of *Freak Orlando*.

While Potter's film rejoins feminist film theory at certain points, redirecting the gaze back on the audience in a way that searches out new spectatorial affiliations, *Freak Orlando* develops a radically aesthetic, pictorial logic in which the grotesque body and the constructed environment are seen metonymically as surface and detail of one another in an elaborate cross-referencing worthy of Arcimboldo, Escher, or Calvino.

Freak City

The opening shot of *Freak Orlando* shows the wandering Orlando (Magadalena Montezuma) coming in from the windy outskirts of a distant city, pausing to drink at the breasts of the Tree of Life Goddess (played by Delphine Seyrig) planted waist deep in the earth, her arms twined with vines and branches. He then walks toward the undersized, fluorescent archway formed by the letters "Freak City" and passes through it. This sequence is repeated in reverse at the film's end.[28] Aptly described as an "apocalyptic dumpscape," this liminal space on either side of the sign represents both the inside and the outside of "Freak City," just as Seyrig's body marks a space above and below ground. The figure of Orlando is split down the middle. The city—a freak city—in the distance, is Berlin.

Ottinger's film is episodic and cumulative rather than in any sense progressive. The five episodes evoke or are set in: 1) a department store in Freak City; 2) outside a medieval basilica; 3) in the streets, walls, and prisons of the Spanish Inquisition; 4) underneath an indus-

Fig. 19   Architecture and the Grotesque in *Freak Orlando.*

trial canopy containing a freak carnival; 5) in a televised contest at the "festival of ugly people," held in Italy. Each episode is historical, even documentary in style, but the materials (literal and figurative) are often surrealistically contemporary and markedly artificial. Sonic and visual features often intersect as in, for example, the cacophony of plastic costumes, muzak, and the mellifluous voice of Seyrig amplified over the department store's public address system in the first episode. The experience of time is similarly askew: The department store man-ager, Herbert Zeus (Albert Heins) sets time in the episode by the advertisement of a "mythological sales week" that, presumably, could last as long as the liturgy of consumerism. Orlando Cyclops and her seven midgets take up too much time in the *fast-soling* section of the store and are run out by Zeus and a band of irate consumers. Trans-gression and punishment are featured in every episode except the last where a mock festival competition—a freak beauty contest—results in some unexpected rewards. As human artifacts placed in specific locations of power and desire, the same or similar actors and characters are moved to suffer and celebrate together in certain configurations, and to round up and persecute one another in others.

The function of architecture is similarly interchangeable: The spectator becomes accustomed to the illogic of architectural spaces which can be occupied differently, depending on the choreography of its inhabitants. Of course, like Marco Polo in Calvino's *Invisible Cities,* who admits to the Kubla Khan that when he speaks of any city, he is speaking of Venice, Ottinger creates a *theatrum mundi* out of Berlin.

Bodily Architecture and Monstrification

In *Freak Orlando,* Ottinger recalls the long tradition of anthropomorphism in architectural theory from Vetruvius onward. In Vetruvius, the body is a model of proportion, completion, and rationality. In contrast, the irregular and often incomplete body of the freak resists the ordering of classical architecture as bodily metaphor, offering instead the uncanny, fragmentary architecture of memory and illusion. Vetruvius, in an oft-cited denunciation of the fantastical, ornamental drawings of the kind associated with the grotto art (hence, grotesque) discovered in the Renaissance around the Domus Aurea in Rome, objected to the association of architecture with irrationality:

> On the stucco are monsters rather than definite representations taken from definite things. Instead of columns there rise up stalks; instead of gables, striped panels with curled leaves and volutes . . . slender stalks with heads of men and animals attached to half the body. Such things neither are, nor can be, nor have been.[29]

He points to monsters, like the "slender stalks with heads of men and animals attached to half a body," and accuses them of "falsehood" because such representations are not architecturally sound and could not, for example, support a roof or statue.[30]

In his very suggestive study of the monstrous in architecture and architectural theory, Marco Frascari emphasizes the role of corporeal fantasy in architectural thinking and process.[31] He traces a countertradition of architectural theory in which buildings and bodies are no longer seen as metaphorical models reinforcing each other's wholeness and rationality, but are metonymically linked by fantastical combinations of imaginative detail derived from cultural, as opposed to natural, reason. If architecture inevitably involves the relationship between structure and detail, then it is unsurprising to find the grotesque architectural detail—the monster—located at the margins and joints of buildings and architectural plans as an articulation of the part to the whole, and as the symptom of the entire complex: "Monsters are located at the edges or the margins of the known world" (Frascari, 16). John Ruskin aptly suggested as a substitute term for the category of decoration in the architectural contract the term "monstrification."[32] A "monstrified" building or landscape would suggest, as fantasies and reveries suggest, an assimilative and transformative relation to reason and the waking state. As the subtitle of Goya's famous allegorical painting *Capricho* (one of Orlando's aliases) reads, *El sueno de la razon produce monstruos* (The dream of reason produces monsters).[33]

Ottinger's film reproduces art, architecture, and the body as monstrifications. Her long shots of distant buildings and extreme close-ups of details, alcoves, and entrances seem to undo the sense of time as progress or as unfolding. History is produced, instead, as a recombination of displaced persons and visual fragments, gathered together in several episodes like booty after an ideological war. Frascari offers the term "architecture of spoils" (*architettura di spoglie*) to categorize fragmentary architecture which takes up the leftovers, the ruins, the incompletions of other buildings and eras. This term seems more suitable than the generic and neutral tag "postmodernist" for describing the aspect of Ottinger's film that refers to the violence contained even in the most formal aspects of the architectural setting. In the most harrowing episode of the film, the Berlin Olympic stadium functions as prison yard for the execution of mutilated prisoners, mental patients, dissidents, heretics and vagrants—all freaks of the Inquisition. Inter-

estingly the artist-dwarf Galli survives to record the events visually, and
he resembles the low-lying stadium with his wide-brimmed hat and
full skirt.[34] The relation of body to building resides typically in the
prosthetic detail and hyperbolized scale created by costuming and
camera work, so that the "natural" freak is reproduced as a cultural
artifact. There is no question of merely assimilating the freak into a
"normal" world in this film. As a grotesque body, the freak is produced
as endlessly perverse, turning away, as Bakhtin suggested, from mirror
images of itself and towards transformation and possible futures.[35]
Like history, the body is shown to be a recyclable *trompe l'oeil*.[36]

The Change

"Taccia di Cadmo e d'Aretusa Ovidio!"
—Dante, *Inferno XXV*[37]

As Dante challenges Ovid in feats of representing metamorphosis,
so Ottinger seems to challenge Browning in the production of cinematic freaks. Episode IV of *Freak Orlando* finds Herr Orlando (alias
Orlando Cyclops, alias Orlando Capricho) at the entrance to a psychi-
atric hospital where he is invited to join a band of sideshow freaks. A
feast is staged under the metal superstructure of an industrial dome.
Like the wedding feast in Browning's *Freaks*, this carnivalesque cele-
bration features the diverse bodily talents of many performers. In
Ottinger's version of the feast, pictorial artifice extends the virtuosity
of the freak performance. To mention only two details, a stunning
female living torso (Therese Zemp) is shown on a Greek pedestal,
crowned by a laurel. Her body, conventionally a half-body, is envi-
sioned as a classical bust—incompletion as a work of art. Of course,
the concept of the classical bust is simultaneously undone. The human
pillar recalls the dreamy, even nightmarish quality of the classical
orders which used the human body as architectural detail. Although
the freak pillar is freestanding, it serves to anchor the communal
scene, a truly decorative and prodigious image of artistic and sexual

Fig. 20   A visual genealogy of Freaks in *Freak Orlando*.

exceptionalism.[38] Freaks are the object of intense, sexual speculation.
As objects of voyeuristic fantasy, they are, in Ottinger's term, "disturbing." In Browning's *Freaks,* the narrative is organized around the
(putatively heterosexual) male body of Hans. The issue is, finally, one
of size: Is he big enough to be a real man? Or is he a baby? The freaks

around the margins of his doomed romance do not have story lines of their own, only jokes and innuendos regarding their sexuality. The Siamese twins in *Freaks*, Daisy and Violet Hilton, are, perhaps, exceptions. The titillating confusions around their unsuccessful marriages and engagements offscreen find their way into several comic scenes. Yet the questions around "Siamese" twin sexuality in Browning's film are strictly patriarchal and domestic: Should a husband have the right to privacy with his wife?[39] Can he prevent her from walking away with her sister? Is the husband of a Siamese twin a bigamist? Is he inevitably the comic, "henpecked" husband because he has to endure the chatter of *two* women? Will the arrival of a fiancé for the sister insure heterosexual symmetry and male dominance?

But what if the other sister is not interested in men? What if the husband were a lesbian transsexual like Freak Orlando? Ottinger's twins Lena and Leni (Delphine Seyrig and Jackie Raynal) are, at first, latter-day versions of Violet and Daisy Hilton. At the freak party, they sing, dance, drink, and flirt outrageously with the newcomer Freak Orlando (Magadelena Montezuma, looking very much as she did in other episodes). When Orlando offers his seal ring to Lena and she accepts, Leni is excluded. Literally, in a two shot of Lena and Orlando dancing, Leni is cut out. When she reenters the frame, it is as a bobbing appendage rather than as a twin partner;[40] in the new economy of the couple as emerging family, she is expendable. When Lena and Orlando become parents and Leni refuses to support Lena's motherhood, Orlando (after much "male" anguish) throws a knife through her heart, inadvertently killing his beloved Lena as well. Freak justice prevails and he is executed. This melodrama of domestic violence is extraordinarily provocative. Shot in the trailer camp, these final scenes show the reluctant but inevitable ritual of male domestic violence in the performance of the knife-thrower act.

The figure of Orlando in *Freak Orlando* is not the eternal youth of Woolf's novel or Potter's film. Freak Orlando confounds gender binaries, but does not transcend the genealogical accumulation of power and violence in her/his travels through the symbolic domains of each

episode. Her/his experience and morality are not better or worse than
the "normal" subject of European cultural histories and travelogues.
The body of Freak Orlando, with all of his/her historical aliases, is not
an heroic exception in either the grand histories, for instance, of the
Inquisition, or the microhistories of marginal subcultures. Sometimes
a leader, sometimes a prisoner, sometimes merely an invited volunteer,
the figure of Orlando folds into the dramas of exclusion and marginalization, finally emerging in the freaks episode as a reluctant but
nonetheless complicitous *paterfamilias.*

The obvious theatricality—the campiness, if you will—of the freak
family derives in part from the multivalence of the butch-femme
aesthetic described by Sue-Ellen Case and others.[41] Certainly, the
gender-layering of *Freak Orlando* privileges lesbianism as style and
bodily surface, and, to the extent that artifice is experiential, it privileges a representation of a lesbian experience.[42] As Frieda Grafe points
out, Magadalena Montezuma's first movements in the film indicate
a woman emphasizing what it is to play a man. I would add that
Montezuma's performance within the film adds an important trajectory in that she plays a woman playing a man *to another woman.*[43]
Orlando's partners in the freak show episode, the flirtatious Lena/Leni,
are super-femmes, double masqueraders of femininity. Like Violet and
Daisy Hilton, they seem doomed to enact the conflict of difference
within the same, until they die together. Death in Ottinger's film seems
to indicate a further transformation: in this case, the trope of the
Siamese twins suggests a more radical female-female sexuality which is
constrained and unrepresentable within the confines even of freak subculture. Freak Orlando's death, an offscreen execution, links the themes
of transformation with exclusion. His disappearance from the screen
signals the end of one male role within the specificities of the freak subculture and gestures to another "off-space" of invisibility and silence.

In *Madame X—eine absolute Herrscherin (An absolute ruler)* (1977),
Ottinger had already greatly expanded the erotic range of male/female
role playing for women. In this feminist swashbuckler which reappro-
priates the male *genre film,* a call goes out to all women to go aboard
The China Orlando, a junk headed for adventures in the South Seas.

Fig. 21   Herr Orlando (Magdalena Montezuma). Courtesy of Ulrike Ottinger.

The sadism of Madame X, a captain (Hook) with a prosthetic hand, intensifies the generic pleasures and dangers of piracy and seduction of native girls.[44] The ritual cruelty, hierarchy, and nonprogressive itinerary around the sea of words and images interrupts the progressive narratives of motherhood, careers, and movement politics, and reinstates difference (power, gender, ethnicity, nationality) as a sexual charge and motivation which demands its own shapes and spaces in a new genealogy of desire.[45]

Yet this high-risk voyage out into the mythic (here, nautical) sublime results in death. Ottinger was criticized by some feminists when the film was first released for its sadomasochistic content and for the (seemingly punitive) deaths of the adventuresome women in the film. In an interview some years later, she related the film's reception to the volatile, early history of the women's movement in Germany: "I tried to explain that, although the deaths in the film are erotically motivated, they also signify changes."[46]

In *Freak Orlando,* change is represented not merely by the voyage in and the voyage out, but in overlapping trajectories. As a radical model of sociality, the freak body is as capacious and extensive as the grotesque body in the model of Bakhtin. It reaches out and makes fantastical connections between and within genders, bodies, costumes, subcultures, architectures, landscapes, and temporalities. The model of the grotesque body in relation to the social group is not, however, democratic or evenhanded in this film. It is constituted and undone by scene after scene of powerful exclusion and death. The repetition of the images of exclusion and marginalization in the figuration of the body and bodily ensembles effects its own kind of social change, albeit in the realm of memory, dreams, and fantasy. As Roswitha Mueller has written, Ottinger's project "does not aim at being marginal but rather to bring the margin into the center, or de-centering the mainstream by introducing the margin on an equal basis." This is, of course, the "equal basis" of language, images, and representation which might be more accurately described as an equivalence in a field of difference. The intensification of the female and grotesque temporarily reshapes male histories, making them concomitantly irregular.[47] It also makes any transcendent model of femaleness or the female body impossible. Impossible bodies are, however, very interesting.

Twins and Mutant Women

David Cronenberg's *Dead Ringers*

"What's going on in there?"
". . . oh, you know, endless renovations"
—David Cronenberg's
Dead Ringers (1988)

IN DAVID CRONENBERG'S BRILLIANT 1988 FILM, *Dead Ringers*, Elliot
Mantle, a gynecologist and an identical twin, is conducting a pelvic
examination on a famous actress who is unable to bear children. With
his fingers expertly tucked inside her body, he marvels at what he can
feel. Neither the film's viewers nor the actress have access to his knowledge of her truly amazing and monstrous anatomy; she is, it turns out,
a mutant woman, a "trifurcate" with three cervical entrances to her
womb. The actress, Claire Niveau (played by Genevieve Bujold), whose
business is appearances and being looked at, is amused that anyone
would be so impressed with the *inside* of her body. "Surely," rejoins the
good doctor, "you have heard of Inner Beauty."

The problem for Dr. Mantle is that this Inner Beauty seems to lack a
corresponding aesthetic discourse; there are no beauty contests for
the insides.[1] "Why," he asks in mock indignation, "do we not have
standards of beauty for the entire body, including the organs?" Claire,
undaunted by the indignities of her lopsided equestrian posture, and
obviously aware of the limited comic role she has been given in this
little spectacle, looks up past the metal stirrups and the bedsheet/cur-
tain draped over her knees and replies, "I have a feeling *you* do, doctor!" And of course, *he* does, not only because he is a man *and* a

gynecologist, but because he and his twin brother, Beverly (both
played by Jeremy Irons), have invented the fabulous Mantle Retractor,
a precise instrument developed through practice on dolls and cadav-
ers, which is put into live women during surgery to make the sexual
organs more accessible.

Gender and professionalism are crucial to the Mantle brothers'
claims to knowledge and to their power over the female body, but it is
their instrument which would seem to give them special claims to elite
medical circles, and especially to the bodies of affluent or famous
women like Claire Niveau.[2] That this instrument is more than a frame
for viewing or feeling the female body is clear; it does not fit into the
live, conscious woman, and it is painful. In any specific case, pre-
dictably, the doctor sees this as the patient's fault (one such patient is
accused by brother Elliott of unnaturalness, of having pain from intercourse with, perhaps, a dog!) The instrument which he uses in this
examination is the solid gold version awarded to the brothers as a trophy of their contribution to gynecology, for setting the standard, as it
were, for the insides. Elliot's logic is clear: "The instrument, Madame,
is solid gold . . . We have the technology . . . the woman's body was all
wrong!" Apart from the "abnormalities" of any particular woman's
body, the abstract, technological, and aesthetic task of the Retractor is
truly creative; it actually reconfigures the pelvis into a more ideal form
for the benefit of the surgeon.

But the Mantle Retractor is not nearly *radical* (a word that repeats
again and again in this film) enough for the formal and psychic challenges which present themselves to Beverly, who in the twins' habitual
division of labor, takes up the practical challenge of his brother's for-
mulations as he grapples with the concept of standards in relation to
bodily anomaly. In line with the fraternal policy of keeping things
simple in their lives and medical practice, Bev finally has only two categories of bodies to deal with, the male twin and the "mutant woman,"
as he designates her.

These categories, both staples of the iconography of the grotesque,
are violently configured in the course of the film as Bev moves back

and forth between his dual identity with his brother (a complementary dyad that relegates the feminine qualities of compassion, practical research, and passivity to Beverly, and the more extroverted
activities of publishing, seduction, and making speeches to Elliot) and
his love affair with the addicted, hysterical, and nonreproductive
Claire Niveau, the paradigmatic "mutant woman." Claire's refusal to
continue sleeping with both brothers, once she understands that there
are *two* of them, in effect "trifurcates" their shared path through life.
Beverly never succeeds in disentangling his professional identity, his
sex life, and his symbiotic relationship with Elliot. The twins' relationship is, for a time, transferred onto Claire, with whom Bev becomes
both more "masculine" and assertive in relation to Elliot, and more
"feminine"—depending, like her, on drugs. Sex between Bev and
Claire is a kind of "playing doctor" with rubber gloves, restraints,
obstetrical positions, drugs, and discussions of her infertility;[3] what
Bev shares with Claire is, in other words, very much the same discourse and objects which he shares with brother Elliot, as if male
twins (seen as a complementary dyad) were commensurate with the
heterosexual couple.

It is interesting that Cronenberg himself has pointed out that he
deliberately made both the brothers heterosexual—rather than relying
on earlier accounts and adaptations of the lives of the famous Marcus
brothers which identify one brother as homosexual—thus keeping the
major reversals in role-playing straight on the axis of gender, at least
early on in the film.[4] At first, it would seem that Beverly simply shut-
tles back and forth between same and different, masculine and feminine, attachment and separation, never breaking out of a set of
normalizing distinctions. For the twin brothers, who have long been
accustomed to sharing female spaces, Claire presents a problem, since
she refuses to be shared by them, and insists on perceiving an unas-
similable difference between them.

It would appear that Beverly's only problem is to choose. But choose
between what? One version of the story would pose the dilemma in
normalizing heterosexual terms as a choice between his weird, claus-

trophobic life with his brother and a loving relationship with a woman. But is Claire a woman? She looks and acts like a woman. Certainly, she is an accomplished *actress* (and her professionalism is underlined repeatedly) who knows how to *perform* womanhood. But Claire's physicality would seem to undermine as much as it supports her identity, since she is portrayed as simultaneously excessive—too much sex, too many cervical openings—and, at the same time sadly lacking, in her inability to bear children. Her body is not adequate; it only approximates femaleness in a culture which identifies the body of the mother with the female body, a fact, not incidentally, that threatens her acting career as much as her private life.[5]

A second movement of the plot would seem to displace Bev's commute between male and female onto the more tortuous paths of the grotesque, where the choice is between one freak or another. The Mantle twins (arguably abnormal *already* as multiple births) come to refer to themselves in the course of the film as Eng and Chang, the historic and spectacularized "Siamese Twins." Similarly, the "normal" monstrosity of intercourse (the beast with two backs) becomes, in Beverly's imagination, "sleeping with a mutant woman."[6] In a fantasmatic scene, Beverly sees Elliot in a dream, watching him in bed with Claire, and Claire separating them by sucking out their connecting organ from the abdomen. In this scene, Claire is the tool for separating Siamese twins, but Beverly begins to conceptualize much more precise instruments.

Grotesque Letters

Torn between Claire and Elliot, and under the influence of drugs which he shares with both of them, Beverly invents a new set of tools, the "instruments for operating on mutant women." He takes his exquisite drawings of these instruments to an artist because they are "too radical" for the large mass-production companies. In a very conspiratorial scene, he asks the artist to produce hand-finished prototypes of the tools. Although the viewer never learns the terms of their deal, it is evident that the artist recognizes the astonishing beauty of

Fig. 22   Claire Niveau (Genevieve Bujold) contemplates one of the "instruments for operating on mutant women" in David Cronenberg's *Dead Ringers* (1988). Courtesy of MOMA Film Stills Archive.

the instruments and that he senses a certain danger and vulnerability in Beverly's request. Seizing his advantage, the artist secretly replicates the tools and exhibits them, carefully aligned on a table, as works of postmodernist art, signing them with his own name and titling them "Gynecological Instruments for Operating on Mutant Women." When Beverly happens to notice them in a gallery window, he breaks into the case and, against the protest of the saleswoman, claims them as his own. In fact, these tools do not belong to either the artist or the doctor; a red dot on the case registers that they have been sold. The citation is not only a self-conscious reproduction of Beverly's words, but it would seem to recall a more distant association. From the opening credits we recognize these tools as belonging to the common history of anatomical drawing *and* the arts.

In the opening credits of the film, the instruments are carefully laid out on a field of vibrant red like a grotesque alphabet, their shapes

Fig. 23   The "Instruments for Operating on Mutant Women" displayed in an art
gallery in *Dead Ringers.*

twisting into delicate curves and flourishes. Although indecipherable
and apparently merely decorative in the framing of the film, these
metal "letters," I will argue, set up the visual logic or system of the plot
and will determine the limits of what the gendered anatomy can be, or
mean, in the hands of the doctor. Alongside these instruments, as in
an illustrated book, are Renaissance drawings of the body, inside out
to the viewer. Most strikingly, these drawings are cross sections of
pregnancy, showing fetal life *in utero* or detached from the mother's
body, fetal twins, their bodies wedged together, as well as miscella-
neous renderings of the reproductive organs. Perched on one drawing
is a tiny gargoyle, as if in the company of fellow monsters.

What these instruments and anatomical figures suggest is the
shared history of the grotesque across art and science, an aesthetic
mediation of the organic and the technological. From the technological to the organic, the leafy tendrils of the anatomical tools outgrow
their instrumentality; from the human body as organism these prosthetic flourishes extend the reach of the clinician. By "reach" I understand—following Foucault's formulation of the absolute gaze which

Fig. 24   A Mantle twin (Jeremy Irons) prepares for surgery.

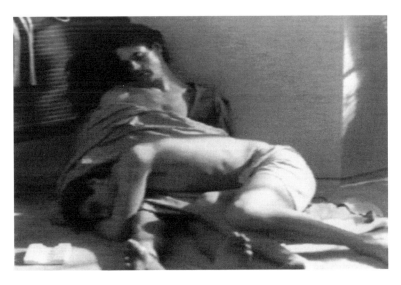

Fig. 25   The concluding image of *Dead Ringers:* a male Pietà.

dominates all other perception—an expanded space for visibility, and hence, power. For Foucault, it is the "glance," a more localized and experimental visual contact, which is caught in the metaphor of the clinical touch.[7]

The prefatorial positioning of the grotesque in the credits recalls its

association with the decorative arts, marginalia, and the detail. In her
study of the detail in art and classical aesthetics, Naomi Schor has
noted this rhetorical linkage of the monstrous and the ornamental.
Citing a treatise of Reynolds, she points out that "the metaphorics of
the detail is heavily freighted with the vocabulary of teratology, the
science of monsters."[8] She emphasizes as typical this passage from
Reynolds, in which he explicitly describes the task of the artist as a
correction of the deformed particular in favor of a Nature that is Ideal:

> . . . he acquires a just idea of beautiful forms; he corrects nature by
> herself, her imperfect state by her more perfect. His eye being able
> to distinguish *the accidental deficiencies, excrescences, and deformi-*
> *ties* of things from their general figures, he makes out an abstract
> idea of their forms more perfect than any one original and what
> may seem a paradox, he learns to design naturally by drawing his
> figures unlike any one object. The idea of the perfect state of nature,
> which the Artist calls the Ideal Beauty, is the great leading principle
> by which works of genius are conducted (Schor, 15).

Using Nature against *herself*, the artist corrects the particular and
"draws his figures unlike any one object," the perfect state of nature
without her imperfections and unnaturalness. As Schor points out,
"the alignment of woman and (devalorized) nature is, of course, not
limited to classical metaphysics or neoclassical aesthetics" (Schor, 16).
The gynecological practice of the Mantle brothers, with its specializa-
tion in female infertility ("we only treat women") and surgical intervention, would seem to lie within this classical paradigm as it intersects
with the new biotechnologies which *focus* on/in bodily details. In the
case of the mutant woman (and arguably all women in the Mantle
brothers clinical practice are mutant) the grotesque detail is identified
with the female genitalia.

Of course, Beverly insists that his instruments belong to medicine,
not to art (even as he insists on the highest level of artistry in their
design and execution). For him, they could not belong to art in the
contemporary sense in which they are appropriated by the artist who
crafted them, who having apparently abandoned the idea of author-

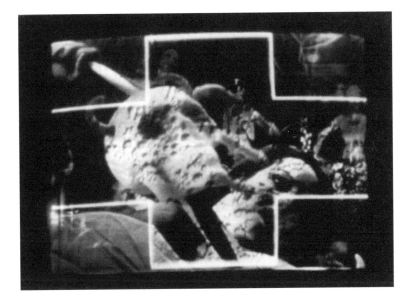

Fig. 26   Orlan, "Successful Operation 1: Death Head Triptych," (Detail).
The performance artist Orlan undergoes and documents plastic surgery
that transforms her face and body in relation to dominant and idealized
images of women. Courtesy of the artist and Penine Hart Gallery.

ship, puts them on the market as his own. But they are connected,
however marginally, to a much more traditional aesthetic which privileges the knowledge and vision of the artist and the artisan. It is
significant that when the strange instruments are brought into the
operating room they are illegible to the surgical nurse (a practitioner
and no aesthete) who can only place them them in an arbitrary
numerical order, like letters in an alphabet. In purely formal terms,
the kinds of shapes and engravings of the tools are repeated in the
reproductions of Renaissance murals on the walls (also red) of the
posh restaurant the Mantle brothers frequent in the film.

Less decoratively, the opening credits link art and the grotesque
with the most grossly material branch of medical science: anatomy
and dissection. Foucault, in *The Birth of the Clinic*, has traced all modern technologies of the body to the anatomical clinic which scrutinized, classified, and finally reorganized "the deep, visible, solid,

enclosed accessible space of the human body" (Foucault, 195).
Through the dark models of pathological anatomy, counter-nature,
and death, the illumined modern body emerges in what he describes
as merely "a syntactical reorganization of disease" in which "the limits
of the visible and invisible follow a new pattern" (Foucault, 195).

In more immediate relation to the grotesque, the art historian Ewa
Kuryluk has remarked on the connection between the earlier, Renaissance "anatomical theater," as the dissecting rooms were sometimes
called, and the artistic imaginings of the grotesque body in illustrations
by Leonardo da Vinci and others, emphasizing the strange juxtapositions of human and animal parts on display. Dissection and surgery
dis-organized the body into many possible systems and components,
and the theater of anatomy added the element of display, which set off
the anatomical specimen as spectacle open to stylization (a comic or
tragic scene of weird juxtapositions of parts). Kuryluk describes these
dissecting rooms as grotto-esque spaces: "In the scientific grotto of the
curiosities, the inside is turned outside and the dark secrets of the
organic become disclosed as the bodily cave is opened up."[9]

What the open body discloses is not as certain as the desire to see
and find *out*. The site of this desire, though not its content, is predictable; that is, the fantasy of abjection described by Julia Kristeva as
"something *horrible to see* at the doors of the invisible—the mother's
body."[10] The distinctions between the body as site and the body as
content, and between the maternal body and the female body, are here
crucial. Although the bodily cave is culturally identified in what I
would describe as a depth model, with the female and the maternal,
gender itself cannot be seen self-evidently therein as a positive shape
or organic truth.

Historically, different things have been seen at the same place. As
Thomas Laqueur documents, the reproductive organs of women, for
instance, were once seen as homologous, if hidden and underdevel-
oped, versions of the male penis and testicles. Looking inside, however
intently, seemed to reveal only the outside of men in the era of this
English rhyme:

For those that have the strictest searchers been
Find women are but men turned outside in.[11]

As Laqueur points out, this seeming interchangeability of form, the
sameness of discernable shape (evident in one of the anatomical drawings in the credits) only emphasized the hierarchized relationship
between the sexes. Anatomically, women were morphologically the
same or similar to men, but inferior to them, as opposed to the later
view of the female body as different and *therefore* unequal.

The more recent view of the organs as replaceable (equal and interchangeable) would seem to have an even greater bearing on the question of what can be seen inside. However, rather than choose between
competing models of gender, representation, and anatomy (all of
which play their part in the film) it seems preferable, preliminarily, to
regard these anatomical caves as inventive spaces where the imagination heats up, rather than as repositories of specimens of the biolo-
gized truth. That the anatomical theater was a continued source of
fantastic inspiration to the artist is evident not only in the work of an
artist like Leonardo, but also in, for instance, the evocation of such a
space in Mary Shelley's *Frankenstein,* where the young scientist finds
inspiration, in the dissecting room and in his "workshop of filthy creation," to patch together a new creature who he intends passionately
to be as beautiful as he is big. The "hideous progeny" is meant to be
an Adonis.[12]

Cronenberg's own twist on this history of aesthetics and medicine
occurs through a constant stylization (with careful art historical allusions) of the professional medical, educational, and private interiors
in which the twins isolate themselves, so that the grotesque elements
are enclosed and circumscribed as "insider" spaces in both the
psychic and disciplinary senses of the word. The dominant color
coding of the film ranges back and forth between red, black and
greys, to blue-grey-greens. The former colors are usually lit quite dra-
matically in sharp contrasts, the latter are associated with diffuse interior light. In an important crossover between the blue/green of

their ultramodern apartment (a kind of Milanese designed fishbowl) and the more historic and archaic associations with redness, the operating teams suit up in liturgical, "cardinal" red instead of the usual dull blue/green.[13]

In the operating room scene, the consequences of crossing these lines of demarcation are represented as truly horrific: a female patient hemorrhages, and Beverly, under the influence of drugs, dives over and into the wreck of her open body, grabbing her oxygen tubes, sucking in air for himself. The scene recalls an early conversation about sexuality and contact between the twins as children, in which one of them points out that in contrast to humans who don't live in the water, "fish don't need sex because they just lay eggs and fertilize them." Immediately, the other twin mentions scuba diving, described as a new technology ("a self-contained underwater breathing apparatus") at which point they ask a knowledgeable little girl to have sex with them *in a bathtub*. She refuses. Until meeting Claire, who is described as "new territory," the twins seem to have mapped out the blue/green aquatic areas of their life together from the red borderlines of the female body, sexuality, and ingestion of food. After Claire, purity and filth, blood and water, order and chaos, become impossibly contaminated in the lives of the twins. Their pristine high tech clinic and apartment are finally cluttered with filth, rotten food, and bodily effluvia. The doorman's question (and who should know more about thresholds)—"What's going on in there?"—is answered by a lie that speaks the truth: "endless renovations."

Twins and Insiders

Some viewers of the film have seen this emphasis on interiors as a privileging of psychic space over the larger, professional and political relations in the field of gynecology. In an issue of the *Canadian Journal of Political Theory* featuring the topic of male hysteria, Frank Burke argues that "the insistence on grounding events within the twinned psyche of Elliott and Beverly repeatedly blunts anything resembling an institutional analysis of the medical profession and makes the film claustrophobic in its rendering of an almost exclusively 'inside' world."[14] He suggests that by grounding the action of the film in sub-jectivity, the misogyny of their gynecogical practice is "reduced to the personal idiosyncracy of two warped but brilliant, coherent, and ini-tially self-determining heroes" (Burke, 32). Further, he argues that Claire is their victim from the moment she is seen "with legs spread apart in a gynecological posture of extreme vulnerability" (Burke, 42). Although I think Burke is certainly right about the blunting of a cer-tain kind of institutional critique, his objections to the film leave in place the opposition between the psyche (twinned, male) and the body of Claire in the gynecological stirrups, an opposition which the film would seem to dislocate at least in part by Claire's anomalousness and, crucially at the end of the film, by putting the male body in the "gynecological posture." While in this gynecological posture, I would argue, subjectivity (still male) is embodied, however temporarily, as a threshhold or boundary condition, and open to negotiation.

Despite the absolutely paradigmatic nature of the gynecological scene as the model of the scopic drive to see, to know, and to control the maternal body as point of origin and separation (with all the vari-ous implications for theories of representation—feminist film theory especially—and social reproduction), perhaps this scene is not so self-evident or revealing, even for purposes of theoretically situating the female.[15] Claire can easily be read as *extremely* vulnerable because she is in this position. But, as a nonreproductive woman and a grotesque, her semiotic potential in this position would seem to exceed the para-meters of the cultural paradigm which lines up the maternal body with the female body. The distinction (to which I will return) between the mother's body and the female body is absolutely crucial to femi-nist cultural criticism and reproductive politics in ways that go far beyond a reading of this film. Here, I will only remark in passing on Claire's seeming invulnerability to intimidation by the doctors in the actual exposure of her vagina and her *extreme* vulnerability to *public* exposure of her internal abnormality because she is an actress, a professional woman. In other words, the usual public/private distinctions are reversed and even untenable for the actress. So, while Cronenberg would seem to ignore some glaring contemporary issues around gender, biotechnology, and reproduction by focusing on the twins, I think the film, in fact, does go some distance in *radically* altering the assumptions about "inside" in relation to the visual field, despite the opening setup of proscenium and perspective which establishes Claire's body as "the looked at" and the doctor as the powerful looker.

Whether this altered perspective is in any sense useful for a feminist agenda is another question. Further, I would suggest that male subjectivity in this film is so hysterical—and I mean this in a topographical sense as being located with and within the hyster—and so repetitive that grotesque twinning and the female grotesque (the "mutant woman") become (almost) identical in the dramatic surgery which ends the film, an ending for the male body and psyche which is not merely a cutting out of the fraternal bond, but a reconfiguraton of the twinned body as a mutant woman, a grotesque rewriting of the script of castration.[16]

At the end of a birthday party to end all birthday parties, a regressive carnival à deux , with cake, no ice cream ("mommy forgot to buy it"), but plenty of drugs and toys, the twins retire to bed. In the series of shots which show them in their skivvies, toddling in step after one another, there is a rare moment of humorous repetition of the kind Bergson describes in his famous essay "On Laughter." Twins, after all, can be hilariously funny as well as disturbingly uncanny. The film, however, as we know from the opening credits, is going in another direction. Under candlelight, and with the soft background music a reviewer flatteringly described as a "post-Wagnerian Liebestod," Beverly takes the "instruments for operating on mutant women," and makes his last surgical intervention straight into the abdomen of an ever nonchalant Elliot. Except for the fact of Jeremy Irons's sustained virtuoso performance, which sets the mouth of the "patient" in a turn unmistakably Elliot's, Beverly can be said to operate on the very image of himself; since Elliot is awake through his anaesthesia, Beverly can see the image of himself looking back as both subject and object at the same time. As a visual instance of reflexive male subjectivity catching itself out (focus on the look and looker rather than the empowered male gaze), the scene could be taken for an enactment or cinematic acknowledgement of the very lack which the cinematic apparatus has taken such pains to cover over in the spectatorial relations which set up the gaze as male and displace lack onto the female body. In an essay on male subjectivity and Fassbinder's cinema, Kaja Silverman has elucidated Lacan's model of specularity in order to emphasize the crucial distinction between the gaze and the look:

> . . . unlike the gaze, the look foregrounds the desiring subjectivity of the figure from whom it issues, a subjectivity which pivots upon lack, whether or not that lack is acknowledged.[17]

The sight of the the male twin separating himself from himself in a castrating gesture, with mixed affect—tearful ("separation can be painful"—Bev) and consolatory ("what's the matter baby brother?"—Elly)—might suggest the kind of male divestiture of mastery and authority that Silverman finds in Fassbinder's exposure of the male look as it "attempts to pass itself off as the gaze" (Silverman, 144). But somehow nothing so "radical" seems to happen. For one thing, the surgical scene is filmed at a respectful distance. The camera never pushes its way towards the dreaded sight of Elliot's eviscerated pelvis, there is no gore, and no bloody internal organs (beautiful or not) reveal themselves as they did in Beverly's dream. Although an organ is seen later in the surgical tray, because it is framed separately, it is somehow no longer Elliot's, though one imagines he might have judged it beautiful. The aftermath of the reconstructive surgery and what might also be called an autopsy (emphasizing the original meaning of the word as *seeing for oneself*) is a kind of purification ritual.[18] Beverly carefully washes, shaves, and dresses his body (which, since it had always stood in for Elliot's, is an extraordinarily ambiguous gesture). On the one hand, he is distinguishing himself from the corpse on the examining table; on the other, he is preparing "the body" for his own burial.[19]

Clean and dressed up, he goes out briefly to call Claire, hangs up, and returns to the clinic where in a final shot his body is shown laid carefully onto the torso of his brother, who is propped up on the floor, in a sitting position, with a sheet artfully draped into soft folds over his chest. Together they form a sculptural figure of great poignancy: religious, mournful, Humanistic, and transcendent—an all-male *Pietà*. The surfaces of drapery and skin blend smoothly and harden over the body, closing it up to the intrusive or unsympathetic spectator. In stark contrast, the viewer can recall the grotesque anatomical drawings with skin flayed and pinned back in four corners to frame rather than to seal the opened body. This classical, humanistic ending excludes Claire, mutancy and, arguably, even twins in the new Oedipal configuration of mother and son.

Although this tragic finale certainly discourages the thrilling possibilities of seeing an inversion of power relations when those doctors who invent the instruments of domination have them turned onto their (or, if we are to hold on to some mark of difference, onto Elliot's) body, the film also offers the more powerful image of Bev just waking up after the surgery. Framed left and foregrounded, he is lying on one gynecological examining table while his brother lies in the background, in the same posture, on another table; out of focus, the image of Elliot only suggests with a splotch of color the bloody spectacle from which Beverly recoils. This is the final shot of a series of gynecological scenes of doctor and patient, but now there are the two doctors or, if you will, two patients. Here is (or might have been) an opportunity to imagine the tables turned on decades of male practitioners whose technologies and instrumentalizations of the female body have resulted in so much pain.[20]

As troubling as such strategies of inversion are in their tendency to reinstate those relations of power which they mean to subvert, it is useful to think of this scene in relation to a shocking news item published in the same year as the film's release. Consider the case of Dr. James Burt, the Dayton, Ohio "love surgeon" who, according to the

New York Times (11 December, 1988) took it upon himself to restructure the insides of hundreds of women—many without their knowledge—to correct the female anatomy which in his words "is structurally inadequate for intercourse." What if *he* were subjected to radical reconstructive surgery, a procedure comparable to his removing the hood of the clitoris, repositioning the vagina, the urethra, and repositioning the walls between the rectum and the vagina, causing scarring, infections, phlebitis, and pain? And what if the dozens of his associates who claimed to "recognize his work" and did nothing to stop it were similarly treated?[21]

More than one woman has fantasized the implications for social organization and culture of men giving birth, or even enduring the medical drill of the gynecogical exam.[22] In *The Woman in the Body*, Emily Martin suggests just such a turnabout as she quotes from an interview with a woman who has been pressured into having a cesarean section:

> If your husband was told that he had to get an erection and ejaculate within a certain time or he'd be castrated, do you think it would be easy? To make it easier, perhaps he could have an I.V. put into his arm, be kept in one position, have straps placed around his penis, and be told not to move: He could be checked every few minutes; the sheet could be lifted to see if any "progress" had been made.[23]

As Martin remarks: "Imagining technology being used to control those who ordinarily use it to control others throws the power relations into focus" (Martin, 58). This is not the same thing as getting even. What such imaginings may most usefully reveal is the utter falseness of the presumed complementarity of the male and female bodies; the ludicrousness of the male body undergoing the gynecological drill shows up more than anything the *asymmetry* of gendered bodies in the same position. It shows up those differences which make the female body a crucial (though presumably not eternal) site of contestation. Martin's anthropological study, which shows that women in general, and working-class women in particular, do resist in various

ways the dominant representations of their bodies because of their
social position, argues forcefully that such altered consciousness is
transformative only in relation to material changes.

Apart from theoretical discussions within feminism of power reversals, there is the important lesson of poststructuralist thought that the
focus on power, or rather the *representation* of the focus on power, can
be an effect of power itself. Jean Baudrillard, for instance, describes as
pure simulation that instance of negative inversion when power seems
to mutilate and annihilate itself:

> Every form of power, every situation speaks of itself by denial, in
> order to attempt to escape, by simulation of death, its real agony.
> Power can stage its own murder in order to rediscover a glimmer of
> existence and legitimacy.[24]

Such a formulation is extremely useful in describing not only the
political effacement of all possible resistance in producing the image
of a gynecologized male body in the closing scene of *Dead Ringers,* but
also in suggesting the limits of such "postpolitical" argumentation. It
could be argued, certainly, that at the performative level, Baudrillard
himself has staged the very simulation he describes, evoking in his
language a drama of theatened loss, "real agony," "death", and "redis-
covery" of power, creating a "glimmer" of sadness, even tragedy, at the
same time as he denies its "existence" within the radically negative
mode of representation he describes.[25] This phrase aptly describes, in
my reading, Cronenberg's closing strategy in *Dead Ringers.*

Returning to the double image of Bev and Elly, men (the two standing for the many) in the gynecological position, how are we to understand the recent convergence of the mass media spectacles of male
hysteria and sacrifice, such as this one, with those more subtle theoretical gestures which also reproduce the appearance of male self-abne-
gation and reconfiguration? The back cover of the *Canadian Journal of
Political and Social Theory* issue on male hysteria[26] offers a kind of
postmodern multiple choice and leaves the reader to choose her/his
favorite explanation:

—Power, fleeing its basis in sexuality generally and male subjectivity specifically, becomes now a *viral* power, a power which speaks
only in the previously transgressive feminist language of absence,
rupture, plurality and the trace. A post-male power which leaves
behind male subjectivity as a hysterical photographic negative of
itself, and which disappropriates women of the privileged ontology
of the Other.

—Or is it just the reverse? Not the decoupling of sex and power, but
a hyper-infusion of power by a male sex which, speaking now only
in the fantasy language of one libido, seeks to hide the privileging
of the phallocentric gaze by theorising the disappearance of power
into seduction. The psychoanalytics of one libido, therefore, as one
last playing-out of old male polyester sex theory, a big zero.

—Or maybe it's neither. Not one libido theory nor its denial, but
the production of neon libidos in the age of sacrificial sex when
sexuality too is both produced by power as *trompe l'oeil* and then
cancelled out. Sacrificial sex, therefore, as a time of the monstrous
double, when all the sex differences are simulated *and* exterminated
in a spiralling combinatorial of cynical signs.[27]

The answer, of course, is all of the above, because this kind of panic-
stricken theory is meant to enact what it is theorizing—an entropic
male hysteria that admits of no outside, certainly no privileged outside point of critique. No positive alterity, no Other.[28] Monstrous
doubles, sacrificial sex, the psychoanalytics of one libido, hysterical
negation, and post-male power, speaking the language of absence and
rupture which once belonged to a "previously trangressive" feminist
language, are all part of the charm of *Dead Ringers,* as is the final
restoration of the consecrated male body in the powerful "tableau
mourant" which ends the film, eliding death and woman.[29]

Mutant Women

The last appearance in the film of the female lead, Claire Niveau,
finds her answering the telephone with a speechless Beverly on the

other end, unable, or unwilling, finally, to make contact. Claire
Niveau's body, defined from its initial framing as mutant, is an unsta-
ble receptor of gender meanings and represents an awkward space for
construing the female as anything but provisional. Her deep, husky
voice, carefully modulated to almost a whisper, is the production of a
disciplined actress who understands the "effects" of the body, and who
keeps an ironic and critical distance from her own appearance.[30] This
relative control over her bodily effects is, of course, greatly constrained by the poor scripts and incompetent costumers which characterize her professional life, and which figure metaphorically in her
everyday amateur performances of the female self.[31] Here, I am thinking, as well, of Genevieve Bujold's limited possibilities in the second
half of Cronenberg's film, in a narrative which has less and less room
for her. Genevieve Bujold/Claire's body is constantly conscripted—in
the medical, theatrical, and sexual scenarios of the film, particularly,
but not exclusively—by those instrumentalities which are custom-
designed for her as mutant woman. She is conscripted in the very
sense that Judge Blackmun used the term in his dissent from the
Supreme Court ruling on abortion which he saw as a move to "clear
the way for the State to conscript a woman's body."[32] Her part in that
gynecological script is, in contrast to her busy professional life, quite
limited and, I would add, inaccessible to the normative narrative productions of the rest of her (work) life. Her grotesque bodily detail is a
thing apart, a part which, in Foucault's terms, is expressible only in
relation to its visibility. For him, what can be seen can be expressed,
and throughout the nineteenth century, the embodied self becomes
more and more expressive. In relation to this part, however, Claire is
cut off from self-expression because it represents a kind of blind spot
in her field of vision. In the classic position described by feminist film
theory, she, unlike the twins, can only see herself being seen and only
up to the vanishing point which is the maternal. Unlike the twins, she
cannot figure or represent the maternal and, hence, is no longer
needed. A line of questioning entirely undeveloped in this film is
whether the nonreproductive female body "part" (two extra doors to

an empty womb) is a particularly dangerous supplement or, in the dominant system of representation which relies on mirroring production, merely a negligible waste, like an abandoned factory.

Of course, the questions do not end here. *Dead Ringers* is relatively low-tech in relation to reproductive technologies and the visual field. In the postmodern visual economy, one might ask if her grotesque reproductive organ might simply be replaced, with its work "sourced out" to another production site, thus ending the conflation of the feminine with the maternal. And, could one not reimagine Beverly, Elliot, and Claire as postmodern, postgender triplets sharing bloodstreams, needles, system environment, and bodily configurations? If sexual reproduction is understood in Donna Haraway's terms, as one design strategy among others, and if corporeal architectures are no longer constrained by any "natural" difference or boundaries, could Claire's mutant anatomy suggest an extra exit, a different way out of maternal visibility and invisibility?[33] Or is this planned obsolescence another modernist ruse for what Rosi Braidotti has identified as the "rehabilitation of one of patriarchy's most persistent fantasies" in "the homologizing of women with a male mode?"[34] Cronenberg's film stops far short of considering the stakes for women in such reconfigurations or fictive tactics. It does, however, remind us that the stakes for women, in the body, are still high.

5

"From the Base Upward"
Trilby's Left Foot, Nationalism, and the Grotesque

> A trapeze, a knotted rope, and two parallel cords supporting each a
> ring, depended from a huge beam in the ceiling. The walls were of
> the usual dull red, relieved by plaster casts of arms and legs and
> hands and feet; and Dante's mask, and Michael Angelo's altorilievo
> of Leda and the swan, and a centaur and Lapith from the Elgin mar-
> bles—on none of these had the dust as yet time to settle.[1]

What a curious habitat was the Bohemian loft at the *fin-de-siècle*,
and how utterly familiar a century later: some exercise equipment, a
few recycled art objects in the form of reproductions or fragments,
and—as "collectibles"—the plaster models of human limbs and extremities used for decoration.[2] Of course, the narrator's satiric comment on the cleanliness of the room frames this scene as something
more or less (depending on your point of view) than postmodernist
kitsch, but belonging, nonetheless, to the modern world's interest in
the pastiches of received culture and the extension of art into life-
style.[3] It seems fitting, if only coincidental, that such "creative clutter"
should gather at the end of both centuries to remind us to sort
through and question what is to be kept and what is to be thrown away
in the bricolage of European culture.

In some ways, the space of Bohemia functioned similarly as a kind
of cultural attic filled with cultural discards—objects and social types
marginal to the formation of the bourgeoisie in the nineteenth century.[4] The eighteenth century had already conceptualized this
Bohemian space to contain the fragile and unruly homeless: gypsies,

the roving bands of *commedia dell'arte* players, acrobats, musicians, Wandering Jews, vagrants, etc.[5] Karl Marx, in a famous passage of *The Eighteenth Brumaire* revises the list:

> . . . ruined and adventurous offshoots of the bourgeoisie . . . vagabonds, discharged soldiers, discharged jailbirds, escaped galley slaves, swindlers, mountebanks, *lazzaroni,* pickpockets, tricksters, gamblers, *maquereaus,* brothel keepers, porter, *literati,* organ-grinders, ragpickers, knife grinders, tinkers, beggars—in short, the whole indefinite, disintegrated mass, thrown hither and thither, which the French term *la bohème.*[6]

In the course of the nineteenth century, this "spectacle of hetero-geneity,"[7] which had been identified by Marx and Engels with an immunity to historical transformation, becomes crucial to the consol-idation of bourgeois art, taste, and life-style. It also moves from a strictly marginal space to literally center stage in the theatricalizations of Henri Murger's *La vie de bohème* in the mid-century, to the era of Puccini's operatic version *La Bohème* in the nineties.[8] Popular enter-tainment, advertising, tourism, and commodification of art, in gen-eral, interacted to produce a fascinating image of the life of the artist in opposition to dominant culture.[9] By the late nineteenth century the perceived degradation and dangers of the Bohemian lifestyle were greatly idealized to produce a refurbished and cleaner Bohemia, avail-able as a "*self-chosen* subculture," now only "loosely associated with marginality, youth, poverty, devotion to art, and a shifting set of rebel-lious behaviors and attitudes."[10]

Bohemia was a social and an imaginative space where a young man could live dangerously for a while and be an artist. Women had their roles in this milieu but not as artists, not as true Bohemians.[11] The *grisette,* the maid, the prostitute, the model, each had an important role to play in the lives of the Bohemians but none that exceeded the bounds of the conventions of gender in nineteenth-century France.[12] As the historian Michael Wilson points out, "the most obvious com-plication of bohemia's transgressive claims" is its construction "around the most conventional, pervasive and invidious norms, those

"AU CLAIR DE LA LUNE"

Fig. 27   Illustration from Georges du Maurier's *Trilby.*

of gender and sexuality" (Wilson, 195). Despite the subordination of women to men, the idealization of the lives of women in Bohemia contained within it a strong and persistent notion of freedom from the domestic and sexual constraints of the bourgeois household.[13] The intense interest in young women, loose in the world, without a bourgeois home, continues throughout the century and the version of this character in the popular novel of George du Maurier, *Trilby*, is in that respect only one of a long series.[14] While there are many other novels that illustrate the themes of this chapter—the grotesque in relation to subculture, the female model and norms of the body, spectacle, and cultural politics—the reception of this novel by young women in the nineties makes it unique. More importantly, the dense mediations of Bohemia as well circulated symbolic capital function within the novel to make its chronological references particularly complex, a feature which accounts, in part, for its association with the subject of the following chapter, Angela Carter's postmodernist novel *Nights at the Circus*.[15]

Trilby

Trilby, a novel with illustrations by the author, began to appear as a serial in *Harper's Monthly* in January 1894. Trilby is the name of the young figure model who falls under the spell of the fiendish musician Svengali, and is transformed into a great virtuoso singer despite the fact that she is tone deaf. A playbill advertising the subsequent stage version starring John Barrymore sensationalizes the plot as "the tale of an evil genius and his beautiful love slave," showing the extent to which the hideous and reviled figure of Svengali with his long, matted hair and unkempt beard, nasty manners, and weird voice eventually took over the reception of the novel.[16] For the student of the grotesque, the appearance of Svengali as a spidery presence lurking in the corners of Bohemian Paris is immediately compelling, for he embodies marginality, mockery and exaggeration, slovenliness, and filth, described in chauvinistic and anti-Semitic associations with Jewishness and with the East. Svengali's body is scrutinized almost as much as Trilby's in the novel and, in one way, even more so, in that she is almost never represented as self-conscious of her body or as self-producing her image. Svengali, on the other hand, is seen in his own mirror, wiping his grimy finger across his forehead and twisting his greasy hair into a particularly offensive tail.[17] Despite the fact that Svengali is set up to be the agent of male seduction and abuse of women in the novel, Svengali and Trilby share many bodily effects and gestures, particularly an uncertain and dangerous social and cultural mobility across the boundaries of nation, class, sexuality, and even gender.[18]

Although Trilby and Svengali captured the popular imagination, they are not, strictly speaking, the main characters in the novel, nor is the tone of the novel uniformly melodramatic or gothic. To the contrary, the narrative begins as a bright, mildly satiric, and leisurely account of life in the Latin Quarter in the mid-nineteenth century for "three nice clean Englishmen" (*TR*, 386): Taffy, the Laird, and Little Billee. Their Englishness is intensified through their association with one another, a fictional instance of that form of male bonding—a deep horizonal comradeship—which Benedict Anderson has described as characteristic of the modern nation state.[19] As the familiar, even hackneyed, plot proceeds, all three young artists come to love Trilby despite her promiscuous past and unconventional manners. As an object of cultural curiosity and desire, she circulates between them in a consolidation of the homosociality described by Eve Kosofsky Sedgwick in *Between Men*.[20] Trilby also, it should be noted, mediates between their little nation and Svengali as the symbolic corridor between the West and the East in the novel.[21] In general terms, their manliness and their Englishness has everything to do with the norms of appearance, cleanliness, speech, and habitation which differentiate them from Trilby and Svengali; but the *kind* of men they are in relation to one another and even the kind of Englishmen they are is established through other norms, including, very importantly, height.[22] Verticality, as figured in the trapeze and the pedestal, quantifies just *how* masculine and how English they are comparatively.

TIT FOR TAT

Fig. 28   Illustration from Georges du Maurier's *Trilby*.

Little Billee (the least masculine) proposes marriage, his mother intervenes to prevent his social ruin, and Trilby disappears until her fabulous reincarnation as "la Svengali." When Svengali dies during one of her performances, Trilby loses her musical powers. She too dies soon afterward, surrounded by the three English friends. The novel ends with an epilogue in which Taffy, now the epitome of the bourgeois English family man, meets up with Svengali's gypsy sidekick, Gecko, for a conversation about the "two Trilbys"—*their* Trilby, the simple girl of the Latin quarter and Svengali's Trilby—before returning to a properly humdrum existence in his perfect English country home.

Thrillbies

According to Du Maurier's son, the plot was offered by the author to his friend, Henry James, who declined. One can only imagine the results of Jamesian treatment, but the version produced by du Maurier himself was astonishingly successful, particularly in the United States, where a cult grew up around the book and produced a body of accompanying materials. This "Trilbyana" included letters from readers, glossaries explaining obscure references and translating the many phrases and dialogues in accented or imprecise French, German, or Latin, critical debates, dramatizations, objects, including sheet music, costume jewelry, novelty food items (e.g., Trilby ice-creams and sausages), contests, amateur musicales, parodies and travesties (called "Thrillbies"), and even circus acts. In 1895, *The Critic* published a collection of Trilbyana which contained the following report:

> Trilby representations have broken out in all sorts of strange places. At the Eden Musee, New York, Miss Ganthony has been restrained from impersonating du Maurier's heroine; and at "The Greatest Show on Earth," Miss Marie Meers who has not been restrained, appears nightly in Trilby costume, *riding bareback (not barefoot)* around the tan-bark of the snappings of ringmaster Svengali's whip (emphasis mine).[23]

The distinction between "bareback" and "barefoot" recalls the crucial issue for contemporary readers of the novel concerning the question of the heroine's virtue. Considering her sexual generosity ("q*uia multum amavit,*" as du Maurier puts it biblically) and the fact of her modelling, in her words, for the "ensemble" or the "altogether," what sort of model in the social and moral sense could she be?[24] It is, of course, a truism of Bohemia that the woman painted as Virtue in the subject paintings which Trilby describes was not likely to be a woman of virtue; this is to compare allegorical and historical contents. But, to put the question in another but not unrelated way as a problem of representation and aesthetic form, what is Trilby, after all, a model *of*, if *not* the barefoot, which is her part *par excellence* in the novel?

As a model of normativity, the severe and penetrating moral, social, and aesthetic judgements seem to converge upon the female body. In this regard, Trilby's body is distinguished by its capacious and accommodating welcome to all comers discursive and otherwise, for she is, as Nina Auerbach has written, a "virtual giantess"—so large that "she can be parcelled into fragments with a self-contained and totemistic value of their own."[25] Given this capaciousness and amazing generativity, where any part may become central, the best tactic might simply be to offer a few footnotes.

Some Footnotes

1. Trilby's foot (her *left* foot, to be exact) is her most classical feature and the feature most represented within the narrative. Her foot is so exquisite, so classically proportioned, that Little Billee is able to draw it from memory after seeing it only once. He simply draws the perfect foot. The drawing of Trilby's foot by the one "real artist" in the group seems to prove the narrator's dictum that you cannot really know how beautiful or how ugly a thing is until you try to draw it.[26] The drawing of Trilby's foot on the wall is an artistic proof of the existence in nature of the classical. This equation of the classical with the natural, which is elaborated throughout the narrative, has as its corollary the dictum that nothing in nature is truly grotesque.

As Trilby makes her first appearance, gleefully kicking off her slippers to show "the delicate lengths and subtly modulated curves and noble straightnesses and happy little dimpled arrangements" of her foot, Little Billee sees the incongruity between this perfection and the rest of her:

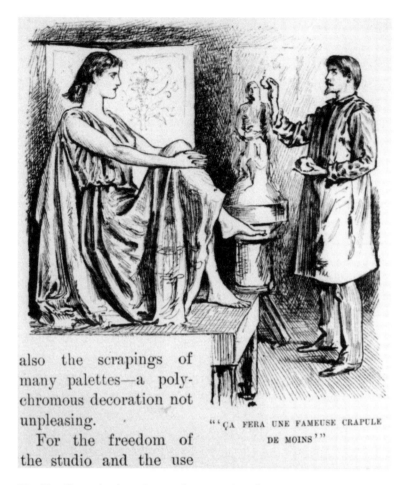

also the scrapings of
many palettes—a poly-
chromous decoration not
unpleasing.   "'ÇA FERA UNE FAMEUSE CRAPULE
    For the freedom of   DE MOINS'"
the studio and the use

Fig. 29   Illustration from Georges du Maurier's *Trilby*.

. . . such a base or pedestal lent quite an antique and Olympian dignity to the figure that seemed just then rather grotesque in its
mixed attire of military overcoat and female petticoat, and nothing
else! Poor Trilby! (*TR*, 18)

Trilby's boyish and irregular features, her robust figure, her big teeth,
and freckled complexion do not fit the artistic frame. The heterogeneity of her body suggests a level of conflict which can only be resolved
by severing her foot from the rest of the "ensemble," so that it can

make its separate way with such timeless mobility that, according to the narrative, it can be found even thirty years later, "facsimilied in dusty, pale plaster of Paris . . . on the shelves and walls of many a studio throughout the world" (*TR,* 18).

2. This foot is gendered. Despite the universality of the classical dream of symmetry, and despite the scale of Trilby's body (much larger than Little Billee's), this foot is eventually revealed as female. This is strikingly evident in the following passage where, as the narrative description moves from praising the wondrous *natural, classic,* and *human* foot to a discussion of the deformity and unnaturalness caused by shoes and boots of "civilized adults," the particular foot is gendered female:

> For when Dame Nature takes it into her head to do her very best, and bestow her minutest attention on a mere detail as happens now and then—once in a blue moon, perhaps—she makes it uphill work for poor human art to keep pace with her.

> It is a wondrous thing, the human foot—like the human hand; even more so, perhaps; but, unlike the hand, with which we are so familiar, it is seldom a thing of beauty in civilized adults who go about in leather boots or shoes.

> So that it is hidden away in disgrace, a thing to be thrust out of sight and forgotten. It can sometimes be very ugly indeed—the ugliest thing there is, even in the fairest and highest and most gifted of her sex; and then it is of an ugliness to chill and kill romance, and scatter young love's dreams, and even break the heart.

> And all for the sake of a high heel and a ridiculous pointed toe— mean things, at the best! (*TR,* 19)

Finally, the shoes and boots are high-heeled and pointed. This most ugly foot ("grewsome, (sic) boot-begotten abominations") which threatens exposure, sexual abjection, and even heartbreak is, in fact, another foot, but one whose proximity to the idealized left foot of Trilby contributes to its meaning in much the same way that the

TRILBY'S LEFT FOOT

Fig. 30 Illustration from Georges du Maurier's *Trilby*.

grotesque constitutes and is constituted by the classical (*TR*, 19).

The introduction of the shoe, and with it history, material production, fashion, and the market completes the logic opposing nature
with culture, classical beauty with deformity, the inner with the outer,
and the hidden with exposed. What we have, in short, is a list of binary
oppositions and two (possibly left) feet. The second, seemingly extra
foot disappears from the narrative but reemerges hilariously in du
Maurier's illustrations of the famous drawings of Trilby's foot.

The first of the two illustrations of Little Billee's famous drawing is
entitled *Trilby's Left Foot,* showing Little Billee and a sculptor friend:
one man drawing, one man looking, and a missing foot. The drawing
seems to be nothing so much as the representation of lack, with two
men (standing for, perhaps, many men) on the side of the gaze and on
the other side, a blank. In this drawing, we may say that Trilby's invisible foot is locatable only in relation to the company of men, an idea
serving to consolidate their own gendered identities. What the artist's
pen has produced is the intact male body; Trilby's left foot is signified
only as lack.

This illustration evokes the Freudian scenario of fetishism as precisely the attempted representation of lack in the service of male disavowal: the foot fetish serving to cover over the recollection of an
earlier perception of the female genitals as mutilated or lacking a
penis. The fetish, as contemporary commentators habitually point
out, is not then to be understood as hiding something (i.e., female
sexuality as a positive term or as a material specificity), but rather hiding the feared no-thing, castration.

Little Billee's drawing, from memory, of Trilby's foot suggests that
the classical foot, with its claims of perfection and universality which
her particular foot comes to model, is available precisely only as an
idealization, even for men. This illustration might be retitled: "Trilby's
Foot: Classicism and Phallic Plenitude."

The second illustration of Little Billee's drawing is set some years
later. The three Englishmen return to the studio and find the old drawing. Again, this second reproduction shows three men facing the wall,
staring intently at Little Billee's drawing which has been framed as a

"souvenir" by one of the former tenants. Little Billee's masterpiece (the drawing is signed with his initials) is something of a joke: the promise of rosy-heeled perfection and perfect symmetry has delivered only a scrawny scribble of a foot, a caricature of classical beauty, a tribute neither to his art school nor to "la grande Trilby." The humor of the drawing is apparently not available to the three Englishmen who are still enormously invested in its artistry. They continue to extol its beauty, deploring the "very vulgar and trivial and coarse" caricatures which surround it, one of which is visible at the right corner of the frame. Only the oak frame separates the chalk sketch of Trilby's foot from the "more or less incomprehensible legends" of the graffiti which are framed in turn by the dirt, stench, and dilapidation of the once charming studio (*TR,* 300).

The horrifying possibility that the "little masterpiece" might perish in the anarchy and filth of its surroundings (an anxiety which operates at the sexual as well as the architectural level) leads the Laird to actually suggest buying a section of the wall and moving it out to a safer location. The fetishizing of the art object in the straight-faced narrative which continues to insist on the beauty of this classical foot almost stifles the visual humor of the foot as grotesque caricature. The illustration might well have accompanied the description of the female foot as bound and deformed by high heels and pointed toes discussed earlier. The drawing seems incompatible with the claims made for Trilby's foot, but it does provide something to cover the wall where her beautiful, stupendous classical foot should have been, but was not, in the first illustration.

This caricature could well be conceptualized in Derridean terms, as a kind of "dangerous supplement," an additional foot representation, compensating for what was supposed to be The Foot, natural and complete unto itself. The concept of the supplement includes, importantly, a sense of mis-fitting. The supplement comes from outside, and is alien rather than complementary; in this regard, it is important to note that these two feet are not a pair. The scribbled foot, which is the mark of the grotesque, belongs as much to the communal graffiti as it does to the private collector or to the gallery. In this case, it resists

"PAUVRE TRILBY"

Fig. 31   Illustration from Georges du Maurier's *Trilby*.

commodification, and the Laird is unable to get the concierge to even quote a price.

As a crucial part of the economy of fetishism, the example of the deformed foot, which has been associated with an historical specificity and with a material production of boots and shoes, threatens

to expose not only the projected image of the female body as mutilated, but the mutilation itself as an historical and cultural event. A
similar process is at work in a much more authoritative text on the
topic. Freud's essay, "Fetishism" ends with an even more startling
grotesque foot image which he calls "a parallel to fetishism in social
psychology . . . the Chinese custom of mutilating the female foot and
then revering it like a fetish after it has been mutilated."[27] As Kaja
Silverman has remarked, this example suggests "that in some situa-
tions the fetish speaks as much to the desire to castrate woman as to
deny her castration."[28] To the extent that this excessive, spectacularized representation operates as violent and conflictual in the social as
well as the psychic field, the orientalist image serves to position the
grotesque as a political and cultural icon of women's oppression. In
Du Maurier's text and illustrations, the grotesque performs a kind of
cultural sign-labor which contributes both to the imaginary form of
classical fetishism and to its de-formity as a representation of real
social relations.

3. Both of the above (feet) have class. As an example of the
European novel's powerful conflation of beauty with morality and
morality with class, Little Billee's half-conscious reflections on the
base (in both the social and the moral sense) are instructive. Briefly,
Little Billee is unable to reconcile Trilby's lack of virtue with her "god-
dess-like extremities" (TR, 48). Her "angel's feet" make him "quite
sick to think she sits for the figure . . . she's quite a lady" (TR, 26).
Interestingly, this preoccupation with "lovely female shapes" as "terrible complicators of the difficulties and dangers of this earthly life"
relates directly to his view of class from the vantage point of what he
imagines as "good people" in the middle: "people . . . whose two parents and four grandparents had received a liberal education and
belonged to the professional class" (TR, 50–51). He scorns the rich (at
least in this youthful Bohemian interlude), seeing them as grotesques
—"bloated dukes and lords," but he cannot bear Trilby's footloose
morality. He wishes she were "a young lady—say the vicar's daughter
in a little Devonshire village—his sister's friend" (TR, 48). In the
words of the ironic and bemused narrator:

And all this melancholy preoccupation, on Little Billee's part, from
the momentary gleam and dazzle of a pair of over-perfect feet in an
over-aesthetic eye, too much enamoured of mere form!

Reversing the usual process, he had idealized from the base
upward! (*TR*, 50)

What is the shame of idealizing "from the base upward?" Georges
Bataille describes this kind of frustrated desire to always elevate
human life as an effect of the constant impetus to divide the world
between the high and the low:

The division of the universe into subterranean hell and perfectly
pure heaven is an indelible conception, mud and darkness being
the *principles* of evil as light and celestial space are the *principles* of
good: with their feet in the mud but their heads more or less in
light, men obstinately imagine a tide that will permanently elevate
them, never to return, into pure space. Human life entails, in fact,
the rage of seeing oneself as a back and forth movement from refuse
to ideal, and from the ideal to refuse—a rage that is easily directed
against an organ as *base* as the foot.[29]

Although these preoccupations are displaced onto the female body, as
foot (and also mouth) in *Trilby*, Little Billee's own body and sexuality
are surely implicated.[30] Unlike Trilby, he is an hysteric when disap-
pointed in love. His body's very diminutive size sets him at the lower
limit of masculinity; twice in the novel Svengali physically attacks him,
whereupon his enormous friend Taffy repels Svengali. He is a natural
friend of women ("darlings young and old") whom he relates to asexu-
ally, as in the novel's illustration *Platonic Love* which shows a man
meditating in a hall of unplayed female violins; in short, in the terms of
the narrator, Billee is "an unmanly kind of duffer" (*TR*, 340).

Similarly, Little Billee is described as having a "homeopathic"
amount of Jewish blood"—making him artistic, sensitive, passionate,
and not too "Angliche" (*TR*, 6). His own bodily configuration contributes greatly to his social mobility, and may account for his preoccupation with Trilby's unwholesomeness. In the most clichéd

anti-semitic fashion, some of his best friends in the capitalist upper classes and in Bohemia (namely Svengali) are Jewish. Because of his class, he is able to accrue a certain cultural capital from his homeopathy; like his association with women, this serves to facilitate his own social and artistic mobility. His inversion of the ideal and the abject is only temporary; once he returns to English society he gets the right side up again and develops his affinity with the upper classes.

Honorine, or The Class Underfoot

Outside the purview of Little Billee's bourgeois sentimentalism, beyond the pale of his consideration of Womanly virtue, lies the body of a seemingly inessential character, Honorine (or Mimi la Salope as she is contemptuously called), who is beaten, exploited financially, and tossed out into the street by Svengali, who threatens to denounce her for prostitution after he has taken all her money for singing lessons. What possible use can this ethnically marked lower-class body have ("a dirty, drabby little doppy-mop of a Jewess, a model for the figure—a very humble person indeed, socially") except to set the lower limits of Trilby's mobility, to prop her up, as it were, onto the stage of bourgeois entertainment and class structure? The displacement of filth, poverty, and immorality onto Mimi, who is cast out into supposed oblivion as a "mere mud-lark of the Paris slums—her wings clipped, her spirit quenched and broken, and with no more singing left in her than a common or garden sparrow," suggests a very fragile line between the public woman in the limelight and the woman in the shadows (*TR*, 65). In the terms of the novel, Mimi does a kind of invisible aesthetic and moral work to facilitate Trilby's fabulous success in the new music halls for mass entertainment.[31]

It is something of an historical irony, however, that the abject figure of Mimi la Salope reemerges in French national culture in the twentieth century in the guise of Edith Piaf and other female singers working in the tradition of the "chanson realiste." The repertoire and performance styles of these singers evoked nostalgically the demimonde of the proletariat, sub-proletariat, pimps, petty criminals, and prostitutes in order to signify a certain authenticity and Frenchness and, arguably, to represent the boundaries of lower/middle class experience.[32]

4. Trilby's foot is historical, one foot among others (on an equal footing?) in the history of reproduction. The studio which she enters in the opening scene is a male bastion with places reserved for sports, such as boxing, fencing, gymnastics and for the general roughhousing of young men who are for a time Bohemians.[33] Because Trilby cannot appreciate music and art, it is said that "fencing and boxing and trapezing were more in her line." This, of course, contributes to one view of her physicality as being on the side of the masculine (*TR*, 46). The most interesting objects in the room in regard to Trilby's foot may be the collection of plaster casts of arms, legs, hands, and feet:

> Along the walls, at a great height, ran a broad shelf, on which were other casts in plaster, terra-cotta, imitation bronze: a little Theseus, a little Venus of Milo, a little discobolus; a little flayed man threatening high heaven (an act that seemed almost pardonable under the circumstances!); a lion and a boar by Bayre; an anatomical figure of a horse with only one leg left and no ears; a horse's head from the pediment of the Parthenon, earless also; and the bust of Clytie, with her beautiful low brow, her sweet wan gaze, and the ineffable forward shrug of her dear shoulders that makes her bosom a nest, a rest, a pillow, a refuge—to be loved and desired forever by generation after generation of the sons of men (*TR*, 2).

These classical reproductions in plaster and terra-cotta are, of all the things in the studio which await her entrance, most like Trilby herself—not only because she exists to be loved and desired by "generation after generation of the sons of men" but because they, too, are models. Furthermore, as models of antiquity in the nineteenth century, there is an interesting parallel between the dwindling status of these reproductions replicated in fragments over four centuries, and Trilby's particular fragmentation, or, as it emerges later in Little Billee's melancholy, a certain ill-defined question of her wholesomeness. In the most literal way, these models are unwholesome and *have* been for a long time. This amazing taxonomy of maimed and battered classical figures (the Bayre animals and Watt's bust of Clytie are the only near-contemporary in the collection) represents the survivors of a century of change in taste and in the technology of reproduction.[34] By the end of the nineteenth century, these copies, which were once the *raison d'être* of art schools, the inspiration for cultural pilgrimages to in-scale "originals" in Italy, were mass produced using new techniques of miniaturization.

According to historians Francis Haskell and Nicholas Penny, the famous firm of Brucciani (mentioned in the novel) opened a hundred foot long public gallery of such casts in Covent Garden in 1864 for commercial purposes, although the firm maintained its ties to the museum.[35] No longer restored by great sculptors or indelibly joined to authentic originals, the classical model in the age of mechanical reproduction was devalued in certain sites; the traveler to Italy was more and more likely to visit early frescoes, paintings, and picturesque landscapes than to search out original statuary with the awe of Montaigne or Goethe.

Nonetheless, these massively familiar items reappeared in new places, at once more public and more private. One direction is underlined by the description of another corner of the studio "filled up as time wore on with endless personal knick-nacks, bibelots, private properties," in short, *kitsch* (*TR*, 3). The move might be characterized as the difference between the souvenir, with its lingering attachment to experience, and the "collectible," which is abstracted and systematized with other like objects.[36] This placement of the object within the studio corresponds to a certain patronizing and ironic domestication of one Trilby O'Ferral whose cultural wildness is a source of superiority and amusement for the three Englishmen, who treat her in that way that Eve Kosofsky Sedgwick has described in another context as an epistemological staging of the "open secret;" *their* Trilby is treated as if they knew something about her that she didn't know about herself.[37] Her cultural value depends on their attitudes and their knowledge. In contrast to this ironic privatization is the spectacular dislocation of the classical model in various sites of an emerging mass-mediated culture:

world fairs, advertising, new musical entertainment fora, photography, and early cinema.

The very last representation of Trilby's foot is seen by the three Englishmen in the shop windows of the Stereoscopic Company on Regent Street. There, among the "presentments of Madame Svengali" in various costumes and poses, they find a picture of her in classical dress, her sandaled left foot thrust forward on a pedestal, "in something of the attitude of the Venus of Milo" (*TR*, 369). Although they have seen La Svengali in performance, it is this photograph which to them identifies the real (their very own) Trilby:

> "Look, Sandy, look—*the foot*! Now have you got any doubts?"
> "Oh yes—those are Trilby's toes, sure enough!" And they all go in and purchase largely (*TR*, 369).

While the mass-reproduction of the image has steadily deprived the Venus of Milo of her aura, this same process has elevated the lowly Trilby (who still organizes her body to foreground the classical foot), and produced her highly profitable aura of celebrity.

From Foot to Mouth: Feminine Performance and the Acoustical Grotesque

> It is a hard thing for music lovers to comprehend, that a man of low and vicious life, and utterly without aspirations, can so express the penetrating beauty that lies in music more than in any other art.
> —Letter to *The Critic*, 1896.[38]

In the Pythagorean Platonic tradition both nature and art contain ideal proportions in three fields: the geometric, the arithmetic, and the musical. Trilby, in effect, violates all three. What reader of the novel can forget her first excruciatingly embarrassing performance of "Ben Bolt" in front of the all-male audience of main characters:

Miss O'Ferrall threw away the end of her cigarette, put her hands on her knees as she sat cross-legged on the model-throne, and sticking her elbows well out, she looked up to the ceiling with a tender, sentimental smile, and sang the touching song,

"Oh, don't you remember sweet Alice, Ben Bolt?
Sweet Alice, with hair so brown? etc. etc."

As some things are too sad and too deep for tears, so some things are too grotesque and too funny for laughter. Of such kind was Miss O'Ferrall's performance of "Ben Bolt."

From that capacious mouth and through that high-bridged nose there rolled a volume of breathy sound, not loud, but so immense that it seemed to come from all round, to be reverberated from every surface in the studio . . . It was as though she could never have deviated into tune, never once have hit upon a true note, even by a fluke—in fact, as though she were absolutely tone-deaf, and without ear, although she stuck to the time correctly enough (*TR*, 23).

This remarkably voluminous, if disharmonious, performance impresses Svengali who soon after seizes the opportunity to examine her mouth, for it is her capacious mouth that is the focus of her musicality. Svengali's inspection, brilliantly illustrated by Du Maurier, shows the bearded maestro peering up into her mouth, throat, and nasal passages with the aid of opera glasses; his running description suggests something between a Victorian medical examination of an hysteric (indeed she had come to him complaining of a neuralgia in her eye), and the inspection of an architectural engineer.[39] The "roof" of her mouth, he exclaims, mixing anatomical, architectural and acoustical metaphors is "like the dome of the Pantheon" and "the bridge" of her nose is "the belly of a Stradavarius" (*TR*, 72). Further, in line with the nationalist themes of the novel, Trilby's inner cavity is surveyed like a topographical map of Europe. He discovers a space so big that there is "room for toutes les gloires de la France, with thirty-two British teeth . . . as big as knuckle bones" (*TR*, 72). The breath produced by her lungs of leather are like those of "a beautiful white heifer fed on the buttercups and daisies of the Vaterland!" (*TR*, 72)

The focus of his examination is on the *immensity* of the inside spaces. Both the grotesque and the sublime potential of her body in performance and as performance is produced by the physical contours of this inner capaciousness. Gender is implicated, not only in the morphology of the female body as inner space but in the paradox of femininity produced as a simultaneous performance of lack ("tone-deaf and without ear") and excess ("so immense that it seemed to come from all around"). The voice production of the diva is engulfing but empty; it awaits the grid of musical proportions.

The move from foot to mouth brings with it a set of striking similarities between Trilby as a model of visual representation and Trilby as a grotesque female performer. Upward mobility, as it were, in the musical field, brings with it a remarkably similar set of constraints, moral accusations, and embarrassments as modelling for individual artists. If we follow Trilby's musical career from this early amateur effort to the triumphs of her appearances in Paris and London, we can identify a trajectory parallel to the visual representations of her left foot through the changing modes of cultural reproduction and mass entertainment in the late nineteenth century. The sketch of her foot framed on the wall of the studio is a reminder not only of the artists' times together but a reminder of *that time* when Trilby exposes herself most fully to the ridicule and condescension of the male artists, especially Svengali, who knows how bad (and how good) she really is. The photograph of her as "La Svengali" in Grecian dress with her foot forward shows her towering majestically above the audience and the musicians. But this representation of classical monumentality is, on closer inspection, as fragile as the foot sketch in the midst of graffiti, for in social and moral terms she teeters perilously between the glory (mass-mediated fame) of the diva and the shame of "little honor"— Honorine. Neither her performance style nor her musical repertoire secure her within the realm of high culture whether understood as an aesthetic or a social field.

Like the representations of her foot, her performance styles may be identified as falling within either the oppositional grotesque, as exemplified by her first totally unmusical rendition of "Ben Bolt," or the hybrid or supplemental grotesque within the classical, exemplified by her triumphant concerts in Paris and London. It would seem that her performances without Svengali's help are all within this first category. Certainly, when left on her own during a public performance, she repeats the humiliating performance of "Ben Bolt" (still in the repertoire to please the English audience) and, again, she sings it "her old way—as she used to sing it in the quartier latin—the most lamentably *grotesque* performance ever heard out of a human throat!" (emphasis mine) (*TR,* 379). Arguably, however, this too is a Svengali production as he sits on the sidelines with a ghastly grimace on his face, enjoying her humiliation in front of the despised English audience.[40]

Trilby's successful performances are in many ways more strikingly grotesque, although du Maurier reserves the word "grotesque" for her failures. Standing in the attitude of Venus of Milo, with her left foot on a pedestal, she is a singing statue, all marble unconscious, her entire body standing as if it were the Pantheon-like mouth. This is the view from afar. A closer description reveals a monstrous physicality in her performance, "her big white teeth glistening as she gently jerks her head from side to side in time to Svengali's baton, as if to shake the notes out quicker and higher and shriller" (*TR,* 332). During the famous Chopin Impromptu, the notes seem to liquify and bubble out of her mouth "like a clear, purling, crystal stream that gurgles and foams and bubbles along (*TR,* 332)." The music coming from Trilby's mouth becomes a spectacular excretion from a bodily monument. Like other models of Greek statuary in this historical era, Trilby's body has become a public fountain.[41] The French audience joins her in transforming the concert hall into a cascade of civic tearfulness ("some five or six thousand gay French people are sniffling and mopping their eyes like so many Niobes"). Niobe, who was turned to rock from which gushed the tears of mourning for her slain children, is the very model of the female fountain as nationalism. Claimed most often

for Italy ("the Niobe of Nations," as Byron called her), the figure of
Niobe in the famous classical statuary group was admired in the early
nineteenth century as a model of stoicism, combining the deepest
pain imaginable (maternal loss) with classical restraint.[42] In contrast,
through the multiplied image of thousands of sniffling French citizens, Niobe is reduced to the emotional equivalent of mass production, banal and ridiculous, like Trilby, who stands for the audience as
the audience stands for her. Along with its association with classical
iconography and style, the fountain has a long economic tradition
from the marketplace to the shopping mall and it is not farfetched to
see Trilby in this guise as another display item promoting mass consumption. In fact this is quite explicit in the text: to drink at this fountain, the Englishmen (all audiences large and small in the novel are
nationally identified) will pay anything:

> There was no sight worth working at in all Paris but Trilby in her
> golden raiment; no other princess in the world; no smile but hers,
> when through her parted lips came bubbling Chopin's Impromptu.
> They had not long to stay in Paris, and they must drink of that bub-
> bling fountain once more—coute que coute! (*TR*, 345)

This point is made again vividly by a consideration of the Svengali
repertoire in relation to the national cultures represented by her audience. Her body had previously been laid out for the viewer like a map
of Europe. Although Trilby is a very public spectacle, her appeal to the
English and French audiences is based on her ability to turn every
musical event into private sentiment and nostalgia.

Her style and repertoire evoke the coziest, domestic scenarios of
national life, establishing a point of class identification so strong that
national differences are temporarily set aside. For instance, during the
performance of the German song "Nussbaum," the French audience
"made up of *the most cynically critical people in the world and the most
anti-German* [emphasis mine], assisting with rapt ears and streaming
eyes at the imagined spectacle of a simple German damsel, a Mäd-
chen, a Fräulein just "verlobte"—a future Hausfrau—sitting under a

walnut tree in some suburban garden—à Berlin!" (*TR*, 323) That the monumental figure of La Svengali herself in the enormous concert hall would contract so neatly, like Alice, to fit the doll's-house scale of bourgeois fantasy, is testimony to the normative capacities of the classical icon in performance and to the ideological compulsion to put the female body back in its domestic place, even as it stretched out over the map of Europe.

There are, however, limits on the mobility of mass entertainers and this, finally, may be the forgotten lesson of Du Maurier's novel. The hierarchies of class and ethnicity structure every aspect of musicality and performance. To the question posed by the American "music-lover" who writes to *The Critic* to inquire how it is that a "man of low and vicious life" like Svengali can "express the penetrating beauty that lies in music more than any art," the musical constraints on the repertoire would indicate that, in fact, he can express musical beauty *only up to the point that is coterminous with his social mobility* at the upper limit of the grotesque. Accordingly to the censorious narrator, Svengali with all his genius cannot perform successfully "the highest and best of all." He must "draw the line just above Chopin. It will not do to lend your own quite peculiar individual charm to Handel and Bach and Beethoven; and Chopin is not bad as a *pis-aller*" (TR, 58). What Svengali as an Eastern European and déclassé Jew may bring to music is "minor literature";[43] that is, a repertoire and musicality which is too marked by the particular or the regional to aspire to the transcendence of the truly classical. Of course, if *Trilby* the novel is to fit anywhere into the canon of literature, it would be precisely in such a category as minor. What is being enacted historically is the shift in popular taste in France and England towards the inclusion and appropriation of marginalized music. Trilby's concerts feature Hungarian musicians, gypsy dances, folk songs, and popular songs from the national cultures of France and England.

Du Maurier's parody of music criticism mocks this bourgeois nationalism even as it participates in the classicism which constitutes it. The cosmopolitan (and bigoted) narrator is at a loss to recover either the twelve crucial articles on the Svengalis by Hector Berlioz or the great Theophile Gautier's "Madame Svengali—Ange, ou Femme" (lost in his collected works); he produces instead the word of a certain ignominious German critic called Herr Blagneur. This nationalist critic attacks as "Svengalismus:" the prima donna, national French taste, and the contamination of classical (German) music by all of the above and by the popular audiences associated with the cafe and the circus:[44]

> Mere virtuosity carried to such a pitch is mere viscosity—base acro-
> batismus of the vocal chords, a hysteric appeal to morbid Gallic
> "sentimentalismus;" and that this monstrous development of a phe-
> nomenal larynx, this degrading cultivation and practice of abnor-
> malismus of mere physical peculiarity, are death and destruction to
> a true music; since they place Mozart and Beethoven, and even *him-
> self* on a level with Bellini, Donizetti, Offenbach—any Italian tune-
> tinkler, any ballad-monger of the hated Paris pavement! and can
> make the highest music of all (even his own) go down with the com-
> mon French herd at the very first hearing, just as if it were some idi-
> otic refrain of the café chantant! (*TR*, 334)

Again, music is figured as a bodily fluid gushing forth from the freak body. Voice produced by the mere accident of grossest anatomy can only be a stunt, and Trilby and the other great divas are stunt singers in this hierarchy of musical taste and musical settings. Svengali's real claim is finally not to a true musical understanding of proportions and composition but of voice and voice alone, which flies from the base upward "making unheard heavenly melody of the cheapest, trivialest tunes—tunes of the café concert, tunes of the nurs-ery, the shop-parlor, the guard-room, the school-room, the pothouse, the slum" (*TR*, 59).[45] Svengali's entrepreneurial genius can be described as mediating high and low culture in just proportion; if he is barred from the upper reaches of musical production and must stop at Chopin, he also sets the lower limit taking in the "cheapest, trivialest tunes" of performance spaces but transforming them in ways that will still exclude the underclasses represented by, for instance, Honorine.[46]

Tuneless and Insane

There is a strong desire on the part of the three Englishmen to end the story of Trilby with a kind of reparation. The reader of the novel, as well, seeks the comforts of a narrative closure. After a last, excruciating public performance of "Ben Bolt" following Svengali's death, Trilby begins to fade away, her now aging body reclaimed by her three friends in a spirit of forgiveness:

> Tuneless and insane, she was more of a siren than ever—a quite unconscious siren—without any guile, who appealed to the heart all the more directly and irresistibly that she could no longer stir the passions (*TR*, 398).

In their view and in the view of some critics, Trilby is "the epitome of the passive, yielding woman . . . who pays for her sins of the flesh, as inevitably she had to, by dying the personification of the contemplative sublime." Citing the passage quoted above, Bram Dijkstra sees in the thematics of her dying body a dangerous fascination "for males of the late nineteenth century—and for women who failed to question its validity."[47]

This characterization of the aesthetic perversions of Trilby's dying is accurate as far as it goes. Her body, which has become progressively thinner and paler throughout the novel, is, in the last scenes, almost transparent. Dijkstra fails to mention, however, the strange circumstances of her actual death, and to note that the version of the dying Trilby as "tuneless and insane" represents the desires of the Englishmen, and is contradicted by the testimony of Svengali's assistant, the lowly Gecko.

Gecko, the gypsy, insists that she was never insane, but that, under hypnotic influence, she became in every sense another person: there were, he insists, "two Trilbys" (*TR*, 457). The description of her death does not provide a resolution to these competing claims, even if we choose to interpret "two Trilby's" as meaning two psyches in one body. In the text, there is more to her dying than meets the eye; for finally, her

death is acoustic. Propped up in bed with a photograph of Svengali, she
begins to sing, without visible breath and without words, the Chopin
Impromptu in A flat that had made her famous. In a Medusean effect,
her startling *vocalise* turns all three men to stone: "Between wonder,
enchantment, and alarm they were frozen to statues" (*TR*, 434). As her
voice grows "louder and shriller, and sweet with a sweetness not of this
earth," her head falls back and she whispers "Svengali" (*TR*, 434). At
least, she is not "tuneless," but the sounds she makes in death are unat-
tributable. The doctor enters moments later, confirms that she is dead,
but estimates that she has been dead at least for "several minutes—perhaps for quarter of an hour" (*TR*, 435). Either she dies singing or she
sings after dying, or both, or neither, since there is Gecko's proto-
Lacanian comment to reckon with that it "takes two to sing like la
Svengali" and that her voice was his unconscious (*TR*, 458).

Like the uncanny, nonidentical resemblance of the dead body to the
live, Trilby's voice is recognizable as her own, and at the same time, it
isn't; certainly, in the terms of the death scene, it is unlocatable in a sin-
gle temporal or acoustical source. In the exemplary text of the uncanny,
Hoffman's *Sandman*, Olympia, the musical performing doll, is nearly
torn apart in a horrifying tug of war between her two creators, the evil
Coppola and Professor Spalanzana. She is last heard of in the sound of
her "dangling feet bumping and rapping woodenly on the stairs."[48] As
with Trilby's voice, some motor mechanism seems still to be working.
Similarly, Trilby's body, figured in her much contested left foot, has
been continuously dislocated in a war of authority and of competing
frames. Far from the aestheticized fadings of Victorian womanhood,
Trilby dies almost too physically, in the midst of a disturbance which is
both material *and* uncanny, an enactment of dying which is similar to
her first performance of "Ben Bolt" except that it is both "too sad for
tears . . . and too grotesque and too funny for laughter."[49]

Verticality and Production

Only within a static and moralizing gaze can Trilby's body be kept
on that late-Victorian ladder from "woman" to "angel," or in the clas-

sical verticality of head to foot of which Little Billee's axis from the base upwards is a mere inversion. As Susan Stewart remarks, the grotesque represents a "jumbling of this order, a dismantling and re-presentation of the body according to the criteria of production rather than verticality[50]. Trilby's foothold on popular culture suggests a more diffuse generativity, a redistribution of the female body which, in the case of young female readers of the novel in the fin-de-siècle, was plea-surable and communal. The young girls who "yearned for feet as graceful as hers, spoke of their own as "Trilbies," wore Trilby slippers, dressed themselves in Trilby hats and coats (decorated with costume jewelry shaped like Trilby's own foot)"[51] were harbingers of the mass culture of the twentieth century, and not merely heirs to the male-authored traditions of aestheticism.

While this chapter has suggested the role of aesthetics and the grotesque in modelling social production, that model is exceeded in class and national terms by the excesses of the category of the grotesque itself, and by new cultural markets and the increasing commodi-fication of culture in those markets. While I would readily admit that such repetition and generativity might seem ideologically dangerous (after all, the Dreyfus affair only a few years later, with its proliferation of images and trinkets, was arguably a mass media carnivalization), this does not mean that Trilbyness signified that the novel "codified for young women everywhere additional extremes of self-destructive be-havior" (Dijkstra, 35). Nor am I suggesting that in the girlish enthusi-asm for Trilby, there emerges a new body politics which would simply ignore the violence of the repeated partitioning and dismemberment of the female body in various cultural contexts. But one should not be forced to surrender the important feminist critiques of partiality and fetishization to conceptualize a re-memberment that would admit, even embrace, incompleteness. Could the images of young women, singing Ben Bolt on a summer's night, with Trilby foot-pins on their dresses, suggest a possible reorganization of the conditions of viewing, as pin-wearers recognized each other in an expanded, if ephemeral (like Trilby's Impromptu) spectacle of community?

6

Revamping Spectacle

Angela Carter's *Nights at the Circus*

I BEGIN WITH THE DESCRIPTION OF A FICTIONAL POSTER depicting a young woman with wings shooting through the air like a rocket, a French circus poster hanging in the London dressing room of a famous aerialiste, "the most famous aerialiste of her day"—her day being the end, "the fag-end, the smoldering cigar-butt, of a nineteenth century which is just about to be ground out in the ashtray of history"[1]—a day, in other words, not unlike our own. In large letters, advertising her engagement in Paris, is her slogan: "Is she fact, or is she fiction?" The poster's sensational image of female flight is marked by a rather unusual angle of viewing:

> The artist had chosen to depict her ascent from behind, bums aloft, you might say; up she goes, in a steatopygous perspective, shaking out about her those tremendous red and purple pinions, pinions large enough, powerful enough to bear such a big girl as she. And she was a *big* girl. Evidently this Helen took after her putative father, the swan, around the shoulder parts (*NC*, 7).

The Helen in question, "Helen of the High-wire," sometimes called "the Cockney Venus," is the fabulous "Fevvers," the central character of Angela Carter's 1984 novel, *Nights at the Circus*.[2] As her stage names indicate (and all her names are stage names), Fevvers straddles high and low culture. A woman with wings, she is no ordinary angel—if there could be such a thing—but rather an exhilarating example of the ambivalent, awkward, and sometimes painfully conflictual configuration of the female grotesque. Everything about this creature is sublime excess: her size, of course, and those wings which strain and bulge beneath her "baby-blue satin dressing gown;" her six-inch-long eyelashes which she rips off gleefully one eye at a time, suggesting not only her deliberate production of unnaturalness, but also the pros- thetic grotesque (a question of give and take); her taste for immense quantities of champagne with eel-pie and a bit of mash; and her over- whelming rancid smell ("something fishy about the Cockney Venus") (*NC*, 8). "Heroine of the hour, object of learned discussion and pro- fane surmise, this Helen launched a thousand quips, mostly on the lewd side" (*NC*, 8).

> Fevvers begins her act under a heap of brightly colored feather behind tinsel bars while the orchestra plays "I'm only a bird in a gilded cage." Vamping, she strains at the bars and mews "part-lion and part-pussy cat" (*NC*, 14).

Walser, the skeptical young American reporter who is assigned to cover her for a paper in the United States, smugly identifies this open- ing bit as "kitsch." With great self-satisfaction, he notes that "the song pointed up the element of the meretricious in the spectacle, reminded you that the girl was rumored to have started her career in freak shows" (*NC*, 14). In fact, Fevvers has performed in meretricious spec- tacles her entire life, beginning with the *tableaux* staged in Ma Nelson's whorehouse and moving on to a less hospitable institution, the Museum of Female Monsters, directed by the gruesome Madame Schreck, who kept her anatomical performers in niches in an under- ground cave, stacked like wine bottles, for private viewings.[3]

In fact, it is debatable whether any performance site is not meretri- cious in this novel for Carter, who described herself as both a feminist and a socialist writer, and who seems to have gone beyond the more individualistic, psychic model of spectacularity which characterizes her short stories, such as "The Flesh and the Mirror," to map an his- torical and even global notion of spectacle similar to that described by Guy Debord in *Society of the Spectacle*. For Debord, "the spectacle is not a collection of images, but a social relation among people, mediated by images."[4] Spectacle in this sense is not an immaterial world apart, but rather the condition, divided, and producing division, of late capitalism:

> the spectacle, grasped in its totality, is both the result and the pro-
> ject of the existing mode of production. It is not a supplement to
> the real world, an additional decoration . . . It is the omnipresent
> affirmation of the choice *already made* in production and its corol-
> lary consumption (Debord, 6).

In a different though not incompatible sense, the concept of the "already made" is central to postmodernist discourse,[5] where it refers to the characteristic mode of cultural reprise or intertextuality of which Angela Carter's work is often taken to be an example.[6] Linda Hutcheon, for instance, in an essay on the politics of parody, cites the production of Fevvers as a feminist parody of Leda and the Swan as an example of subversive repetition.[7] Describing *Nights at the Circus*, she writes:

> The novel's parodic echoes of *Pericles, Hamlet,* and *Gulliver's Travels* all function as do those of Yeats' poetry when describing a whorehouse full of bizarre women as "this lumber room of femi-
> ninity, this rag-and-bone shop of the heart"; they are all ironic fem-
> inizations of traditional or canonic male representations of the so-called generic human-Man. This is the kind of politics of repre-
> sentation that parody calls to our attention (*NC*, 98).

In *Nights at the Circus* alone, dozens of other examples of intertexts from high and low culture might be cited, and not all of them by any means as central to the European canon as Shakespeare, Swift, or Yeats.[8] Allusions abound to the twentieth-century artistic and political avant-gardes, to Andrei Bely's *Petersburg*, to Freud, Poe, Bakhtin, and to the Marquis de Sade who remains perhaps the most striking influence throughout Carter's work.[9] Equally important, popular cul-
ture, which had once produced its own version of critical parody in carnival, reappears and is transformed in modes of display, perform-

ance, and reproduction which characterize its institutionalization in the European circus, museums, journalism, and advertising. Nor does Carter limit herself to male producers and performers. In what may be my favorite bit of intertextual play, Fevvers looks into the mirror as she prepares to go on stage in St. Petersburg and delivers Mae West's famous line, "Suckers," from *I'm No Angel* (1933), which features the great female impersonator dressed in circus garb as a lion tamer in an imposture of dominance and control.[10] This Hollywood image of Mae West as a "double-bluff" dominatrix is refigured in the excesses and obvious artifice of Fevvers' body and her act.[11] The cinematic frame is transposed to the frame of the mirror, an historical backward slide from high technology to the artisanal production of the female body "making-up."

Female narcissism itself as a canonical representation of the feminine is parodied and revised in the frames, mirrors, and circus rings which accompany the hyperbole of self-consciousness that is female masquerade. Carter returns again and again in her writing to female narcissism as a scene of failed transcendence.

"Flesh and the Mirror"

In the short story, "Flesh and the Mirror," Carter's unnamed European heroine returns to Japan from a trip to England to find her lover absent. Of course, she is not alone, because someone is always looking: "I am told that I look lonely when I am alone." To overcome the particular loneliness of this looked-at-ness, she sets out to restage the scene.[12] Again, in a paradigmatic, imperialist gesture of recentering, she uses the "enigmatic transparency" and "indecipherable clarity" ("Flesh and the Mirror," 69)[13] of Japan literally to "reorient" herself, as subject and center of the world:

> And I moved through these expressionist perspectives in my black
> dress as though I was the creator of all and of myself, too, in a black
> dress, in love, crying, walking through the city in the third-person
> singular, my own heroine, as though the world stretched out from

my eye like spokes from a sensitized hub that galvanized all to life
when I looked at it ("Flesh and the Mirror," 68).

Yet even as a perfect heroine of her own little black costume drama,
she is excruciatingly embarrassed by her acute consciousness of the
old scripts she is using ("And wasn't I in Asia? Asia!") and the old,
ridiculed models ("Living never lived up to the expectations I had of
it—the Bovary syndrome.") Back in another hotel room with a
stranger, the center is lost as the coordinates of the self disappear into
a psychotic or "magic" mirror above the bed, the mirror without an
embodied self: ("I was the subject of the sentence written on the mirror. I was not watching it.") The ambiguity of the mirror in this story
is that it provides, on the one hand, a possible identity, and that, on
the other, it binds the heroine to the mirror as flesh to image so that
real experience takes place "elsewhere," when as in blindness or a kind
of death, she is not able to look.

> Mirrors are ambiguous things.The bureaucracy of the mirror
> issues me with a passport to the world; it shows me my appearance.
> But what use is a passport to an arm chair traveler? Women and
> mirrors are in complicity with one another to evade the action
> I/she performs that she/I cannot watch, the action with which I
> break out of the mirror, with which I assume my appearance
> ("Flesh and the Mirror," 71).

Breaking out of the mirror, if only provisionally, effects a self-
estrangement; in the terms of the story, she feels as if she had "acted
out of character" and that her "fancy-dress disguise" had led her to a
"modification of myself that had no business at all in my life, not in
the life I had watched myself performing" ("Flesh and the Mirror,"
72). In this story, all she can do is "light a fresh cigarette from the butt
of the old one" ("Flesh and the Mirror," 72) in a gesture of involuntary
repetition, and leave this room for another room where, after a while,
the estrangement she has felt from her lover, her country, her body,
and herself, appear normal. The difference is that the normal now is
recognized as merely the habitual and the performative: *"The most*

difficult performance in the world is acting naturally, isn't it?" ("Flesh and the Mirror," 77, emphasis mine).

The heroine of *Nights at the Circus* begins in some ways where the heroine of "Flesh and the Mirror" leaves off, trying to act natural which, in her case, will mean acting flamboyantly artificial. Like all of Carter's creations she loops and somersaults backward as well as forward in the plot, expanding the spatial dimensions of female spectacularity but never leaving the mirror entirely behind. Female narcissism is still a dilemma in this book, but Fevvers, without reading Simone de Beauvoir, knows at least that she is not born a "natural" woman. In fact, she is not even born, but hatched. The lack of human origins confounds the expectations of Walser, who wonders why all of London isn't searching, as he is, for her belly button. But Fevvers "does not bear the scar of loss." "Whatever her wings were, her nakedness was certainly a stage illusion."[14] Her body is not lacking but her trajectory, as I will describe it in relation to her act, is out of sync with the conventions of what is called human development. She starts and stops in the intervals between points, hovering on the brink of possibility, instead of going forward.[15]

Wings of Change

> A Klee painting named *Angelus Novus* shows an angel looking as though he is about to move away from something he is fixedly contemplating. His eyes are staring, his mouth is open, his wings are spread. This is how one pictures the angel of history. His face is turned toward the past.[16]

> Never mind the diabolical explanations of air-foil you get in Pan-Am's *multilingual INFORMATION TO PASSENGERS, I happen to be convinced that only my own concentration (and that of my mother—who always expects her children to die in a plane crash) keeps this bird aloft.*
> — Amanda Wing in Erica Jong's *Fear of Flying.*

In an interview,[17] Carter identifies a crucial intertext which I would like to follow up in discussing Fevvers as a female grotesque, a passage

written by the poet Guillaume Apollinaire which she had previously
quoted in her controversial nonfiction work, *The Sadeian Woman:*

> It was no accident that the Marquis de Sade chose heroines and not
> heroes," said Guillaume Apollinaire. Justine is woman as she has
> been until now, enslaved, miserable, and less than human; her
> opposite, Juliette, represents the woman whose advent he antici-
> pated, *a figure of whom minds have as yet no conception, who is rising
> out of mankind, and will have wings and who will renew the world*
> (emphasis mine).[18]

Although Carter's critics have sometimes confused her own views of
the "praxis of femininity"[19] with Sade or Sade's heroine, Juliette, who
wraps herself in the flags of male tyranny to avoid victimization, Carter
is quite explicit about Juliette's limits as a model of the future for
women.[20] "She is, just as her sister is, a description of a type of female
behavior rather than a model of female behavior and her triumph is
just as ambivalent as is Justine's disaster." If Juliette is a New Woman,
"she is a New Woman in the model of irony."[21] What Juliette gains in
the way of freedom is the ability to occupy space, "transforming herself
from pawn to queen . . . and henceforth goes wherever she pleases on
the chess board. Nevertheless, there remains the question of the presence of the king, who remains the lord of the game." Juliette masters
the destructive techniques of power, inflicting suffering rather than
suffering herself; yet although she seeks to avoid the fate of her sister at
all costs, the two figures of femininity are inversely connected to pain,
pleasure, and death. The difference may be that Justine's narrative of
female suffering and submission may seem more representative of an
essentialistic formulation of feminine identity and the "condition of
women," whereas Juliette's behavior is far in excess of any possible
identification with other women because disavowal of any shared
"femininity" is a condition of her dominance and her freedom.[22]

Nights at the Circus is unique in its depiction of relationships
between women *as* spectacle, *and* women as producers *of* spectacle. To
the extent that female countercultures are depicted in the novel, they
are placed within larger social and economic histories and fictions. The

point I want to make here is simply that to the extent that value is contested in the production of images of women in this novel, it is contested socially. One body as production or performance leads to
another, draws upon another, establishes hierarchies, complicities, and
dependencies between representations and between women. Conflict
is everywhere. Female figures such as Madame Schreck, "the scarecrow
of desire," organize and distribute images of other women for the
visual market. Her disembodied presence suggests the extreme of
immateriality and genderless politics; she may, as the narrator suggests,
be only a hollow puppet, the body as performance *in extremis*.[23]

It is with great irony that Carter reproduces aspects of Juliette and
the libertarian tradition in *Nights at the Circus*. In a series of critical
counterproductions of the affirmative woman "who will have wings
and who will renew the world," Fevvers is born and born again, as an
act (in the theatrical sense) of serial transgression. I have described
Fevvers as the figure of ultimate spectacularity, a compendium of
accumulated cultural clichés, worn and soiled from circulation. Yet,
poised as she is on the threshold of a new century, her marvelous
anatomy seems to offer endless possibility for change. Seeing her
wings for the first time, Ma Nelson, whose whorehouse gives Fevvers a
comfortable girlhood, identifies in "the pure child of the century that
just now is waiting in the wings, the New Age in which no woman will
be bound down to the ground" (*NC*, 25).

Ironically, in the context of the whorehouse, this means only that
Fevvers will no longer pose as Cupid with a bow and arrow, but will
now act as the Winged Victory, a static performance of her femininity
"on the grand scale," but hardly a pure or transformative vision. The
magnificent Nike of Samothrace from the second century B.C., long
thought to be the greatest example of Hellenistic sculpture, is de-
servedly famous for its activation of the space around it. Standing
eight feet tall, the figure of the victorious goddess leans out into the
spatial illusion of onrushing air, still in motion, barely touching the
ground. This icon of classical culture was much reproduced as a collectible souvenir and model of classicism. Through the techniques of

miniaturization and reproduction described in chapter three, Nike reemerged in the late nineteenth century as Victorian bric-a-brac. It is in this guise that she is reproduced and reenlarged by the young Fevvers, whose domestic portrayal (on the whorehouse mantel) of this art object-souvenir in the *tableau vivant* for male visitors would seem merely to set the terms for their accession to, and repeatable acquisition of, the other women who service them. Like Trilby, Fevvers poses as the advertisement and model for similar commodities; not exactly a prostitute herself, she nonetheless installs the myth of femininity as virgin space in the displaced aura of the art work, while suggesting the comfort of the already-used, the "sloppy seconds" of womanhood waiting, for a price, in the upper chambers.

The Pose

The redundancy of such posing, its mimetic charge, is always already excessive, as Craig Owens[24] has pointed out in one of the most interesting essays on contemporary mimesis and the pose.[25] Owens tentatively isolates two different perspectives on the question of the pose: the social and the psychosexual. As an example of the social perspective, he cites the work of Homi Bhabha on the mimetic rivalry of colonial discourse as an "ironic compromise" between what Bhabha describes as "the synchronic *panoptical* vision of domination—the demand for identity, status—and the counter-pressure of the diachrony of history—change, difference."[26] From the social perspective, Fevvers' first pose looks down (here, from a domestic perch) as if reversing the power relations of the panoptical gaze with the power of aerial surveillance. The compromised circumstances of her pose within the topography of the "house" (already a mock family space, headed by a Madame) contributes further to the irony of the *tableau*.[27]

From the psychosexual perspective, this pose reveals the constraints of the masquerade of femininity, as described and analyzed by Mary Ann Doane.[28] Although Doane's first essay on masquerade had focused on female spectatorship rather than female spectacle, it would appear, as she acknowledges in her second essay on the topic, that the concept of masquerade is more promising as a way to understand femininity as spectacular production.

> To claim that femininity is a function of the mask is to dismantle the question of essentialism before it can even be posed. In a theory which stipulates the claustrophobic closeness of the woman in relation to her own body, the concept of masquerade suggests a "glitch" in the system . . . Masquerade seems to provide that contradiction insofar as it attributes to the woman the distance, alienation, and divisiveness of self (which is constitutive of subjectivity in psychoanalysis) rather than the closeness and excessive presence which are the logical outcome of the psychoanalytic drama of sexualized linguistic difference. The theorization of femininity as masquerade is a way of appropriating this necessary distance or gap, in the operation of semiotic systems, of deploying it for women, of reading femininity differently ("Masquerade Reconsidered," 37).

But this shift leaves some problems unsolved. The theoretical drawbacks of appropriating the psychoanalytical model of masquerade as if it were the definitive feminist answer to the constraints of gender (or worse, as if the dismantling of essentialist models of femininity could *tout court* dispel the effects of the imposition of gender, making feminism unnecessary) are, in my view, increasingly evident in the disavowal of the female body as a site of political activism.

In the case of Fevvers as Winged Victory, there is redoubled irony in her grotesque body (already redundant with wings *and* arms) in exposure and retreat as her arms are released to represent the complete "original" of a dismembered female figure, an ideal of Beauty, while her feathery humps are spread out to the viewer only to be taken as useless, arty, attachments:

> Well, Ma Nelson put it out that I was the perfection of, the original of, the very model for that statue which, in its broken and incomplete state, has teased the imagination of a brace of millennia with its promise of perfect, active beauty that has, as it were, been mutilated by history (*NC,* 37).

To the redundancy of arms and wings, Ma Nelson (alias Admiral Nelson) adds even more; to complete the picture, she places a sword in the hands of Victory ("as if a virgin with a sword was the fittest guardian angel for a houseful of whores.") This finally is too much for the clients: "Yet it may be that a *large* woman with a *sword* is not the best advertisement for a brothel. For slow, but sure, trade fell off from my fourteenth birthday on" (*NC*, 32). Although blame for the demise of the whorehouse falls, in the last analysis, on the bad influence of Baudelaire ("a poor fellow who loved whores not for the pleasure of it but, as he perceived it, the *horror* of it"), business falls off when young men become impotent at the sight of the big girl becoming a big woman with too many appendages and a phallus—a Medusa with her own sword. And, of course, she has received the sword from a symbolic mother who is giving her best part, in the theatrical sense, to complete the pose of the living statue. Ma Nelson, a cross-dresser and a Madame, is also (not surprisingly) a feminist:

> "Yet we were all suffragists in that house; oh, Nelson was 'Votes for Women', I can tell you!"

> "Does that seem strange to you? That the caged bird should want to see the end of cages, sir?" queried Lizzie, with an edge of steel in her voice.

Lizzie's questions and commentary, which repeatedly interrupt the autobiographical narrative that Walser hopes will pin down the truth about Fevvers, suggest an interrogation of female biography modeled on the stories of Cinderella or Snow White, filled with evil mothers and sisters and a Prince. Fevvers herself describes her coming of age as an apprenticeship in being looked at: "Is it not to the mercies of the eyes of others that we commit ourselves on our voyage through the world." And she does not wait for a Prince to take her away; on the contrary, her greatest fear is that his kiss would harden the white powder on her face and "seal me up in my *appearance* forever!" (*NC*, 39). Her way out, as it were, is in the company of the other women who, if

Fevvers is to be believed, were, when not working, learning to read and play instruments. Lizzie describes a world of female sociality set in a liminal time when, as with the French clock she carries with her, it is always noon or midnight—the time of change and of revolution. The portrait of the artist as a young mannequin ends with the Winged Victory keen on learning how to fly.

> We all engaged in our intellectual, artistic or political—Here Lizzie coughed—pursuits and, as for myself, those long hours of leisure I devoted to the study of aerodynamics and the physiology of flight ... (*NC,* 40).

Flying:
Lessons of Class, Gender, and Sexuality

How did Fevvers really learn to fly? The Oedipal Walser, always searching for origins and empirical certainties, can only assume that a male impresario, some Svengali or other, has created Fevvers and her act. He cannot fathom the collaboration of Fevvers and her inseparable companion and foster mother, Lizzie, and it is this disbelief that leads him to wonder whether, after all, underneath the layers of masquerade, Fevvers may not be a man, throwing all questions of identity, authenticity, and origins onto the axis of gender.

> "Don't excite yourself, gel," said Lizzie gently. Fevvers' chin jerked up almost pettishly.
> "Oh, Lizzie the gentleman must know the truth!"
> And she fixed Walser with a piercing, judging regard, as if to ascertain just how far she could go with him. Her face, in its Brobdingnagian symmetry, might have been hacked from wood and brightly painted up by those artists who build carnival ladies for fairgrounds or figureheads for sailing ships. It flickered through his mind: Is she really a man? (*NC,* 35).

The figure of the aerialist, as I indicated in the first chapter in considering the work of Balint, Starobinski, and others, has repeatedly produced the question of gender for the male viewer. The female aerialist as masculinized or ambiguous in relation to gender appears in historical sources, as well as fiction and visual representation. Arthur Munby's famous photographs and diaries of Victorian working girls includes female gymnasts and acrobats whose masculine qualities he never fails to note.[29] Although, as Stallybrass and White have noted, Munby's voyeurism is usually characterized by the "conjunction of the maid kneeling in the dirt and the standing voyeur" (from high to low), the gaze upward (from low to high) can produce a similar effect: on the one hand, a reinforcement of male power and social standing and on the other a temporary reversal so that the male viewer appears childlike or at least diminished.[30] From Huysmans's Miss Urania to Cleopatra, the "big woman" in Tod Browning's *Freaks*, the aerialist and the female acrobat have been women represented through the eyes of a dwarfed, clownish, or infantilized man. In an unusual reversal, George Grosz's *Seiltänzerin* (1914), an aerial drawing of a female tightrope walker, shows a demonic clown looking up from far below at the large, muscular figure straddling the rope between her thighs as she strains to raise herself up onto one leg. This grotesque caricature of the Romantic ideal of ethereal Womanhood suggests, as well, an altered masculinity in the balance.

Carter's production of Fevvers as the aerial diva, enigmatic regarding gender, is only the latest version of this image, produced typically by male artists but occasionally and with surprising results by twentieth-century women artists and writers. The figure of the trapeze artist Frau Mann (alias the Duchess of Broadback) who appears in the first chapter of Djuna Barnes' *Nightwood*, is the repressed, lesbian prefiguration of a Fevvers—a possible body.[31] Her body is strong and muscular, and in the air, it appears "much heavier than that of women who stay on the ground." It is a body shaped through her work and the technology of aerial performance. Her legs, for instance, "had the specialized tension common to aerial workers; some of the bar was in her wrists, the tan bark in her walk." Like Fevvers, her very flesh seems sewn into her performance costume, making an artifice of nudity;

Frau Mann, however, goes a bit further in this regard than Fevvers, in that her costume reweaves the crotch in a textual rezoning of the body as off-limits to men.

> The stuff of her tights was no longer a covering, it was herself; the span of the tightly stitched crotch was so much her own flesh that she was as unsexed as a doll. The needle that had made one the property of the child made the other the property of no man (Barnes, 13).

Nudity and clothing are a continuous surface, flattening the image of Frau Mann's body, and in a reversal of the usual fetishistic practice as described by Freud, redesigning the "phantasmagoric division between an inside and an outside" which characterizes the representation of the female body as invested with mystery or threat.[32] Whether this feminine surface sufficiently interferes with the (male) fetishist's desire to know and therefore have, or whether "the needle" in question is the projection of a lesbian morphology, there is definitely a *different* line of viewing and a different spectatorship suggested than that represented by Walser's suggestion that Fevvers really needs a tail: "Physical ungainliness in flight caused, perhaps, by the absence of a *tail*—I wonder why she doesn't tack a tail on the back of her cache-sexe; it would add verisimilitude and, perhaps, improve the performance."

The comparison of *Nights at the Circus* with Barnes' *Nightwood,* written in 1936, reveals a commonality of surrealist techniques and themes, as well as a mutual interest in the dispersion of carnivalesque materials in new social formations. *Nightwood* was introduced in the thirties by an extremely anxious T. S. Eliot, who feared that the characters in the novel would be regarded "as a horrid sideshow of freaks."[33] His evocation of the freak show as the trope to be shunned would seem to substantiate Allon White's claim that the remnants of carnival as cultural history reemerge as "phobic alienation" in bourgeois neurosis, since "bourgeois carnival is a contradiction in terms."[34] The metaphor of the freak show in Eliot's introduction (clearly a reference to the lesbian and transsexual themes of the novel) resonates oddly with the first chapter, "Bow Down," in which Felix (Baron Volkbein) is introduced as a dévoté of the circus and popular theater. The high/low dichotomies of class and gender give way as the "carnival of the night" temporarily subsumes difference. Volkbein's attachment to "that great disquiet called entertainment" mirrors his own aristocratic yearnings: "In some way they linked his emotions to the high and unattainable pageantry of kings and queens" (Barnes, 11). The entertainers, of course, in the carnivalesque tradition, mimic the pomp and titles of the upper classes. Felix's pleasure in the mock ritual of the "bow down" to the demimonde is palpable. At once degrading and liberatory, his social and sexual dissolution amidst the carnival of *Nightwood* recalls Aschenbach's encounters with the grotesque figures in *Death in Venice:*

> He moved with a humble hysteria among the decaying brocades and laces of the *Carnavalet;* he loved that old and documented splendour with something of the love of the lion for its tamer—that sweat-tarnished spangled enigma that, in bringing the beast to heel, had somehow turned toward him a face like his own ... (Barnes, 11).

> The emotional spiral of the circus, taking its flight from the immense disqualification of the public, rebounding from its illimitable hope, produced in Felix longing and disquiet. The circus was a loved thing he could never touch (Barnes, 12).

In contrast, Walser is a male spectator oblivious to the transcendent powers of the circus. Though Carter's deeply historic novel is set at the end of the nineteenth century, Walser is much younger than the Baron, as a representative of the bourgeoisie. Of course, he is first of all an American on the brink of the "American Century," filled with all the common sense and the imperialistic instincts required to make him an ideal employee for Colonel Kearney (a P. T. Barnum clone). Secondly, he is a journalist and a professional debunker, sent to reveal the secrets of the trade, to sort, discard, and exploit the travesties of the circus as he will later plunder ethnographic materials in his ethnocentric explorations of other cultures. No aesthete or modernist intent on looking up to women or lamenting old myths, he tries instead, in what to him is the most effective democratic mode, to bring Fevvers down to his scale.

As model spectator, Walser is continuously in the dark when it comes to issues of gender and generation, especially the aspects of female homosociality which dominate the London section of the book. He cannot tolerate sexual ambiguity and he cannot recognize or place "older" women, particularly in foreign national contexts. The dialogical narrative of Lizzie and Fevvers, with its dissonant tonality, silences, and contradictions makes him increasingly anxious to place Fevvers and to illuminate those aspects of her anatomy and her story which are extraneous or implausible. The story of her first flight, which is simultaneously the story of her surrogate mother, Lizzie, and her "natural" mother, London ("London, with one breast, the Amazon queen") is told as a night fable (*NC,* 36). The nocturnal carnival which occasions intimations of the sublime for Felix borders on the terrifying for Walser, whose imagination is easily overwhelmed: "Although he was not an imaginative man, even he was sensitive to that aghast time of night when the dark dwarfs us" (*NC,* 37). Fevvers, if she is (and she certainly is in some sense) a bird, is not a natural flier:

> Like Lucifer, I fell. Down, down, down I tumbled, bang with a bump on the Persian rug below me, flat on my face amongst those blooms and beasts that never graced no natural forest, those creatures of dreams and abstraction not unlike myself, Mr. Walser. Then I knew I was not ready to bear on my back the great burden of my unnaturalness (*NC,* 30).

She learns to fly through cultural imitation (a fake Titian of Leda and the Swan), some library books, risks and falls, a momentary sense of hovering ("that sensation that comes to us, sometimes on the edge of sleep") (*NC,* 31), and finally, through the help of Lizzie's knowledge gleaned from observing pigeons learning to use their "aerial arms," she lets Lizzie push her into the air, risking not only death but the "terror of irreparable *difference*" (*NC,* 34).[35] She flies for the first time through

the dark, into a liminal space in the hours before dawn on Midsummer's Night, and then back to work, posing as Winged Victory.[36]

The elevation of the grotesque body to the nocturnal sublimity of a
midsummer's night is accomplished with great effort, and, like the
narrative itself, it works as a collaborative effort between Fevvers and
Lizzie. The model for flight is a lowly pigeon but the experience and its
description are meant nonetheless to be sublime. Fevvers' flying style
is as eclectic, grand, and ungainly as her voice and as indeterminate
with regard to its origins. Walser's description of her voice reflects his
own skepticism regarding the narrative of her first flight.

> Her voice . . . her cavernous, somber voice, a voice made for shout-
> ing about the tempest, her voice of a celestial fishwife. Musical as it
> strangely was, yet not a voice for singing with; it comprised dis-
> cords, her scale contained twelve tones. Her voice with its warped,
> homely Cockney vowels and random aspirates . . . Yet such a voice
> could almost have had its source, not within her throat but in some
> ingenious mechanism or other behind the canvas screen, voice of a
> fake medium at a seance (*NC*, 43).

This "throwing" of the female voice is an extremely telling acoustical image.[37] It is reminiscent of *Trilby* and of the seemingly disembodied telephone voice of Claire Niveau in Cronenberg's *Dead Ringers*.
Located at the site of "perhaps, the most radical of all subject divisions—the division between meaning and materiality," the voice is
that place of excess which precedes and follows the organization of
meaning (Silverman, 44). The spatial image of the *thrown voice* further stretches the gaps or intervals between the body and language,
like one of Fevvers' long, antisocial yawns. The body which produces
this voice is not identical with it, any more than the sounds produced
are identical in any positive sense with meaning. In relation to music
as organized sound, "this voice is not for singing," meaning that it is
"noisy" in the technical sense and exceeds the regimes of canonical
Western music. As an instance of cultural noise, this voice, which is
the voice of the novel as well as the voice of Fevvers, contains within it
a particularly resonant blend of modernist scales, class and regionally

inflected vowels and aspirates, and the "rough music" of carnival.[38] The "grain" of this voice, to use Roland Barthes expression, suggests a different cultural as well as a different musical history in which, as he suggested, "we would attach less importance to the formidable break in tonality accomplished by modernity."[39] Deeply historical as well as radically modernist in its trajectory, the voice of the "celestial fish-wife"—the sonic female grotesque *par excellence*[40]—flies from the cavern, above the tempest, and to the heavens and down again to Cockney London, somber, full, and in its own way sublime.

To recapitulate briefly the relationship between the aerial sublime and the female grotesque, I want to return to Fevvers in the midst of her circus act. By way of reference, I turn to the paradigm of the trapeze act as analyzed by Paul Bouissac in his work on the semiotics of the circus. Once in the air, the act is a negotiation, with interruptions, between two stations, with a certain expenditure of energy by the velocity of flight (up to 60 mph), permitting the human body to offer a certain illusion of suspension. Bouissac fails to note that in the case of the female performer, her negotiation of space is often interrupted by a male performer who catches her. Fevvers in the air, however, travels alone.

An additional model of normativity for the flying act is provided by Thomas Aquinas who notes, writing of "real" angels, "their motion can be as continuous or as discontinuous as it wishes. And thus an angel can be in one instant in one place and at another instant in another place, not existing at any intermediate time." I am assuming that in relation to identity, Fevvers has equal claim to either of these models yet no full claim at all to either, since her act seems to dissimulate failure to occupy either time or space in these modes. Quoting the novel, from the point of view of the informed male spectator:

> When the hack *aerialiste*, the everyday wingless variety, performs the triple somersault, he or she travels through the air at a cool sixty miles an hour; Fevvers, however, contrived a contemplative and leisurely twenty-five, so that the packed theater could enjoy the spectacle, as in slow motion, of every tense muscle straining in her

Rubenseque form. The music went much faster than she did; she
dawdled. Indeed, she did defy the laws of projectiles, because a pro-
jectile cannot *mooch* along its trajectory; if it slackens its speed in
mid-air, down it falls. But Fevvers, apparently, pottered along the
invisible gangway between her trapezes with the portly dignity of a
Trafalgar Square pigeon flapping from one proffered handful of
corn to another, and then she turned head over heels three times,
lazily enough to show off the crack in her bum (*NC,* 17).

For Walser, semiotician and connoisseur of the hoax, it is precisely
the limitations of her act which allow him momentarily to suspend
disbelief and grant her a supernatural identity, for no mere mortal
could effect such incompetence in the air without dire consequences.
Walser observes:

> For, in order to earn a living, might not a genuine bird-woman—in
> the implausible event that such a thing existed—have to pretend
> she was an artificial one? (*NC,* 17)

What is more interesting to me than this sophisticated insight
which, after all, only goes so far as to permit him the pleasure of a
naive spectator's night at the circus, is that Fevvers reveals what angels
and circus stars normally conceal: *labor* and its bodily effects in the
midst of simulated play and the creation of illusion. Her body dawdles
lazily (the hardest work of all in the air) and yet, unlike her angelic sisters, she never seems to occupy discrete spots on her trajectory; she
does not rest. She vamps in the musical sense, filling in the intervals
with somersaults. The one time she is static in the air, perched on the
swing, the rope breaks and she is stranded. What is revealed in her
routine is at one level economic: the Victorian working girl is not the
angel (in the house), and the novel is in many ways about working
girls.[41] This is not to say that here finally a materiality has emerged
from underneath an illusion, that with the appearance of work, we
have a ground, that we are no longer, so to speak, in the air. Rather, I
would read Fevvers' act as a reminder that the spectacle which con-
ceals work is itself produced, and revamping spectacle shows up and
diverts this cultural production.

The Intergenerational Body (Politic)

Carter herself has remarked that "the creation of Fevvers necessi-
tated the creation of her foster mother, Lizzie, a gnarled old leftist."
Throughout the novel, Lizzie undercuts the high-flying rhetoric of the
new age woman while working behind the scenes to effect a revolution. Her own body is unfetishized. She exists unadorned as a kind of
maid or sidekick in the drama of the star performer, but her work is
nonetheless indispensable. As a couple, Lizzie and Fevvers produce a
real challenge to the male and heterosexual gaze of Walser, who is confused both by their narrative mode and by their apparent physical
incompatibility, which he can only articulate as a question of scale,
measured in height. From a distance, he sees them as "a blond, heroic
mother taking her daughter home from some ill-fated expedition up
west, their ages obscured, their relationship inverted."

Together, they figure an intergenerational grotesque of the kind
which Mikhail Bakhtin evokes in his paradigm of the grotesque terra-
cotta images of senile, pregnant hags. When Lizzie first sees that her
young ward has wings, she does not uncritically welcome the new in
the guise of youth, as Ma Nelson does; rather, she historicizes *herself,*
and sees in Fevvers the "Annunciation of my own Menopause." When
the figurative biological clock is communal, birth and rebirth are
dialectical. This parody of the annunciation is of the critical variety
which Linda Hutcheon has described in her work on postmodernism
as signalling "how present representations come from past ones, and
what ideological consequences derive from both continuity and
difference" (Hutcheon, 93). The consequences of such an intergenerational conception is that the new is not immediately and transparently
identified with the young. This interrupts the logic of what Debord
describes as "false choice in spectacular abundance," the creation of
arbitrary contrasts and competitions which seem natural or self-evident. Among these false choices is a certain commodification of generational difference:

> Wherever there is abundant consumption, a major spectacular
> opposition between youth and adults comes to the fore among the

false roles—false because the adult, master of his life, does not exist
and because youth, the transformation of what exists, is in no way
the property of those who are now young, but of the economic system, of the dynamism of capitalism. *Things* rule and are young.[42]

Again, my point is not to deny that there are such things as aging
and generational difference; rather, the spectacle of the new is produced and can therefore be counterproduced. As Fevvers and Lizzie
together reconfigure "the pure child of the new century," the "new"
becomes a possibility that already existed, a part of the aging body in
process rather than the property (like virginity) of a discrete and static
place or identity. What appeals to me about this vamping onto the
body (to use the word in a slightly archaic sense) is that it not only
grotesquely de-forms the female body as a cultural construction in
order to reclaim it, but that it may suggest new political aggregates—
provisional, uncomfortable, even conflictual, coalitions of bodies
which both respect the concept of "situated knowledges" and refuse to
keep every body in its place.

It is tempting to read this novel and even Carter's entire *oeuvre*
as a progression, as one critic sees it, from the alienation of the femininity of the "coded mannequin" to the liberatory prospects of the
woman with wings.[43] Indeed, towards the end of the novel, Fevvers
looks forward to the day when "all the women will have wings, the
same as I":

> The dolls' house doors will open, the brothels will spill forth their
> prisoners, the cages, gilded or otherwise, all over the world, in
> every land, will let forth their inmates singing together the dawn
> chorus of the new, the transformed (*NC*, 285).

But Carter never lets this optimistic progressivism stand unchal-
lenged:

> "It's going to be more complicated than that," interpolated Lizzie.
> "This old witch sees storms ahead, my girl. When I look to the
> future, I see through a glass, darkly. You improve your analysis, girl,
> and *then* we'll discuss it" (*NC*, 285–286).

Lizzie's view of the future is not forward-looking but rather—like the angel of history in a powerful and much-quoted passage from Walter Benjamin—a look backwards to see the future in the past, not as "sequence of events" but as "a catastrophe which keeps piling wreckage upon wreckage" (Benjamin, 257). To Lizzie and to the angel of history, "a storm is blowing from Paradise" (*NC*, 257). And there is no going back. In Benjamin's image, borrowed from Klee's painting *Angelus Novus,* the angel is caught by the storm with his wings blown open; the storm "propels him into the future to which his back is turned, while the pile of debris before him grows skyward. *This storm is what we call progress*" (emphasis mine) (Benjamin, 258).

Only if Lizzie's stormy comments are read as merely cynical or extraneous can the exchange be made to stand for a developmental antithesis in Carter's writing rather than an apocalyptic intersection of incommensurate discourses, resulting in a "blow-up" of the narrative and a breakup of two women's narrative partnership. To side provisionally with Lizzie, who represents an ever-present but minority voice in the novel, it is more complicated than that.

I would prefer to read their differences as part of an ongoing dialogue, filled with conflict and repetition—a difficult friendship and an improbable but necessary political alliance.[44] At this point in the novel, the conversation is about losses and making do. Fevvers has "mislaid her magnificence on the road from London; one wing is bandaged and the other has faded to drab. She is no longer commercially viable. God knows if she will ever fly again." Lizzie's anarchic power, "her knack for wreaking domestic havoc," is lost. As the designated heroine of the novel, Fevvers is trading in her wings for marriage with what she hopes will be a transformed Jack Walser ("I'll sit on him, I'll hatch him out. I'll make him into the New Man, in fact, a fitting mate for the New Woman"). And Lizzie, of course is skeptical: "'Perhaps so, perhaps not,' she said, putting a damper on things."[45] For Lizzie, it is necessary to think twice "about turning from a freak into a woman" (*NC*, 283).[46]

This exchange between Lizzie and Fevvers is, like everything in the novel, inconclusive. As Susan Suleiman has written, Carter's strategy

"*multiplies* the possibilities of linear narrative and of 'story,' producing a dizzying accumulation that undermines the narrative logic by its
very excessiveness."[47] There is always something left over, something
as untimely as subjectivity itself, that forms the basis of a new plan,
perhaps another flight.

Like Fevvers' excessive body itself, the meaning of any possible flight
lies in part in the very interstices of the narrative, as the many-vectored
space of the here and now, rather than a utopian hereafter. The end of
flight in this sense is not a freedom from bodily existence but a rechart-
ing of aeriality as a bodily space of possibility and repetition:

> There is a feeling of absolute finality about the end of a flight through
> darkness. The dream of flight is suddenly gone before the mundane
> realities of growing grass and swirling dust . . . Freedom escapes you
> again, and the wings which were a moment ago no less than an eagle's
> and swifter, are metal and wood once more, inert and heavy.[48]

Notes

Notes to Introduction

1. Stephen Jay Gould, "Living with Connections: Are Siamese Twins One Person or Two?" *Natural History* (November 1982), p. 20.

2. Originally published in *Feminist Studies/Critical Studies,* ed. Teresa de Lauretis (Bloomington: Indiana University Press, 1986).

3. Laura Mulvey, "A Phantasmagoria of the Female Body: The Work of Cindy Sherman," *New Left Review,* no. 188 (July/August 1991), p. 146.

4. The question of "the body" and whether it has been been "played out" in some theoretical sense in relation to feminism is the central topic of many books and articles. In the course of this study, I refer to many of them, but I am also aware that many others, no doubt, are about to be published at the time of this writing. For collected essays on women and the body, see the special edition of *Hypatia,* ed. Elizabeth Grosz, vol. 6, no. 3 (Fall 1991), and *The Female Body in Western Culture,* ed. Susan Rubin Suleiman (Cambridge, Massachusetts and London: Harvard University Press, 1986). See also, *Body Guards: The Cultural Politics of Gender Ambiguity,* ed. Julia Epstein and Kristina Straub (New York and London: Routledge, 1991).

5. On this topic, see also Ewa Kuryluk, *Salome and Judas in the Cave of Sex: The Grotesque—Origins, Iconography, Techniques* (Evanston, Illinois: Northwestern University Press, 1987). Kuryluk points out that the late Roman grotesques were "attached to femininity, which was present in the caves in manifold ways" (18). There is a crucial difference, of course, between attachment and identification.

6. For an excellent account of this early history of the grotesque, see Geoffrey Galt Harpham, *On the Grotesque: Strategies of Contradiction in Art and Literature* (Princeton: Princeton University Press, 1982), especially chapter two.

7. As quoted in Harpham, pp. 30–31.

8. Naomi Schor, *Reading in Detail: Aesthetics and the Feminine* (New York: Methuen, 1987), p. 16.

9. On this topic, see especially, Sarah Kofman, *Nietzsche et la scène philosophique* (Paris: Editions Galilée, 1986), and Luce Irigaray, *Marine Lover of Friedrich*, trans. Gillian Gill (New York: Columbia University Press, 1991); see also, the collection of essays in *Nietzsche, Feminism and Political Theory*, ed. Paul Patton (New York: Routledge, 1993).

10. Friedrich Nietzsche, *The Gay Science*, trans. with commentary by Walter Kaufman, (New York: Vintage Books, 1974), p. 38.

11. My discussion of the grotesque is generally limited to the Western European tradition. Many excellent studies exist or are in the works on the grotesque which focus on literature outside the this tradition. In American studies, there is the extremely important literature of the "Southern grotesque." On this topic, see especially Patricia Yaeger, *Dirt and Desire: The Grotesque in Southern Women's Writing* (forthcoming); see also, for example, Mae Henderson, "Toni Morrison's *Beloved*: Remembering the Body as Historical Text" in *Discourses of Sexuality: From Aristotle to AIDS* (Ann Arbor: The University of Michigan Press, 1992), pp. 312–342. For a cross-cultural application of Bakhtin in film, see Robert Stam, *Subversive Pleasures: Bakhtin, Cultural Criticism, and Film* (Baltimore and London: The Johns Hopkins University Press, 1989).

12. Arthur Conan Doyle, *The Complete Sherlock Holmes* (Garden City, New York: Doubleday, 1930), p. 869.

13. Mikhail Bakhtin, *Rabelais and His World*, trans. Helene Iswolsky (Bloomimgton: Indiana University Press, 1984). Future references to this book will be identified as *RW*.

14. Wolfgang Kayser, *The Grotesque in Art and Literature*, trans. Ulrich Weisstein (Bloomington: Indiana University Press, 1963).

15. Sigmund Freud, "On the Uncanny," in *The Standard Edition of the Works of Sigmund Freud*, vol. 17, ed. and trans. James Strachey (London: Hogarth Press and the Institute for Psychoanalysis, 1953–1974), pp. 233–238.

16. Peter Stallybrass and Allon White, *The Politics and Poetics of Transgression* (Ithaca: Cornell University Press, 1986), p. 16; see also, Peter Stallybrass, "Marx and Heterogeneity: Thinking the Lumpen-proletariat," *Representations* 31 (Summer 1990), pp. 69–95, and Allon White, "Hysteria and the End of Carnival: Festivity and Bourgeois

Neurosis" in Nancy Armstrong and Leonard Tennenhouse, eds., *The Violence of Representation* (London: Routledge, 1989).

17. See the entry on *anaclisis* in Jean Laplanche and J. B. Pontalis, *The Language of Psychoanalysis*, trans. Donald Nicholson-Smith (New York and London: W.W. Norton, 1973), pp. 29–31.

18. Julia Kristeva, *La Révolution du langage poétique* (1974) and *Powers of Horror: An Essay on Abjection*, trans. Leon S. Roudiez (New York: Columbia University Press, 1982).

19. Kristeva, *The Powers of Horror*, p. 208.

20. Michel Foucault, *Discipline and Punish: The Birth of the Prison*, trans. Alan Sheridan (New York: Vintage Books, 1979), p. 184.

21. Georges Canguilhem, *On the Normal and the Pathological*, trans. Carolyn R. Fawcett with an introduction by Michel Foucault (Dordrecht, Holland and Boston: D. Reidel Publishing Co., 1978), p. xix.

22. See Teresa de Lauretis, *Technologies of Gender: Essays on Theory, Film, and Fiction* (Bloomington and Indianapolis: Indiana University Press, 1987).

23. This is a very limited list inherited mostly from the nineteenth-century repertoire of exhibitions. The pseudo-sciences of phrenology and phys-iognomy were much more detailed in their categorizations of female appearance. With the new "sciences" of eugenics and criminology, these earlier types were attached to expanded theories of social de-viance. See for instance, Cesare Lombroso and William Ferrero, *The Female Offender* (London: T. Fisher Urwin, 1895). For an account of the importance of appearance in diagnosing mental illness in women, see Elaine Showalter, *Women, Madness, and English Culture, 1830–1980* (New York: Pantheon, 1985), pp. 84–98. See also, Bram Dijkstra, *Idols of Perversity: Fantasies of Feminine Evil in Fin-de-siècle Culture* (New York and Oxford: Oxford University Press, 1986).

24. On this topic, see Lisa Tichner, *The Spectacle of Women: Imagery of the Suffrage Campaign 1907–14* (Chicago: The University of Chicago Press, 1988), p. 167–174. For images of the most recent wave of women's liber-ation, see Susan J. Douglas, *Where the Girls Are: Growing Up Female With the Mass Media* (New York: Time Books, 1994).

25. On performance and gender, see, for instance, *Making A Spectacle*, ed. Lynda Hart (Ann Arbor: University of Michigan Press, 1989), and

Peggy Phelan, "Feminist Theory, Poststructuralism and Performance," *TDR* (Spring, 1988), pp. 107–127; see also, *Performing Feminisms,* ed. Sue-Ellen Case (Baltimore: The Johns Hopkins University Press, 1990).

26. Donna J. Haraway, *Simians, Cyborgs, and Women: The Reinvention of Nature* (New York: Routledge, 1991). See, for instance, as an example of the postmodern grotesque, the description of the interspecies encounter from Octavia Butler's science fiction work *Dawn: Xenogenesis* (New York: Warner Books, 1987), involving the heroine, Lilith Iyapo, a young Black woman survivor of a nuclear war, and the Oankali, an alien species. "Without human sensory organs, the Oankali, the alien species that originally believed humanity was intent on committing suicide and so would be far too dangerous to try to save. Without human sensory organs, the Oankali are primatoid Medusa figures, their heads and bodies covered with multi-talented tentacles like marine invertebrates. These humanoid serpent people speak to the woman and urge her to touch them in an intimacy that would lead humanity to a monstrous metamorphosis" (227).

27. These "odd boundary creatures" are, literally, *monsters,* a word that shares more than its root with the word "demonstrate."

Notes to Chapter One

1. Roswitha Mueller, ed., *Ulrike Ottinger: A Retrospective* (n.p.: The Goethe Institutes in the United States and Canada, 1990), p. 5.

2. Luce Irigaray, *Speculum of the Other Woman,* trans. Gillian C. Gill (Ithaca, New York: Cornell University Press), p. 236.

3. Sigmund Freud, "On the Uncanny," in *The Standard Edition of the Works of Sigmund Freud,* Vol. 17, ed. and trans. James Strachey (London: Hogarth Press and the Institute for Psychoanalysis, 1953–1974), pp. 233–238. In this section of the essay, Freud is commenting on *Die Elisire des Teufel,* a novel by E. T. A. Hoffman, whom he regards as "the unrivalled master of the uncanny in literature."

4. As Earhart tells it, almost everything came in handy eventually: cooking lessons, the influenza epidemic, riding horseback, automobile repair, medicine, French literature, social work at Denison House in Boston, photography, a knowledge of the underground passageways of Columbia University, and the stairwells to the top of the library dome (a knowledge she used to witness the eclipse of the sun in 1925).

5. Amelia Earhart, *The Fun of It: Random Notes of My Own Flying and of Woman in Aviation*(New York: Brewer, Warren, and Putnam), 1932, p. 36.

6. On social stigmas, see Mary Douglas, *Risk and Blame: Essays in Cultural Theory* (London and New York: Routledge, 1992), p. 36. Douglas' work complicates the social strategy which would work progressively towards de-stigmatization as a removal of earlier or "primitive" modes of explanation and exclusion in the presence of perceived social dangers, suggesting that these strategies are caught between an "innocent" vision of a society devoid of all exclusionary behavior and a desire to not notice difference: "An individualist culture finds ways of making its disadvantaged members disappear from sight. To stop stigmatizing would be another way of making them invisible." For another view, see for instance, Sandor Gilman, *Difference and Pathology: Stereotypes of Sexuality, Race, and Madness* (Ithaca: Cornell University Press, 1985).

7. Michel de Certeau, *The Practice of Everyday Life,* trans. Steven Rendall (Berkeley and London: University of California Press, 1982), p. xix. In contrast, a "strategy" is "the calculus of force-relationships which become possible when a subject of will and power (a proprietor, an enterprise, a city, a scientific institution) can be isolated from an 'environment.' A strategy assumes a place that can be circumscribed as *proper (propre)* and thus serve as the basis for generating relations with an exterior distinct from it . . ." (xix). For another example of "tactical" stunts, see Meaghan Morris, "Great Moments in Social Climbing: King Kong and The Human Fly" in *Sexuality and Space* (New York: Princeton Architectural Press, 1992), pp. 1–51.

8. The term "biographeme" is Roland Barthes' via Nancy Miller, *Getting Personal: Feminist Occasions and Other Autobiographical Acts* (New York and London: Routledge, 1991), p. 27, n2.

9. Maud Ellmann, *The Hunger Artists: Starving, Writing, Imprisonment* (Cambridge, Massachusetts: Harvard University Press, 1993), pp. 3–4.

10. In reference to Catherine Gallagher's work on the large body and political economy, Eve Kosofsky Sedgwick remarks that the representational labor of the large body is a kind of "employment" from which is extracted a double and contradictory value: "Visible on the one hand, in this scene, as a disruptive *embolism* in the flow of economic circulation, the fat female body functions on the other hand . . . as the very *emblem* of that circulation," Eve Kosofsky Sedgwick and Michael Moon, "Divinity: A Dossier, a Performance Piece, a Little-Understood

Emotion" in *Discourse: Theoretical Studies in Media and Culture*, vol. 13, no. 1 (Fall–Winter 1990–1991), p. 14. The dialogue between Moon and Sedgwick goes a distance in circulating the sign of the fat woman outside the dominant representational economy as a borrowed or donated signifier.

11.   On this issue see especially, Susie Orbach, *Fat Is A Feminist Issue: The Anti-Diet Guide to Permanent Weight Loss* (New York: Berkeley, 1987).

12.   As Ellmann points out, fat has gone from being a sign of affluence to a sign of poverty in the last century (3). See also, Caroline Bynum, *Holy Feast and Holy Fast: The Religious Significance of Food to Medieval Women* (Berkeley: University of California Press: 1987), and Joan Brumberg, *Fasting Girls: The Emergence of Anorexia Nervosa as Modern Disease* (Cambridge, Massachusetts: Harvard University Press, 1988).

13.   Many of these performance artists are represented in *Angry Women*, ed. Andrea Juno and V. Vale (San Francisco: Re/Search Publications, 1991). Elinor Fuchs has attempted to break through the usual feminist oppositions in relation to pornography and the sex debates in her important essay on the obscene theater, one of the few pieces to activate the categories of class and venue in considering the transgressive potential of performers like Annie Sprinkle and Karen Finley. Fuchs begins with an acknowledgement of the ambivalence produced as female spectators and performers are split apart in the desocialization which occurs when pornography moves to "legitimate" theatrical venues and audiences. This ambivalence becomes productive in her analysis at both social and psychological levels, suggesting a future "merger" between "good" and "bad" girls, and between sexually and socially divided populations of women. In my view, the grotesque body politic is one useful model for reconfiguring this spectatorship, since it resists the homogenization of other mergers. See her "Staging the Obscene Body" in *TDR: The Drama Review: A Journal of Performance Studies*, vol. 33, no. 1 (Spring 1989). In the same issue, see Jill Dolan, "Desire Cloaked in a Trenchcoat," on lesbian spectatorship and the script of "Dress Suits to Hire" by Holly Hughes, Peggy Shaw, and Lois Weaver, and the discussion of it by Kate Davy, "Reading Past the Heterosexual Imperative."

14.   On women, technology, and modernism, see Andreas Huyssen, *After the Great Divide: Modernism, Mass Culture, Postmodernism* (Bloomington: Indiana University Press, 1986).

15.   For an excellent account of Earhart in relation to liberal feminism in this era, see Susan Ware, *Still Missing: Amelia Earhart and the Search for Modern Feminism* (New York and London: W.W. Norton, 1993).

16. Susan Bordo, *Unbearable Weight: Feminism, Western Culture, and the Body* (Berkeley, Los Angeles, and London: University of California Press, 1993), p. 14.

17. Quoted in Ware, p. 204.

18. Muriel Rukeyser, *Theory of Flight* (New Haven: Yale University Press, 1935), p. 35.

19. On feminism and the discourse of liberation, see also, Patricia Yaeger, *Honey-Mad Women: Emancipatory Strategies in Women's Writing* (New York: Columbia University Press, 1988).

20. Jessica Benjamin, *Bonds of Love: Psychoanalysis, Feminism, and the Problem of Domination* (New York: Pantheon Books, 1988), p. 127. Using Winnicott, Benjamin goes on to develop the concept of containment, while I am more interested in risk-taking tactics and trajectories outward bound; nonetheless, I share her commitment to reworking these metaphors to model female agency.

21. Alice A. Jardine, *Gynesis: Configurations of Woman and Modernity* (Ithaca and London: Cornell University Press, 1985), p. 25.

22. See Rosi Braidotti, *Patterns of Dissonance: A Study of Women in Contemporary Philosophy* (New York: Routledge, 1991). For an important study of modernism and the avant-garde in relation to gender, see Susan Rubin Suleiman, *Subversive Intent: Gender, Politics, and the Avant-Garde* (Cambridge: Harvard University Press, 1990), p. 276.

23. Not all male writers find the crisis of reason sad. For an extremely interesting reading that takes into account feminist epistemology, see Iain Chambers, *Border Dialogues: Journeys in Postmodernity* (London and New York: Routledge, 1990).

24. Fredric Jameson, *Postmodernism, Or, The Cultural Logic of Late Capitalism* (Durham: Duke University Press, 1991), p. 154.

25. On this topic, see, for instance, *Feminism and Postmodernism*, ed. Linda J. Nicholson (New York: Routledge, 1990). See also, Linda Hutcheon, *The Politics of Postmodernism* (London: Routledge, 1990).

26. For an excellent critique of the antifeminism or prefeminism which emerges from some of these postmodernist positions, see Tania Modleski, *Feminism Without Women: Culture and Criticism in a "Postfeminist" Age* (New York and London: Routledge, 1991), pp. 3–23.

27. See Celeste Olalquiaga, *Megalopolis: Contemporary Cultural Sensibilities* (Minneapolis: University of Minnesota Press, 1992).

28. David Harvey, *The Condition of Postmodernity* (Oxford and Cambridge, Massachusetts: Basil Blackwell, 1989), p. 91, and quoted in Mark Wigley, "Theoretical Slippage: The Architecture of the Fetish" in *Fetish: The Princeton Architectural Journal*, no. 4 (1992), p. 94. I am indebted to Wigley but also to my students, who never fail to make the same point in their discussions of the book. See also, Rosalind Deutsche "Men in Space," *Strategies*, no. 3 (1990).

29. See Harvey, pp. 57–59.

30. See Harvey, chapter four.

31. See Slavoj Žižek, *The Sublime Object of Ideology* (London and New York: Verso, 1989). See also, Jean-François Lyotard, "Can Thought Go On Without a Body?," *Discourse* 11, no. 1 (Fall–Winter 1988–1989).

32. See Modleski, pp. 104–109.

33. See Mary Russo, "Female Grotesques: Carnival and Theory" in Teresa de Lauretis, ed., *Feminist Studies/Critical Studies* (Bloomington: Indiana University Press, 1986), pp. 213–229.

34. On Freud's essay "On the Uncanny" see especially Hélène Cixous, "Les fictions et ses fantômes," *Poétique* 3 (1972), pp. 199–216; see also, Samuel Weber, "The Sideshow, or Remarks on a Canny Moment" *MLN* 83 (December 1973), pp. 1102–1133.

35. Freud, "On the Uncanny," pp. 235–263.

36. Thomas Weiskel, *The Romantic Sublime: Studies in the Structure and Psychology of Transcendence* (Baltimore and London: The Johns Hopkins University Press, 1976), p. 46.

37. See, for instance, Suzanne Guerlac, "Delights of Grotesque and Sublime," *Diacritics* 14 (Summer 1984), pp. 47–53; Frances Ferguson, "The Nuclear Sublime" *Diacritics* 14 (Summer 1984), pp. 4–10; Neil Hertz, *The End of the Line* (New York: Columbia University Press, 1985); Jean-François Lyotard, *The Postmodern Condition* (Minneapolis: University of Minnesota Press, 1979) pp.77–81 and his "The Sublime and the Avant-Garde" *Paragraph* 6 (October 1985), pp. 1–18; Raimonda Mondiano,"Humanism and the Comic Sublime: From Kant to Friedrich Theodor Vischer," *Studies in Romanticism*, vol. 26 (1987), pp. 231–244; Allan Stoekl, "The Performance of Nausea," *The Yale Journal of Criticism*, vol. 1 (Spring 1988), pp. 1–22.

38. Patricia Yaeger, "Toward a Female Sublime," in *Gender and Theory: Dialogues on Feminist Criticism*, ed. Linda Kauffman (London: Basil Blackwell, 1989). See also the reply to her article by Lee Edelman: "At

Risk in the Sublime: The Politics of Gender and Theory" in the same volume. See also, Gary Shapiro, "From the Sublime to the Political: Some Historical Notes," *New Literary History* 16, no. 2 (Winter 1985), pp. 213–235.

39. On Freud, temporality, and modernity, see Mary Ann Doane, "Technology's Body: Cinematic Vision in Modernity," *differences* 5 (Summer 1993), pp. 10–12.

40. Mikhail Bakhtin, *Rabelais and His World*, trans. Helene Iswolsky (Bloomington: Indiana University Press, 1984), p. 37. (Identified as *RW* hereafter).

41. For a Bakhtinian critique of Freud, see V. N. Volosinov, *Freudianism: A Critical Sketch*, trans. I. R. Titunik, ed. in collaboration with Neal H. Bruss (Bloomington and Indianapolis: Indiana University Press, 1976); for a discussion of this work as a disputed text, see p. xiii.

42. See n. 35 above.

43. Katerina Clark and Michael Holquist, *Mikhail Bakhtin* (Cambridge and London: Harvard University Press, 1984), p. 206.

44. Michael Balint, *Thrills and Regressions* (New York: International Universities Press, 1959), p. 26.

45. See Julia Kristeva, *Desire in Language: A Semiotic Approach to Literature and Art*, ed. Leon S. Roudiez (New York: Columbia University Press, 1980).

46. Kristeva, p. 78. See also, Julia Kristeva, "Women's Time," trans. Alice Jardine and Harry Blake in *Feminist Theory: A Critique of Ideology*, ed. Nannerl O. Keohane, et al. (Chicago: University of Chicago Press, 1982), pp. 31–55. My own view of "generation" in relation to gendered space is elaborated in chapter 6 in relation to Angela Carter.

47. For an excellent overview of Kristeva's work in relation to the social in general, and to feminism in particular, see Ann Rosalind Jones, "Julia Kristeva on Femininity: The Limits of a Semiotic Politics," *Feminist Review* 18 (Winter 1984), pp. 56–73; see also, Jacqueline Rose, *Sexuality in the Field of Vision* (London: Verso, 1986), pp. 141–164; and Toril Moi, *Sexual/Textual Politics: Feminist Literary Theory* (London and New York: Routledge, 1988).

48. Sandor Ferenczi, *Thalassa* (New York: The Psychoanalytic Quarterly, 1937).

49. My emphasis here is on the cultural contents of Balint's formulation in relation to modernity rather than on the feminist discussion of the

phallus in Lacanian terms. On this topic, see especially Jane Gallop, *Thinking Through the Body* (New York: Columbia University Press, 1988) and *Reading Lacan* (Ithaca: Cornell University Press, 1985); see also the contributions of Parveen Adams, Charles Bernheimer, Kaja Silverman, and Judith Butler in *differences* 4/1 (Spring, 1992).

50. Peter Stallybrass and Allon White, *The Politics and Poetics of Transgression* (Ithaca: Cornell University Press, 1986), p. 190.

51. Juliet Mitchell, *Women, the Longest Revolution: Essays in Femininsm, Literature and Psycho-analysis* (London: Virago, 1984), p. 291.

52. See Laura Mulvey, "Changes," *Discourse* 7 (Fall 1985), pp. 11–30. See also her *Visual and Other Pleasures* (Bloomington: Indiana University Press, 1989). For a discussion of the acrobatic sequence in *Riddles of the Sphinx*, see Kaja Silverman, *The Acoustic Mirror: The Female Voice in Psychoanalysis and Cinema* (Bloomington: Indiana University Press, 1988), p. 139.

53. Kristeva also makes the association between the confusion of spectator and performer with Nietzsche. She writes:

     A carnival participant is both actor and spectator; he loses his sense of individuality, passes through a zero point of carnivalesque activity and splits into a subject of spectacle. . . .

     Within the carnival, the subject is reduced to nothingness, while the structure of *the author* emerges as an anonymity that creates and sees itself created as self and other, as man and mask. The cynicism of this carnivalesque scene, which destroys a god in order to impose its own dialogical laws, calls to mind Nietzsche's Dionysianism" (Kristeva, *Desire in Language,* p. 78).

54. Naomi Ritter makes this connection between the aerialist and Nietzschean transcendence in "Art and Androgyny: the Aerialist," *Studies in Twentieth-Century Literature,* vol. 13, no. 2 (Summer 1989), p. 175.

55. See Laura Mulvey, "Pandora: Topographies of the Mask and Curiosity," in *Sexuality and Space,* ed. Beatriz Colomina (New York: Princeton Architectural Press, 1992), pp. 53–71. See also Tom Gunning, "An Aesthetic of Astonishment: Early Film and the (In)credulous Spectator," *Art and Text* 34 (Spring 1989), pp. 31–45. In her discussion of early cinema and popular exhibition in Naples, Giuliana Bruno suggests the fascinating connections between the freak show and high culture in relation to the famous Jusepe de Ribera painting, *Magdalena Ventura*

with her Husband and Son—popularly known as The Bearded Woman (in "Spectatorial Embodiments: Anatomies of the Visible and the Female Bodyscape.") In the Italian context, the overlapping discourses of aesthetics, anatomy, and criminology, are developed in Cesare Lombroso and William Ferrero, *The Female Offender* (London: T.F. Unwin, 1895).

56. See Teresa de Lauretis, "Eccentric Subjects: Feminist Theory and Historical Consciousness," *Feminist Studies* 16 (1990), pp. 115–150; see also, *Technologies of Gender: Essays on Theory, Film, and Fiction* (Bloomington, and Indianapolis: Indiana University Press, 1987).

57. De Lauretis, *Technologies of Gender*, p. 26.

58. I am referring here not to Judith Butler's very significant intervention in *Gender Trouble* (New York: Routledge, 1990), but to what seems to me a widespread misreading of her work that suggests that the instability of gender as a category relying on performative repetition somehow relieves one of the constraints of that category, or that to acknowledge the oppressions of gender asymmetry rather than willing them away is to be heterosexist. See also her recent *Bodies That Matter: On the Discursive Limits of Sex* (New York and London: Routledge, 1993).

59. With or without Foucault, the practice of feminism in the last twenty-five years has encountered, if not understood, oppression as working in a social field defined by its diversity, multiplicity, and the interrelated-ness of its discourses and practices, including racism, classism, and sexual discrimination. My own view of this recent history is that it is characterized by uneven development and that many significant microhistories are covered over in academic accounts of feminism as progressively moving from one fairly intact and exclusive model to another, as in feminism to "postfeminism," or, as Tania Modleski puts it, from feminism to "gynocidal feminism." See her "Postmortem on Postfeminism" in *Feminism Without Women: Culture and Criticism in a "Postfeminist" Age*, n. 26 above (pp. 3–22). For an early and rather cranky assessment of the "Anglo-American" vs. "French Feminist" divide, see my "Notes on Postfeminism" in *The Politics of Theory*. See also, Toril Moi, *French Feminist Thought* (New York: Blackwell, 1987), and especially Jane Gallop, *Around 1981: Academic Feminist Literary Theory* (New York: Routledge, 1992); Chris Weedon, *Feminist Practice and Poststructuralist Theory* (Oxford: Basil Blackwell, 1987); *Gender and Theory: Dialogues on Feminist Criticism*, ed. Linda Kaufman (Oxford: Basil Blackwell, 1989), especially the essay by Barbara Christian.

60. Sandra Bartky, *Femininity and Domination: Studies in the Phenom-enology of Oppression* (New York: Routledge, 1990), p. 43. Within psy-choanalysis, strictly speaking, this is already impossible.

61. On this topic, see Sarah Kofman, *The Enigma of Woman: Woman in Freud's Writings*, trans. Catherine Porter (Ithaca: Cornell University Press, 1985).

62. Peggy Phelan, *Unmarked: The Politics of Performance* (London and New York: Routledge, 1993), p. 27.

63. Charles Ludlum's performance of the dying heroine in *Camille* would be my favorite example of a subversion of the icon of the dying woman.

64. J. K. Huysmans, *Against the Grain*, trans. John Howard (New York: Dover, 1969).

65. For an excellent treatment of this topic in relation to performance and sexuality, see Mark Franko "Where He Danced: Cocteau's Barbette and Ohno's Water Lilies," *PMLA*, vol. 107, no. 3, pp. 594–607. I am grateful to him for alerting me to Cocteau's essay and to the complications of the "male gaze" across the feminist and gay male fields of vision.

66. As Franko observes, for Cocteau the theatricality of Barbette's sexual enigma occurs backstage when Barbette cross-dresses and becomes a woman (Franko, 196).

67. Djuna Barnes, *Nightwood* (New York: New Directions, 1937), p. 13.

68. Jean Starobinski, *Portrait de l'artiste en saltimbanque* (Geneva: Editions d'art Albert Skira, 1970), p. 55 [translations in the text mine].

69. As quoted by Catherine Clément, *Opera or the Undoing of Women*, trans. Betsy Wing (Minneapolis: University of Minnesota Press, 1988), p. 78. In a short chapter entitled "Girls Who Leap into Space," Clement locates operatic jumping with the seduction of the young female or her undoing through dangerous liaisons or disastrous marriage. Partic-ularly interesting for the above discussion is her reading of Mimi in *La Bohème* as a girl Pierrot. Clement's book is staged as a relentless, histri-onic critique, leaving room for counterproductions of the operatic, as for example, Sally Potter's reworking of *La Bohème* in her experimental film *Thriller*. As Susan McClary points out in her introduction to Clement, many women composers and performance artists, including Diamanda Galás, Ma Rainey, Bessie Smith, Janika Vandervelde, and Madonna have extended the gender boundaries of bourgeois musical production. In fact, the hyperbole of opera has made it wonderfully susceptible to appropriations across gender and sexuality for some

time. See for instance, Charles Ludlum's Ridiculous Theater productions, like *Der Ring Gott Farblonjet* (1977) and *Galás*. See also, the recent book by Wayne Koestenbaum, *The Queen's Throat* (New York: Poseidon Press, 1993).

70. See Bram Dijkstra, *Idols of Perversity: Fantasies of Feminine Evil in Fin-de-Siècle Culture* (New York and Oxford: Oxford University Press, 1986).

71. Slavoj Žižek, *Looking Awry: An Introduction to Jacques Lacan Through Popular Culture* (Cambridge and London: MIT Press, 1991), p. 84.

72. Judith Mayne, *The Woman at the Keyhole: Feminism and Women's Cinema* (Bloomington: Indiana University Press, 1990).

73. See Kaja Silverman, *Male Subjectivity at the Margins* (New York and London: Routledge, 1992).

74. See Judith Butler's critique of Slavoj Žižek in chapter seven of *Bodies that Matter* (see n. 58 above).

75. Phelan's example is the group of artists and activists calling themselves the "Guerrilla Girls," who anonymously draw attention to the discriminatory practices of the art world with their posters and masked stunting (Phelan, p. 19).

76. Sue-Ellen Case, "Tracking the Vampire," *differences* 3/2 (Summer 1991), pp. 1–22.

77. Eve Kosofsky Sedgwick, "Socratic Raptures, Socratic Ruptures: Notes Toward Queer Performativity," in *English Inside and Out: The Places of Literary Criticism,* ed. Susan Gubar and Jonathan Kamholtz (London and New York: Routledge, 1993), p. 125.

78. See Gilles Deleuze and Felix Guattari, *Kafka: Toward a Minor Literature,* trans. Dana Polan (Minneapolis: University of Minnesota Press, 1986).

79. Franz Kafka, "A Report to an Academy," *Franz Kafka: The Complete Stories,* ed. Nahum N. Glatzer (New York: Schocken Books, 1971), pp. 253–254.

Notes to Chapter Two

A version of this paper was presented at "Feminist Studies: Reconstituting Knowledge," a conference held at the Center for Twentieth Century Studies, organized by Teresa de Lauretis. It was published subsequently in *Feminist*

Studies/Critical Studies, Teresa de Lauretis, ed. (Indiana: 1986). Because I return to many of the issues raised in this article in the course of this book, I have confined my revisions to updating some of the footnotes.

1. Mikhail Bakhtin, *Rabelais and His World,* trans. Helene Iswolsky (Bloomington: Indiana University Press, 1984). An earlier edition of this translation was published in 1968 by MIT Press. References to *Rabelais and His World* will be identified as *RW* and included in the text. Also important for discussions of language and carnival are *The Dialogical Imagination: Four Essays,* ed. Michael Holquist (Austin: University of Texas Press, 1981), and *Problems of Dostoevski's Poetics,* trans. R. W. Rotsel (Ann Arbor: University of Michigan Press, 1973). For other works attributed to Bakhtin, see P. N. Medvedev and M. M. Bakhtin, *The Formal Method in Literary Scholarship: A Critical Introduction to Sociological Poetics,* trans. Albert J. Wehrle (Baltimore: The Johns Hopkins University Press, 1978), and V. N. Volosinov, *Freudianism: A Marxist Critique* (New York: Academic Press, 1976).

2. See Peter Stallybrass and Allon White, *The Politics and Poetics of Transgression* (Ithaca: Cornell University Press, 1986), which contains a rigorous historical and critical introduction to carnival as political discourse.

3. See Julia Kristeva, *La Révolution du language poétique: l'avant-garde à la fin du 19e siècle: Lautréamont et Mallarmé* (Paris: Seuil, 1977) and *Polylogue* (Paris: Seuil, 1977); and Teresa de Lauretis, *Alice Doesn't: Feminism, Semiotics, Cinema* (Bloomington: Indiana University Press, 1984), and *Technologies of Gender: Essays on Theory, Film, and Fiction* (Bloomington and Indianapolis: University of Indiana Press, 1987).

4. See Mary Douglas, *Purity and Danger: An Analysis of Concepts of Pollution and Taboo* (London: Routledge and Kegan Paul, 1966); Victor Turner, *From Ritual to Theatre: The Human Seriousness of Play* (New York: Performing Arts Journal Publications, 1982) and *The Ritual Process: Structure and Anti-structure* (Chicago: University of Chicago Press, 1968); and Clifford Geertz, *The Interpretation of Cultures* (New York, Basic Books, 1973).

5. Natalie Zemon Davis, "Women on Top" in her *Society and Culture in Early Modern France* (Stanford: Stanford University Press, 1965), p. 131.

6. Davis, p. 148. As Davis points out, this image of the "strong woman" is problematic: "The unruly woman not only directed some of the male festive organizations; she was sometimes their butt. The village scold or

the domineering wife might be ducked in the pond or pulled through the streets muzzled or branked or in creel" (p. 140).

7. On grotesque images of suffragettes, see Lisa Tichner, *The Spectacle of Women: Imagery of the Suffrage Campaign 1907–14* (Chicago: University of Chicago Press, 1988), pp. 167–174. For grotesque types in second-wave feminism, see Susan J. Douglas, *Where the Girls Are: Growing Up Female With the Mass Media* (New York: Time Books, 1994).

8. Since the original publication of this article, the interest in cross-dressing has grown exponentially. For an excellent overview and bibliography, see Marjorie Garber, *Vested Interests: Cross-Dressing and Cultural Anxiety* (New York and London: Routledge: 1992).

9. Work of this type has greatly increased in the last five years. See, for instance, *New Cultural History*, ed. Lynn Hunt (Berkeley: University of California, 1989); Joan Wallach Scott, *Gender and the Politics of History* (New York: Columbia University Press, 1988); Carroll Smith-Rosenberg, *Disorderly Conduct: Visions of Gender in Victorian America* (New York: Oxford University Press, 1986); Carlo Ginzburg, *Clues, Myths, and the Historical Method*, trans. John and Anne C. Tedeschi (Baltimore: The Johns Hopkins University Press, 1989); and Roger Chartier, *Cultural History: Between Practices and Representation*, trans. Lydia G. Cochrane (Ithaca: Cornell University Press, 1988).

10. See Maurice Agulhon, *Marianne into Battle: Republican Imagery and Symbolism in France, 1789–1880* (Cambridge: Cambridge University Press, 1981), and Eric Hobsbawm, "Man and Women in Socialist Iconography," *History Workshop: A Journal of Socialist Historians*, no. 6 (Autumn 1978), pp. 107–121. See also replies to Hobsbawm by Maurice Agulhon and by feminist historians Sally Alexander, Anna Davin, and Eve Hostettler in *History Workshop*, no. 8 (Autumn 1978), pp. 167–183. For an interesting exchange on the topic, see Neil Hertz, "Medusa's Head: Male Hysteria under Political Pressure," *Representations* 4 (Fall 1983), pp. 55–73, and the comments that follow it by Catherine Gallagher and Joel Fineman.

11. See Victor Turner, "Frame, Flow and Reflection: Ritual and Drama as Public Liminality," in *Performance in Postmodern Culture*, ed. Michel Benamou and Charles Caramello (Madison: Coda Press, 1977), pp. 35–55. As Turner puts it, "The danger here is not simply that of female 'unruliness.' This unruliness itself is the mark of the ultraliminal, of the perilous realm of possibility of 'anything *may* go' which threatens any social order and seems more threatening, the *more* that order *seems* rigorous and secure . . . The subversive potential of the carnivalized femi-

nine principle become evident in times of social change when its manifestations move out of the liminal world of Mardi Gras into the political
arena itself" (pp. 41–42); and Emmanuel Le Roy Ladurie, *Carnival at
Romans,* trans. Mary Feeneg (New York: Braziller, 1979).

12. Paul Céline, quoted in Julia Kristeva, *Powers of Horror: An Essay on
    Abjection,* trans. Leon S. Roudiez (New York: Columbia University
    Press, 1982), p. 169.

13. See also Kristeva, chapter eight, "Those Females Who Can Wreck the
    Infinite" (pp. 157–73).

14. "His fascination with Jews, which was full of hatred and which he main-
    tained to the end of his life, the simple-minded anti-Semitism that
    besots the tumultuous pages of the pamphlets, are no accident; they
    thwart the disintegration of identity that is coextensive with a scription
    that affects the most archaic distinctions, that bridges the gaps insuring
    life and meaning. Céline's anti-Semitism, like political commitment,
    for others—like, as a matter of fact, any political commitment, to the
    extent that it settles the subject within a socially justified illusion—is a
    security blanket" (Kristeva, 136–37).

15. Writing or "literature" is a "vision of the apocalypse that seems to me
    rooted no matter what its socio-historical condition might be, on the
    fragile border (borderline cases) where identities (subject/object, etc.)
    do not exist or only barely so—doubly, fuzzy, heterogeneous, animal,
    metamorphosed, altered, abject" (Kristeva, 207).

16. Stallybrass and White, p. 21.

17. See especially chapters three, five, and six.

18. Michèle Richman, "Sex and Signs: The Language of French Feminist
    Criticism," *Language and Style* 13 (Fall 1980), pp. 62–80.

19. Richman, p. 74. The work of Luce Irigaray and Michèle Montrelay is
    especially important to this discussion.

20. The dangers of essentialism in posing the female body, whether in rela-
    tion to representation or to "women's history," have been well-stated, so
    well-stated in fact that "anti-essentialism" may well be the greatest inhi-
    bition to work in cultural theory and politics at the moment, and must
    be displaced. The hyperboles of masquerade and carnival suggest at
    least some preliminary "acting out" of the dilemma, and perhaps a
    moving beyond the Lacanian psychoanalytic model of femininity as
    lack. For an account of debates around essentialism and the female
    body in film, see Constance Penley's chapter "Feminism, Film Theory,

and the Bachelor Machine," in *The Future of an Illusion* (Minneapolis: University of Minnesota Press, 1989). For a more recent exchange of views on this topic, see *differences*, vol 1, no. 2 (Summer 1989) (*The Essential Differences: Another Look at Essentialism*) with contributions by Teresa de Lauretis, Naomi Schor, Luce Irigaray, Diana Fuss, Robert Scholes, Leslie Wahl Rabine, Ellen Rooney, and Gayatri Spivak. See also, Diana Fuss, *Essentially Speaking: Feminism, Nature and Difference* (New York and London: Routledge, 1989). For a "personal" account of critical debates in the eighties, see Nancy K. Miller, *Getting Personal: Feminist Occasions and Other Autobiographical Acts* (New York and London: Routledge, 1991).

21. Catherine Clément, quoted in Richman, p. 69.

22. Luce Irigaray, *The Sex Which is Not One*, trans. Catherine Porter (Ithaca, New York: Cornell University Press, 1985), p. 76.

23. Jacques Lacan, *Feminine Sexuality: Jacques Lacan and the "Ecole Freudienne,"* ed. Juliet Mitchell and Jacqueline Rose, trans. Jacqueline Rose (New York: W. W. Norton, 1982), p. 84.

24. Mary Anne Doane, "Film and Masquerade: Theorizing the Female Spectator, *Screen* vol. 23, no. 3/4 (September/October 1982), pp. 74–87, and "Women's Stake: Filming the Female Body," *October* 17 (Summer 1981), pp. 23–36. For her reconsideration of masquerade, see "Masquerade Reconsidered" in *Femmes Fatales: Feminism, Film Theory and Psychoanalysis* (New York and London: Routledge, 1992); See also Kaja Silverman, "Histoire d'O: The Construction of a Female Subject," in *Pleasure and Danger: Exploring Female Sexuality,* ed. Carole S. Vance (Boston: Routledge and Kegan Paul, 1984), pp. 320–349, and "Changing the Fantasmatic Scene," *Framework* 20 (1983), pp. 27–36. For a discussion of masquerade in relation to postmodernism, see Craig Owens, "Posing" in *Difference: On Representation and Sexuality Catalog* (New York: New Museum of Contemporary Art, 1985).

25. Doane, "Film and Masquerade," p. 87.

26. Gayatri Spivak, "Displacement and the Discourse of Woman," in *Displacement: Derrida and After,* ed. Mark Krupnick, Center for Twentieth Century Studies, Theories of Contemporary Culture Vol. 4 (Bloomington: Indiana University Press, 1983), p. 186.

27. As Spivak quotes Derrida, "she is twice model, in a contradictory fashion, at once lauded and condemned ... (First), like writing ... But, insofar as she does not believe, herself, in truth ... she is again the model, this time the good model, or rather the bad model as good

model: she plays dissimulation, ornament, lying, art, the artistic philosophy" (Spivak, 171).

28. Dick Hebdige, *Subculture: The Meaning of Style* (London: Methuen, 1979); Homi Bhabha, "Of Mimicry and Man: The Ambivalence of Colonial Discourse," *October* 28 (Spring 1984), pp. 125–133. Conversely, both Hebdige and Bhabha have largely ignored gender difference.

29. Elaine Showalter, "Critical Cross-Dressing: Male Feminists and the Woman of the Year," *Raritan,* vol. 3, no. 2 (Fall 1983), pp. 130–149.

30. James Creech, Peggy Kamuf, and Jane Todd, "Deconstruction in America: An Interview with Jacques Derrida," *Critical Exchange* 17 (Winter 1985), p. 30. I wish to thank Theodore M. Norton for alerting me to the hilarious possibilities of this interview.

31. Derrida says, "So let's just say that the most insistent and the most organized motif in my texts is neither feminist nor phallocentric. And that at a certain point I try to show that the two are tantamount to the same thing" (Creech, et al., p. 31).

Notes to Chapter Three

1. Cynthia Macdonald, "Celebrating the Freak," *(W)holes* (New York: Alfred A. Knopf, 1980) copyright 1980 by Cynthia McDonald. Reprinted by permission of Alfred A. Knopf, Inc., p. 14.

2. Jimi Hendrix, *Axis: Bold as Love* (Reprise Records compact disc 6281–2).

3. Frederick Drimmer in his popular account of freak performers, suggests that a protest against the use of the word freak, supposedly organized by Annie Jones, the Bearded Lady, was in fact a publicity stunt by Barnum and Bailey. The circus used other words like "curiosities," "prodigies," and "strange people" at various stages of the circus' history. Carnivals and local fairs were perhaps more driven to continue the use of the term "freaks" in their sideshows to increase publicity. Drimmer prefers "very special people." In contrast, I use the word "freaks" to indicate an historical *difference* produced through social relations of ownership, violence, exploitation, and (occasionally) self-naming. "Special" would not do justice to this history, although it is a much more comfortable term. See Frederick Drimmer, *Very Special People: The Struggles, Loves, and Triumphs of Human Oddities* (New York: Amjon Publishers, Inc., 1973), pp. 10–11. See also Daniel P. Mannix, *Freaks: We Who Are Not as Others* (San Francisco: Re/search Publications, 1976).

4. Katherine Dunn, *Geek Love* (New York: Warner Books, 1990).

5. Patricia Bosworth, *Diane Arbus: a Biography* (New York: Avon Books, 1985), p. 365.

6. Leslie Fiedler, *Freaks: Myths and Images of the Secret Self* (New York: Simon and Schuster, 1978).

7. Mikhail Bakhtin, *Rabelais and His World*, trans. Helene Iswolsky (Bloomington: Indiana University Press), p. 53. Future references to this work will be identified as *RW*.

8. Susan Stewart, *On Longing: Narratives of the Miniature, the Gigantic, the Souvenir, the Collection* (Durham and London: Duke University Press, 1993), p. 109.

9. Guy Debord, *Society of the Spectacle* (Detroit: Black and Red, 1983), p. 1.

10. Robert Bogdan, *Freak Show: Presenting Human Oddities for Amusement and Profit* (Chicago and London: University of Chicago Press, 1988), p. 97.

11. Bogdan, pp. 94–116. As Bogdan points out, the medicalization of freaks was accompanied by a commercial degradation of their presentation. As freaks were viewed less as exotic visitors fit to be received by the Queen than as medical accidents or anomalies, their paraphernalia was less elaborate and their audiences less affluent. Symptomatically, "the carefully posed, professional-quality photographic images that the freaks sold were replaced by poor quality postcards" (p. 116). Although his classification of freak presentation is useful in reminding the reader or viewer that the freak is a cultural representation, these categories overlap consistently, and the history of carnivals and freak shows does not show an even development. Also, his account would be interestingly complicated by a consideration of early cinema.

12. I am thinking of a recent tabloid cover story which featured a picture of Hillary Clinton with an oversized baby-alien whom she was supposedly adopting in secret, with the "secret service" preparing a hidden nursery.

13. Wini Breines, *Community and Organization in the New Left: 1962–1968* (New York: Praeger, 1982), p. 6. Breines writes that "the term *prefigurative politics* is used to designate an essentially anti-organizational politics characteristic of the movement, as well as parts of new left leadership, and may be recognized in counter institutions, demonstrations, and the attempt to embody personal and anti-hierarchical values in politics ... The crux of prefigurative politics imposed substantial

tasks, the central one being to create and sustain within the live practice of the movement, relationships and political forms that "prefigured" and embodied the desired society."

14. Sheila Rowbotham, *Woman's Consciousness, Man's World* (Harmonds-worth: Penguin Books, 1973), p. 27.

15. Friedrich Nietzsche, *The Genealogy of Morals*, trans. Francis Golffing (New York: Anchor Books, 1956), pp. 201–202.

16. Anthropologists sometimes refer to this aspect of the social body as the "grid," as opposed to the inside/out differences which define the "group" from other social groups. For classic exposition of these terms, see Mary Douglas, *Natural Symbols: Explorations in Cosmology* (New York: Vintage Books, 1973).

17. As a model of community, differences in movements, gestures, dress, etc., are not merely tolerated; they are refined into different modes of not only performance in the theatrical sense, but into different modes or techniques of ordinary bodily functions like eating. As I argue, Browning draws the line at sexuality/gender, and represents only very constrained options in terms of how one is a man or a woman in the film.

18. In an earlier scene, which takes place *outside* the freak show, in the country, Madame Tetralini, the monster-nanny, begs the men who stumble upon the group to recognize them as children—homogenizing them into the human race, while excluding them from anything but a marginal place within it. Later, the much diminished body of Cleopatra is exhibited in a crib like a baby freak (not a Man), a "chick."

19. This recalls the career of Ophuls' Lola Montes, who is finally contained in a circus act controlled by the male narrator.

20. Michel Foucault, *The History of Sexuality, Vol. I: An Introduction*, trans. Robert Hurley (New York: Vintage Books, 1980).

21. Allon White, "Pigs and Pierrots: The Politics of Transgression in Modern Fiction" *Raritan*, vol. 2, no. 2 (Fall 1982), p. 53.

22. For an excellent general discussion of Ottinger's work in relation to feminism and women filmmakers, see Roswitha Mueller "Interview with Ulrike Ottinger," *Discourse* 4 (Winter 1981–1982), pp. 108–126. On Foucault and *Freak Orlando* as a "history of the world," see especially p. 115.

23. Erica Carter, "Interview with Ulrike Ottinger," *Screen Education* 41 (Winter–Spring 1982), pp. 36–37.

24. Perhaps the most striking example of the collage style of mixing the everyday and the mythic is in the department store episode in a "prehistorical period." In this scene, the materials, costumes, and liturgical time represented by "mythological sales-week" produce the chiasmas of a ritual of consumerism in the consumption of ritual.

25. Virginia Woolf, *Orlando: A Biography* (Harmondsworth, Penguin Books, 1970).

26. The emphasis on clothes and fashion in Woolf's novel as an expression of Orlando's personal charm, versatility, and upper-class modernity is not a feature of Ottinger's film. Interestingly, Bloomingdale's Department Store featured a high-fashion "Orlando" theme to honor Sally Potter's lavishly costumed 1992 version which is much closer to the novel. For a discussion of *Orlando* in relation to cross-dressing, see Marjorie Garber, *Vested Interests: Cross-Dressing and Cultural Anxiety* (New York: Routledge, 1992, reprinted Harper Perennial, 1993), see especially pp. 134–135 and 311–312. For a general discussion of cross-dressing and modernity, see Sandra M. Gilbert and Susan Gubar, *No Man's Land 2: Sexchanges* (New Haven and London: Yale University Press, 1989). For earlier versions of this work, see Sandra M. Gilbert, "Costumes of the Mind: Transvestism as Metaphor in Modern Literature," *Critical Inquiry,* vol. 7, no. 2 (Winter 1980), pp. 391–417, and Sandra Gubar, "Blessings in Disguise: Cross-Dressing as Re-dressing for Male Modernists," *Massachusetts Review* (Autumn 1981). See also Carroll Smith-Rosenberg, *Disorderly Conduct: Visions of Gender in Victorian America* (New York: Oxford University Press, 1985).

27. Quoted in Gilbert and Gubar, p. 344.

28. Not only do actors play multiple roles in the film, but as in this scene with Delphine Seyrig, parts of their bodies are cast, further confusing the categories of "real freaks" and "normal" or artificial freaks.

29. Vetruvius quoted in Geoffrey Galt Harpham, *On the Grotesque: Strategies of Contradiction in Art and Literature* (Princeton: Princeton University Press, 1982), p. 26.

30. "For how can a reed actually sustain a roof, or a candelabra the ornaments of a bagle, or a soft and slender stalk a seated statue, or how can flowers and half-statues rise alternatively from roots and stalks?" (Vetruvius quoted in Harpham, p. 26)

31. Marco Frascari, *Monsters of Architecture: Anthropomorphism in Architectural Theory* (Savage, Maryland: Rowman and Litchfield Publishers, 1991). I am grateful to Arielle Saiber for bringing this study to my attention.

32.   "Many forms of so-called decoration . . . ought in truth be set down in
      the architects contract, as for *Monstrification*," (John Ruskin quoted in
      Frascari, p. 31). Frascari comments on Ruskin as follows: "From this
      point of view, architecture is not a specific body of works, or a sequence
      of aediculas or edifices; neither is it a collation of the products of a pro-
      fession. Rather, it is an intellectual representation resulting from the
      traces of semiotic practices, ie., the manipulation of signs in accordance
      with 'cultural reasons' (p. 31).

33.   For a discussion of Goya's *Capricho* paintings in relation to architec-
      tural monstrosity, see Frascari, pp. 84–86.

34.   In one frame, a tall phallocrat in a pointed hat stands near the dwarf
      artist Galli, with the 1932 Berlin Olympic stadium as a background.
      The "stylite" hat mimics the tall, chimney-like entry to the stadium
      behind them, while the broad flat hat and wide skirt mimic the stunted
      look of the base of the stadium. Again, Ottinger's emphasis is on the
      artificial, specifically the prosthetic, bodily detail. This frame is repro-
      duced in the catalogue, *Ulrike Ottinger: A Retrospective* (n.p., Goethe
      Institute, 1990).

35.   This is the difference between bourgeois realism in Bakhtin and gro-
      tesque realism: grotesque realism does not merely affirm the status quo.

36.   In discussing a later film, *Ticket of No Return,* Thomas Elsaesser
      describes Ottinger's cinema as "the *mise en scène* of perversion," to sig-
      nal a move towards a more radical aestheticism and away from the "cin-
      ema of experience." See Thomas Elsaesser, *New German Cinema: A
      History* (New Brunswick: Rutgers University Press, 1989), pp. 199–201.

37.   Dante Alighieri, *The Divine Comedy,* trans. Charles S. Singleton
      (Princeton: Princeton University Press, 1970), p. 97.

38.   As one German critic wrote, the film "redistributes the balance between
      real and artificial monstrosity." Neither category is more plausible than
      the other. Frieda Grafe, *Suddeutsche Zeitung* 7/8 (November 1981),
      quoted in *Ulrike Ottinger: A Retrospective* (see n. 34 above).

39.   As opposed to the more "exotic" construals of freak sexuality in
      pornography.

40.   In fact, she resembles the two-headed girl in an earlier episode, since
      she seems to have surrendered her bottom half to her sister and to her
      sister's "marriage."

41.   Sue-Ellen Case, "Toward a Butch-Femme Aesthetic," in *Making a
      Spectacle: Feminist Essays on Contemporary Women's Theatre,* ed. Lynda
      Hart (Ann Arbor: University of Michigan Press, 1989), pp. 282–300.

42. For a discussion of Ottinger's cinema in relation to the "the aesthetic of the experience of artifice" see Elsaesser (n. 36 above).

43. In the first scene, Orlando walks toward the figure of the goddess of the tree of life buried in the ground; like her, Orlando is a representation of a woman on top with no bottom in sight. In a larger sense, it might be argued that Ottinger's cinema plays to the experience of a specific "lesbian" viewing pleasure. For an interesting discussion of the theoretical and psychoanalytic issues involved in such a model of spectatorship, see "Ambiguities of 'Lesbian' Viewing Pleasure," in the excellent anthology *Body Guards: The Cultural Politics of Gender Ambiguity,* ed. Julia Epstein and Kristina Straub (New York: Routledge, 1991).

44. A very interesting theoretical frame for discussing *Madame X* might be the controversial "philosophy of difference" put forward by certain Italian feminists, since it addresses female power and hierarchy in relation to the symbolic role of the female leader. In English, see The Milan Women's Bookstore Collective, *Sexual Difference: A Theory of Social-Symbolic Practice,* trans. Patricia Cicogna and Teresa de Lauretis (Bloomington and Indianapolis: Indiana University Press, 1990). See especially the excellent introduction by Teresa de Lauretis, pp. 1–21. See also, Renate Holub, "The Politics of Diotima," *Differentia* 6 (1991), pp. 161–173.

45. This nonprogressive and utopian itinerary is made explicit in the speech by Josephine Collage (Yvonne Rainer), who plays a famous international avant-garde artist in the film. Rainer, who scripted her own speech is, of course, a celebrated member of the avant-garde.

46. Carter, p. 34. The controversy over *Madame X* is resonant with the "sex wars" within feminism in the United States. The 1982 Scholar and the Feminist IX conference held at Barnard College, "Towards a Politics of Sexuality," crystallized many of the debates around female eroticism and pornography. For an account of the debates and an excellent selection of writings on the topic, see *Pleasure and Danger: Exploring Female Sexuality,* ed. Carole S. Vance (Boston, London, and Melbourne: Routledge & Kegan Paul, 1984).

47. See, for instance, the groups of men who appear sequentially as male flagellants, Nazis, gay leather-boys, etc.

Notes to Chapter Four

1. For a discussion with Cronenberg about the idea of visceral beauty in his other films, see Michel Ciment, "Entretien avec David Cronenberg," *Positif* 337 (1989), pp. 33–44.

2. For the Mantle Brothers, a fascination with instruments seems to have always preceded their understanding of biology and reproductive practices. In the childhood scene which opens the film, the young twins compare information about aquatic sex life which requires no actual male/female contact. This conversation leads them to an exchange about scuba diving which is, for them, tantamount to an "underwater breathing apparatus," and to their unsuccessful attempt to persuade a young girl to join them in the bathtub. Her very savvy refusal ("you don't even know what fucking is!") points to their subsequent triumphs as inventors of the Mantle Retractor, an invention which is based upon a certain willful *ignorance* of the female body and a preference for tools.

3. Obviously, the spectacle of shared sex and intravenous drugs suggests the portrayal of AIDS in the 90s and the identification of that disease with deviance and monstrosity in the media. Claire's identity as an actress links her to that other female stand-in, the prostitute, who is the paradigmatic polluted and polluting woman. As Andrew Parker points out in an article on an early Cronenberg film, *Rabid,* the horror genre and related popular narratives, provided the cultural imagery, themes, and fictions, to support the representation of the AIDS epidemic as a menace to the body politic, so it is not surprising to see this convergence. See Andrew Parker, "Grafting David Cronenberg: Monstrosity, AIDS Media, National/Sexual Difference," *Stanford Humanities Review,* vol. 3, no. 1 (Winter 1993), pp. 7–19. See also, Simon Watney, "The Spectacle of AIDS," *October* 43 (Winter 1987) and Leo Bersani, "Is the Rectum a Grave?" in the same issue. See also, Judith Williamson, "Every Virus Tells A Story" in Erica Carter and Simon Watney, eds., *Taking Liberties: AIDS and Cultural Politics* (London: Serpent's Tail, 1989). For an excellent, recent study of a horror subgenre in relation to representation, gender, and sexuality, see Carol Clover's *Men, Women, and Chainsaws: Gender in the Modern Horror Film* (Princeton: Princeton University Press, 1992.) See also, for a discussion of the difficulties of classifying Cronenberg's films, Noel Carroll, *The Philosophy of Horror, or Paradoxes of the Human Heart* (New York: Routledge, 1990).

4. In his interview with Michel Ciment (see n. 1 above), Cronenberg says that he thought having one brother homosexual seemed psychologically false. "I could imagine", he says, "two heterosexual twins or two homosexual twins but not that distinction." Later in the same interview, he remarks that twins seem to him the perfect metaphor for the relationships of the couple such as husband and wife, or parent and child, which are intense and claustrophobic.

5. Claire's inability to bear children is set up in the film as a public relations issue: the melodramatic version of the story—beautiful actress brokenhearted over not having a child of her own—has already been published in the tabloids. The grotesque version, detailing her "mutancy," would ruin her career.

6. The threat of sleeping with a mutant woman is used to warn off his imagined rival, who answers the telephone at the Niveau suite while she is on location reshooting a television series. Since the thought of sleeping with a mutant would supposedly repel a "normal" man, Cronenberg, consistent with the heterosexist bias of the film, has her homosexual manager answer. The joke being that he is then totally "freaked" out by the very thought.

7. "The glance does not scan a field: it strikes at one point, which is central or decisive; the gaze is endlessly modulated, the glance goes straight to its object. The glance chooses a line that instantly distinguishes the essential; it therefore goes beyond what it sees; it is not misled by the immediate forms of the sensible, for it knows how to traverse them; it is essentially demystifying . . . The glance is of the non-verbal order of *contact* perhaps, but in fact a more *striking* contact, since it traverses more easily, and goes further beneath things. The clinical eye discovers a kinship with a new sense that prescribes its norm and epistemological structure; this is no longer the early straining to catch a language, but the index finger palpatating the depths. Hence, that metaphor of touch by which doctors will ceaselessly define their glance." Michel Foucault, *The Birth of the Clinic: An Archeology of Medical Perception,* trans. A. M. Sheridan Smith (New York: Pantheon Books, 1973), p. 122. For further discussion of the visible and the tangible, see Gilles Deleuze, *Foucault,* trans. and ed. Sean Hand (Minneapolis: University of Minnesota Press, 1988), p. 59.

8. Naomi Schor, *Reading in Detail: Aesthetics and the Feminine* (New York and London: Methuen, 1987), p. 16.

9. Ewa Kuryluk, *Salome and Judas in the Cave of Sex: The Grotesque— Origins, Iconography, Techniques* (Evanston, Illinois: Northwestern University Press, 1987), p. 28.

10. Julia Kristeva, *The Powers of Horror: an Essay on Abjection,* trans. Leon S. Roudiez (New York: Columbia University Press, 1982), p. 155.

11. Thomas Laqueur, "Orgasm, Generation, and the Politics of Reproductive Biology," in *The Making of the Modern Body: Sexuality and Society in the Nineteeth Century,* ed. Catherine Gallagher and Thomas

Laqueur (Berkeley and Los Angeles: University of California Press: 1987.), p. 2.

12. Mary Shelley, introduction to the third edition of *Frankenstein, or the Modern Prometheus,* ed. James Rieger (Indianapolis and New York: Bobbs-Merrill, 1974), p. 229. *Frankenstein* depends, of course, on eighteenth century scientific discourses of galvanization. Unlike most of Cronenberg's other films, the treatment of biographical material on the brothers is, however, finally humanistic and tragic.

13. Critics of the film have noted the relationship between the aquatic color schemes of the apartment and clinic and the early conversation of the boy twins concerning procreation underwater. See, for instance, Francois Ramasse, "La chair dans l'ame (Faux Semblants)," *Positif* 337 (Spring 1989), p. 32. The fishbowl atmosphere is, of course, another turn on the theme of the inside out, a staple of Cronenberg's films.

14. Frank Burke, "How'd You Like to Disappear?: Theorizing the Subject in Film," *Canadian Journal of Political and Social Theory/ Revue canadienne de theorie politique et social* vol. 13, no. 1–2 (1989), p. 32.

15. See Marcie France, "The Camera and the Speculum: David Cronenberg's *Dead Ringers,*" PMLA (May 1991), pp. 459–470.

16. I am indebted to Michael Silverman for this reading of the surgery scene as a reconfiguration of the twin as mutant woman. On male hysteria in this film, see also Barbara Creed, "Phallic Panic: Male Hysteria and *Dead Ringers,*" *Screen* vol. 31, no. 2 (Summer 1990), pp. 125–146.

17. Kaja Silverman, *Male Subjectivity at the Margins* (New York and London: Routledge, 1992), pp. 142–143. In arguing that feminist film theory has not gone far enough in emphasizing that "the gaze" cannot, strictly speaking, be owned or controlled by anyone (male or female) to the extent that they themselves would escape specularity, Silverman offers Fassbinder's cinema as a countermodel exposing the vulnerability of male subjectivity in relation to the gaze. As she observes, "changing the images or screens through which we see the male subject . . . is waged very much at the level of corporeal representation, suggesting that although the phallus is not the penis, it nonetheless derives its material support from that organ." In defiance of the criticism of Fredric Jameson and many others reproaching feminists for having (naively) tended to confuse the penis with the phallus, Silverman has carefully reread Lacan who himself on occasion defined the phallus as "the image of the penis." Also, for an excellent discussion of the

"tabooed referentiality" of the body in Lacanian theory, see Andrew Parker's provocative "Mom," in *The Oxford Literary Review*, vol. 8, no. 1–2 (1986), pp. 96–104.

18. See Mary Douglas, *Purity and Danger* (London, Boston, and Henley: Routledge and Kegan Paul, 1969). Also, Julia Kristeva, *Powers of Horror*, pp. 65–67, and on the corpse or bodily remainder as impure, pp. 108–111.

19. The Christian motifs of this sequence include not only the final shot of the brothers configured as a Pietà, but a shot of Elliot layed out like the deposition from the Cross.

20. Still the standard reference on this issue, see Barbara Ehrenreich and Deirdre English's *For Her Own Good: 150 Years of the Experts' Advice to Women* (Garden City and New York: Anchor Books, 1979). See also Ann Oakley, *The Captured Womb: A History of the Medical Care of Pregnant Women* (London and New York: Basil Blackwell, 1984). On the new reproductive technologies, see Gena Corea, et al., *Man-Made Women* (Bloomington: Indiana University Press, 1987) and *The Mother Machine: Reproductive Technologies from Artificial Insemination to Artificial Wombs* (New York, Harper and Row, 1986).

21. According to the *New York Times* (Sunday, December 11, 1988), Dr. Burt practiced his "crude experimentation" for over 22 years. Although the Ohio State Medical Board formally charged him with "gross immorality" and "grossly unprofessional conduct" in performing his reconstructive surgery, it was more than 12 years after his book *Surgery of Love* had been published, detailing the procedures he had used on hundreds of women. The failure of his many colleagues to question his procedures, which were quite recognizable in their effects, was described by a spokesman for the medical board as "a breakdown in the reporting system." Why most of the women who suffered from the complications of the surgery did not protest is dramatized in the film in the conversation between the doctors and their patients, in particular on the topic of "trust." The women who have sued Dr. Burt report being told that their Fallopian tubes were "rotting" and one woman describes herself after surgery as a "freak."

22. The cosmetic surgeries counterproduced by the performance artist Orlan reverse these relations. For a fictional inversion, see Angela Carter *The Passion of the New Eve* (London: Virago Press, 1982). The novel features a female grotesque called "Mother," with four breasts, who is an extremely gifted plastic surgeon, specializing in sex-change operations. She turns Evelyn into the new Eve.

23. See Emily Martin, *The Woman In the Body: A Cultural Analysis of Reproduction* (Boston: Beacon Press, 1987), p. 58. A major theme of Martin's book is how metaphors of production and failed production structure medical discourse around the female body as factory, worker, etc., and how such views of women's bodies also imply a managerial separation of laborer and labor, laborer and product, and, of course, laborer and doctor/manager.

24. Jean Baudrillard, *Simulations* (New York: Semiotext(e), 1983), p. 37.

25. Baudrillard, p. 12. I find this rhetorical nostalgia typical of Baudrillard's work where, despite claims to the contrary, there is, in his words, a "resurrection of the figurative where the object and substance have disappeared." The theatricality and a "resurrection of the figurative where the object and substance have disappeared" are reenacted even as they are denied.

26. For a consideration of Cronenberg in relation to national (Canadian) identity, see A. Parker (see n. 3 above).

27. *The Canadian Journal of Political and Social Theory/Revue canadienne de theorie politique et social,* volume 13, no. 1–2 (1989).

28. For a male "outsider's" reworking of the gynecological scene and sexual reconfiguration, see Charles Ludlum's "Bluebeard," in *The Complete Plays* (New York: Harper and Row Publishers, 1989), p. 115–143.

29. My point is not that every all-male pietà is ideologically closed or repressive, but that this classical, humanistic *tableau* sublates the grotesque, the visceral, and the female. In contrast, see the collection of gay male pietàs in Juan Davila and Paul Foss, *The Mutilated Pieta* (Surrey Hills, NSW: Artspace, 1985) (I wish to thank Sean Holland and Robert Schwartzwald for this reference); see also, Leo Steinberg, *The Sexuality of Christ in Renaissance Art and in Modern Oblivion* (New York: Pantheon, 1983).

30. For instance, her scene in the dressing room as she ironically describes the painted bruise on her face as "what glamor looks like."

31. As many critics of the film have noted, Claire is written out of the psychic struggle of the twins except as the necessary mediating third term in their relationship; still, Cronenberg gives space to her professional life and to her relationships with her agent, manager, and costumer. In the terms of the film, however, this arena of partial self-determination only makes the contrast with her gynecologicial identity more tragic.

32. Webster v. Missouri. In the same spirit, a placard at the July 4, 1989 rally in Boston, protesting the decision, read: "I love America, but keep your laws off my uterus."

33. See Donna Haraway, "The Biopolitics of Postmodern Bodies: Deter-minations of Self in Immune System Discourse," *differences*, vol 1, no. 1 (Winter, 1989), pp. 3–45.

34. Rosi Braidotti, "Organs without Bodies," *differences*, vol. 1, no. 1 (Winter, 1989), p. 157.

Notes to Chapter Five

1. George Du Maurier, *Trilby*, (New York: Harper and Brothers Publishers, 1894), p. 1. Hereafter, referred to in the text as *TR*.

2. Other furnishings in the room include kitchen utensils, oil paintings of nudes, copies of Renaissance paintings, and a "model throne."

3. See Pierre Bourdieu, *Distinction: A Social Critique of the Judgement of Taste*, trans. Richard Nice (Cambridge, Massachusetts: Harvard University Press, 1984).

4. See, for instance, Jerrold Siegel, *Bohemian Paris: Culture, Politics, and the Boundaries of Bourgeois Life, 1830–1930* (New York: Viking, 1986).

5. See Marilyn Brown, *Gypsies and Other Bohemians: The Myth of the Artist in Nineteenth-Century France* (Ann Arbor: University of Michigan Research Press, 1985), p. 3.

6. Karl Marx, *The Eighteenth Brumaire of Louis Bonaparte* (New York: International Publishers, 1963), p. 75.

7. See Peter Stallybrass, "Marx and Heterogeneity: Thinking the Lumpen-proletariat," *Representations* 31 (Summer 1990), pp. 69–95.

8. Siegel, pp. 45–53.

9. For an account of cultural production as resistance in this period, see Richard Terdiman, *Discourse/Counter-Discourse: The Theory and Practice of Symbolic Resistance in Nineteenth-Century France* (Ithaca: Cornell University Press, 1985).

10. Michael Wilson, "'Sans les femmes, qu'est-ce qui nous resterait': Gender and Transgression in Bohemian Montmartre," in *Body Guards*, ed. Julia Epstein and Kristina Straub (New York: Routledge, 1991), p. 195. See also his *The Commerce of Bohemia: Marginality, Masculinity, and Mass Culture in Fin-de-siècle Paris* (forthcoming).

11. The lives of the *grisettes* (named probably after the grey clothing typically worn) were difficult and far from the romantic characterization of Mimi in *Bohème*, although as Jerrold Siegel points out, "from a middle-

class perspective" their lives "often seemed attractive, independent, and free from constraint" (Siegel, 40).

12. For an excellent discussion of gender and Bohemia, see Michael Wilson, n. 10 above.

13. Both Siegel and Wilson emphasize the ideological nature of this perceived freedom.

14. In Trilby, the narrator emphasizes the nostalgia of his description of the room, recalling that Du Maurier himself had studied art in Paris. On the other hand, Du Maurier also acknowledged the influence of Murger. Perhaps, as one commentator writes, ". . . here is a case of life imitating art and then art imitating an amalgam of the two." See Richard Kelly, *George Du Maurier* (Boston: Twayne Publishers, 1983), p. 89. On Du Maurier's career and *Trilby*, see John Masefield and Daphne Du Maurier, "Introduction to Peter Ibbetson and Trilby," in *Novels of George Du Maurier* (London: The Pilot Press, 1947), pp. i–xii.

15. Carter's novel also features a female performer who was once a model, although she operates in a different, but carnivalesque subculture and with real independence.

16. See the *Trilbyana Collection*, Houghton Library, Harvard University.

17. The important exception is the short episode when Trilby is between men. After jilting Little Billee, she makes her way back to Paris, hair shorn and dressed as a working-class boy. Despite the fact that she begins her long march to escape Svengali, who is supposedly coming after her, she ends up at his door (*TR*, 389–390).

18. Of course, it is the very thought of their bodies together that makes the book, in part, a horror tale. For a discussion of various perspectives on the figure of Svengali, see Kelly pp. 117–118. He notes that the illustration of Svengali resembles the drawing by Cruikshank of Fagin from *Oliver Twist*.

19. Benedict Anderson, *Imagined Communities: Reflections on the Origin and Spread of Nationalism* (London: Verso, 1983), p. 16. See also, the introduction to *Nationalism and Sexualities*, ed. Andrew Parker, Mary Russo, Doris Sommer, and Patricia Yaeger (Routledge: New York and London, 1992), pp. 1–18.

20. Eve Kosofsky Sedgwick, *Between Men: English Literature and Male Homosocial Desire* (New York: Columbia University Press, 1985).

21. As Siegel emphasizes in his history of Bohemian Paris, the question of boundaries and nationhood, even if figurative, was important from

Murger's time. The irony is that Svengali and the gypsy musicians are not afforded citizenship in the Bohemia of the Englishmen.

22. On ways of "having" gender and nationality, see Eve Kosofsky Sedgwick, "The Age of Wilde" in *Nationalisms and Sexualities* (see n. 19 above), pp. 239–240.

23. Quoted in *Trilbyana: The Rise and Progress of a Popular Novel* (New York: The Critic, 1895) p. 21. *The Critic* (New York: Good Literature Publishing Co.) was published monthly between 1884 and 1906.

24. "I'm posing for Durien the sculptor, on the next floor. I pose to him for the altogether." "The altogether?," asked Little Billee. "Yes, *l'ensemble*, you know—head, hands, and feet—everything—especially feet" (*TR*, 18).

25. Nina Auerbach, *Woman and the Demon: The Life of a Victorian Myth* (Cambridge, Massachusetts and London: Harvard University Press, 1982), p. 17.

26. Only Trilby's face is completely visible for scrutiny at this point. It is described as "too" everything: "the eyes were too wide apart, the mouth too large, the chin too massive, the complexion a mass of freckles" (*TR*, 15). The observation that "you can never tell how beautiful (or how ugly) a face may be till you have tried to draw it" (*TR*, 15) not only alludes to the old Vetruvian models of symmetry, but also to the Romantic ideal of the artist as *revealing* Beauty hidden in the particulars. Trilby reveals her foot, out from underneath the pair of huge male slippers, but only Little Billee can create her foot in his perfect drawing.

27. Sigmund Freud, "Fetishism" in *The Standard Edition*, vol. 21 (London: Hogarth Press, 1961), p. 157.

28. Kaja Silverman, *The Acoustic Mirror: The Female Voice in Psychoanalysis and Cinema* (Bloomington: Indiana University Press, 1988), p. 22.

29. Georges Bataille, "The Big Toe" in *Visions of Excess: Selected Writings 1927–1939*, trans. and ed. Allan Stoekl (Minneapolis: University of Minnesota Press, 1985), pp. 20–21.

30. On Little Billee, see Eve Kosofsky Sedgwick, *Epistemology of the Closet* (Berkeley and Los Angeles: University of California Press, 1990), pp. 193–195.

31. For a discussion of the types of performance and performances in this period, see Francois Caradec and Alain Weill, *Le café-concert* (Paris: Hachette/Massin, 1980).

32. Peter Stallybrass and Allon White make a similar point in more general terms: "The bourgeois subject continuously defined and redefined itself through the exclusion of what it marked out as "low"—as dirty, repulsive, noisy, contaminating. Yet the very act of exclusion was constitutive of its identity. The low was internalized under the sign of negation and disgust . . . These low domains apparently expelled as 'Other,' return as the object of nostalgia, longing, and fascination." *The Politics and Poetics of Transgression* (Ithaca: Cornell University Press, 1986), p. 191.

33. For an example of this mix of the sporting and the cultural see *TR*, pp. 46–47.

34. Thanks to Mary Anne Ferguson for identifying and tracking down these objects in the New York Public Library.

35. Francis Haskell and Nicholas Penny, *Taste and the Antique: The Lure of Classical Sculpture 1500–1900* (New Haven and London: Yale University Press, 1981), p. 121.

36. See Susan Stewart, *On Longing: Narratives of the Miniature, The Gigantic, the Souvenir, the Collection* (Baltimore and London: The Johns Hopkins University Press, 1984). See also Jean Baudrillard, *For a Critique of the Political Economy of the Sign* (St. Louis: Telos Press, 1981).

37. See Eve Kosofsky Sedgwick, *The Epistemology of the Closet* (see n. 30 above).

38. Letter to *The Critic*, 1896, in the *Trilbyana Collection*, Houghton Library, Harvard University.

39. See for instance, Freud's account of "Irma's Injection" in *The Interpretation of Dreams*, ed. James Strachey (New York: Avon Books, 1965). Nina Auerbach has also noted the relationship between Trilby and Freud's Dora, in *Woman and the Demon: The Life of a Victorian Myth* (Cambridge, Massachusetts: Harvard University Press, 1982), pp. 16–17.

40. Svengali dies with this hideous expression on his face as he watches Trilby on stage.

41. Although Trilby is a very public spectacle, her appeal to the English and French audiences is based on her ability to turn every musical event into private sentiment or nostalgia: "So that the tears that are shed out of all these many French eyes are tears of pure, unmixed delight in happy reminiscence! (Chopin, it is true, may have meant something quite different—a hot-house, perhaps, with orchids and arum lilies and tuberoses and hydrangeas—that is neither here nor there)" (*TR*, 331–332).

42. See, for instance, the episode in Madame de Stael's novel *Corinne ou l'Italie,* where Corinne contemplates the statue of Niobe and concludes that she is not capable of such sublime restraint.

43. See Gilles Deleuze and Felix Guattari, *Kafka: Toward a Minor Literature,* trans. Dana Polan (Minneapolis: University of Minnesota Press, 1986).

44. Their debut is compared to opening night at the Cirque des Bashi-baboucks (*TR,* 332).

45. The limits of the Svengalis as a musical couple are clear along the lines of class, but those marks of gender, ethnicity, and class which mark and limit their music also enable their success and absorption into bourgeois national culture, at least as a novelty act.

46. The same can be said of his gender positioning; clearly and tyrannically domineering as the Man who controls Trilby, he nonetheless serves to keep out and abuse Gecko, the gypsy.

47. Bram Dijkstra, *Idols of Perversity: Fantasies of Feminine Evil in Fin-de-Siècle Culture* (New York and Oxford: Oxford University Press, 1986), pp. 34–35.

48. E. T. A. Hoffman, *The Tales of Hoffman,* trans. Michael Bullock (New York: Ungar Publishing, 1963), p. 29.

49. This performance is, of course, not hers alone, for her body has transgressed its boundaries.

50. Susan Stewart, *On Longing: Narratives of the Miniature, the Gigantic, the Souvenir, the Collection* (Durham and London: Duke University Press, 1993), p. 105.

51. James D. Hart quoted in Dijkstra, p. 35.

Notes to Chapter Six

1. Angela Carter, *Nights at the Circus* (London: Chatto and Windus, The Hogarth Press, 1984). All subsequent references are to this edition as *NC.*

2. I am indebted to three extraordinary students who worked with me on senior theses which focused on the work of Angela Carter: Linda McDaniel and Jennifer Hendricks of Hampshire College, and Meg O'Rourke of Mt. Holyoke.

3. The topography of the Madame Schreck episode owes much to Edgar A. Poe, but there are historical precedents for the anatomical museum.

See, for instance, Christiane Py and Cecile Vedart, "Les Musées d'anatomie sur les champs de foire" *Actes de la recherche en sciences sociales*, no. 60 (November 1985), p. 3–10.

4. Guy Debord, *Society of the Spectacle* (Detroit: Black and Red, 1983), p. 1.

5. Fevvers construes her own primal scene from a possibly fake and certainly filthy ("as though through a glass darkly") painting of the Leda and the Swan by Titian (*NC*, 30).

6. For an extremely important discussion of feminist writing in relation to the historical avant-garde in general and Dada/Surrealist parody in particular, see Susan Rubin Suleiman, *Subversive Intent: Gender, Politics, and the Avant-Garde* (Cambridge, Massachusetts and London: Harvard University Press, 1990).

7. Linda Hutcheon, *The Politics of Postmodernism* (London and New York: Routledge, 1983).

8. For a discussion of intertextuality and politics in her work, see Angela Carter, "Notes From the Front Line," in Michelene Wandor, ed., *On Gender and Writing* (London: Pandora, 1983), p. 71.

9. In her interview with Helen Cagney Watts, Carter herself says that Sade was a primary influence. Helen Cagney Watts, "Angela Carter: An Interview with Helen Cagney Watts," in *Bête Noire* (August 1987), p. 162. In relation to Sade, see also David Punter, "Angela Carter: Supercessions of the Masculine," in his *The Romantic Unconscious: A Study of Narcissism and Patriarchy* (New York: New York University Press, 1990), pp. 28–42.

10. Carter writes about Mae West, in *Nothing Sacred* (London: Virago, 1982). This impersonation of the impersonator is Fevvers' (and Carter's) stock-in-trade.

11. The "double bluff" was not only sexual (a woman playing a man playing a woman playing a man), but also existential: she plays on the "freedom" given to older women. As Carter points out, Mae West started her Hollywood career in middle age. Her self-display played on the masquerade of youthfulness, the freedom of the discard who has nothing left to lose, and the impersonation of male power. "She made of her own predatoriness a joke that concealed its power, whilst simultaneously exploiting it. Yet she represented a sardonic disregard of convention rather than a heroic overthrow of taboo." (*The Sadeian Woman and the Ideology of Pornography* [New York: Pantheon Books, 1978], p. 62).

12. Angela Carter, "The Flesh and the Mirror," in *Fireworks: Nine Profane Pieces* (London and New York: Penguin Books, 1987), p. 67.

13. See, for instance, Roland Barthes, *Empire of Signs,* trans. Richard Howard (New York: Hill and Wang, 1982).

14. This question is posed first to Walser by an Indian fakir. Walser sees his journalistic quest as a compilation of "Great Humbugs of the World" (*NC,* 11).

15. As a male and heterosexual witness to Fevvers' naked artificiality, it is Walser's impossible task to "cover Fevvers' story" which means to expose her fiction.

16. Walter Benjamin, "Thesis on the Philosophy of History," in *Illuminations,* trans. Harry Zohn (New York: Schocken Books, 1969), p. 257.

17. See "Angela Carter, an Interview with Helen Cagney Watts," in *Bête Noire* (August 1987), pp. 161–175.

18. Angela Carter, *The Sadeian Woman,* p. 79.

19. See, for instance, Andrea Dworkin, *Pornography: Men Possessing Women* (New York: Perigree Books, 1979.), pp. 84–85. The phrase "praxis of femininity" is Carter's (*The Sadeian Woman,* p. 78).

20. For an excellent discussion of Justine and Juliette in relation to criticism of Carter, see Elaine Jordan, "The Dangers of Angela Carter" in *New Feminist Discourses: Critical Essays on Theories and Texts* (London and New York: Routledge, 1991), pp. 119–131. I am in agreement with Jordan's "defense" of Carter (not, as she says, that Carter needs defending). For another view of Carter on Sade, see Susanne Kappeler, *The Pornography of Representation* (London: Polity Press, 1986), pp. 133–137. See also Andrea Dworkin cited in previous note. For a critical overview of the pornography debates within feminism, see B. Ruby Rich "Feminism and Sexuality in the 1980s" in *Feminist Studies,* vol. 12 (1986).

21. Carter, *The Sadeian Woman,* p. 79. For another influential and provocative account of the interests and pitfalls of Sade for contemporary feminists, see Jane Gallop, *Thinking Through the Body* (New York: Columbia University Press, 1988); see also, her *Intersections: A Reading of Sade with Bataille, Blanchot, and Klossowski* (Lincoln: University of Nebraska Press, 1981).

22. In relation to Juliet's character, Carter is quite unambiguous: "A free woman in an unfree society is a monster," (*The Sadeian Woman,* p. 27; also, quoted in Jordan, p. 121). Jordan makes the excellent point that

both figures of antithetical feminity point towards something else in Carter and are meant to show up the limitations of these types as models of resistance.

23. For a very different use of the iconography of the emaciated female body, see for instance the puppetry of Lotte Prinzel, or in the context of feminist art, see Valie Export's performance work described in "Persona, Proto-Performance, Politics," *Discourse* 14/2 (Spring 1992), pp. 26–35.

24. Craig Owens, "Posing," in *Difference: On Representation and Sexuality Catalog* (New York: New Museum of Contemporary Art, 1985), pp. 7–17.

25. Owens identifies the pose as both an "imposition" and an "imposture." Since, in his view, sexuality is imposed (culturally) we might characterize Fevver's installation of femininity as a reimposition.

26. Owens also mentions the work of Dick Hebdige on the self-display of punk subculture. Of course, the social and the psychosexual merge in many examples of posing in contemporary cultural production. Jennie Livingston's very successful documentary film on camp balls and "vogueing," *Paris is Burning,* has racial, class, and sexual dimensions. Like Fevvers and the other women exhibits and performers in *Nights at the Circus,* the young performers in her film band together in "houses" which take the names of commercial fashion houses.

27. Ma Nelson has a further distinction. She cross-dresses as Admiral Nelson, commanding the whorehouse like a tight ship: "It was a pirate ship, and went under false colours . . . It was from the, as it were, topsail or crow's nest that my girl made her first ascent" (*NC,* 32). The Winged Victory of this barge, of course, is a ship's figurehead.

28. See Mary Ann Doane, *Femmes Fatales: Feminism, Film Theory, Psychoanalysis* (New York and London: Routledge, 1991), especially pp. 17–43. Doane's influential 1982 essay, "Film and Masquerade: Theorizing the Female Spectator" is reprinted in this collection along with the recent, "Masquerade Reconsidered." The first essay represents an attempt to dislodge the psychoanalytic discussion of masquerade as the norm of femininity and to see it, rather, as a defamiliarization and a "way out." Her second essay emphasizes the theoretical constraints and the socio-political implications of the concept of sexuality as masquerade in Riviere and Lacan. In relation to feminist theory and theories of the feminine, see especially her reply to Tania Modleski (pp. 40–43). Modleski's critique of Doane is contained in *The Women Who Knew Too Much: Hitchcock and Feminist Theory* (New York: Methuen, 1988), pp. 25–28.

29. Munby indicated in his diary that he intended to write a paper on female gymnasts. His interest in their sexuality is evident in most entries. For instance: "The only clothing she had on was a blue satin doublet fitting close to her body and having very scanty trunk hose below it; her legs, cased in fleshings, were as good as bare, up to the hip: the only sign of a woman about her was that she had a rose in her bosom, and another in her short curly hair . . ." (Entry dated 7 September, 1868) quoted in Michael Hiley, *Victorian Working Women: Portraits from Life* (Boston: David R. Godine, 1980), p. 116. See also, D. Hudson, *Munby: Man of Two Worlds: The Life and Diaries of Arthur J. Munby* (London: John Murray, 1972).

30. Stallybrass and White point out that the contradiction between the high social standing of the upper-class male and the low class standing of the maid is complicated by the physical comparisons of his weakness and her strength, and his childishness in relation to her role as nurse. Of course, a point to be made here is that Munby is controlling both the sight-lines and the social configuration.

    The Politics and Poetics of Transgression, (Ithaca: Cornell University Press, 1986), pp. 155–156. See also, L. Davidoff, "Class and Gender in Victorian England: The Diaries of Arthur J. Munby and Hannah Cullwick," *Feminist Studies,* vol. 5, no. 1, pp. 89–141.

31. Djuna Barnes, *Nightwood,* with an introduction by T. S. Eliot (New York: New Directions, 1961).

32. For an important, recent consideration of fetishism and the depth model of the female body in relation to curiosity, see Laura Mulvey, "Pandora: Topographies of the Mask and Curiosity" in *Sexuality and Space,* ed. Beatriz Colomina (New York: Princeton Architectural Press, 1992), pp. 58–59.

33. Barnes, xvi. Although Eliot does not mention the lesbian texts and in his plea that the book not be read as a "psychopathic study," his insistence that the "miseries that people suffer through their particular abnormalities of temperament" be understood not on the surface but in light of "the deeper designs . . . of the human misery which is universal."

34. Allon White, "Hysteria and the End of Carnival: Festivity and Bourgeois Neurosis," in *The Violence of Representation: Literature and the History of Violence,* ed. Nancy Armstrong and Leonard Tennenhouse (New York: Routledge, 1989), pp. 156–170.

35. She fears that her first flight will be her last and that she will pay for her hubris with her very life (*NC,* 36).

36. Fevvers herself interrupts the sublime narrative of night flight with the ongoing account of her working life (*NC*, 37).

37. See Kaja Silverman, *The Acoustic Mirror: The Female Voice in Psycho-analysis and Cinema* (Bloomington: Indiana University Press, 1988).

38. For a study of noise and cultural production in relation to carnival and twentieth century music, see Mary Russo and Daniel Warner, "Rough Music," *Discourse* 10.1 (Fall–Winter 1987–88), pp. 55–76. See also Jacques Attali, *Noise: The Political Economy of Music* (Minneapolis: University of Minnesota Press, 1985).

39. Roland Barthes, *Image-Music-Text,* trans. Stephen Heath (New York: Hill and Wang, 1977), p. 189.

40. The figure of the fishwife suggests the marketplace speech of carnival, the revolutionary power of the women of the French revolution, and the "fishwives" of Marx's *Eighteenth Brumaire.* Carter also elicits the olfactory image of fishy women in descriptions of Fevvers "perfume" in the first chapter.

41. For an account of the female circus performer as Victorian working girl, see Michael Hiley, *Victorian Working Women: Portraits From Life* (Boston: David Godine, 1980). The figure of the female acrobat raises the predictable questions of gender and propriety: "Ought we forbid her to do these things? . . . And, though it is not well to see a nude man fling a nude girl about as she is flung, or to see her grip his body in mid-air between her seemingly bare thighs. I think that an unreflecting audience takes no note . . . and looks upon these things and looks at him and her only as two performers. Still, the familiar interlacing of male and female bodies in sight of the public, is gross and corrupting, though its purpose be mere athletics" (p. 119).

42. Guy Debord, *Society of the Spectacle* (Detroit: Black and Red, 1983), p. 27.

43. Paulina Palmer's "From 'Coded Mannequin' to Bird Woman: Angela Carter's Magic Flight," in *Women Reading Women's Writing* (New York: St. Martin's Press, 1987), argues that the tension which exists between an impulse to analyze and demythologize gender and the impulse towards utopian celebrations of woman-centered culture is reflected in two "stages" of Carter's work. From Palmer's perspective, the image of the puppet or "coded Mannequin" is "replaced by the image of Fevvers' miraculous wings which she observes make her body 'the abode of limitless freedom' and the egg from which she claims to have been hatched." Hoffmann, Freud, and the uncanny are associated with texts

published prior to 1978, those "marred by an element of distortion," and those later texts, including *The Bloody Chamber* and especially *Nights at the Circus*, are associated with "the expression of emotions which have a liberating effect." As an opening illustration of this dichotomy, she cites a passage (which I would agree is crucial) from the conclusion of the novel, in which Fevvers, for the last time, gives an "enthusiastic if cliché-ridden speech heralding the new age of women's liberation" (Palmer, 179).

44. The claim that "an emergence of a female counter-culture is celebrated" in the novel (Palmer, 180) is, in my view, true only as a prefigurative *possibility.* And many female types and institutional contexts are represented in the novel, implicating any definition of female counterculture in the histories and metahistories of violence and oppression by and of women. Fevvers herself eats caviar in a grand hotel, at the expense of the peasant woman, Baboushka. Countess P., Olga Alexandrovna, and Madame Schreck all partake in criminality and destruction.

45. The prospects for life with Walser, the New Man, have seemed dim for most of my students. Although I have suggested alternative readings, on the numerous occasions when we have discussed his transformations as successively a brash American journalist, a fellow traveller with the clowns, a surrealistic anthropologist who "goes native," and a new age man, students tend to see him in all these roles as a "jerk"—something closer to the bad alternatives in Tania Modleski's *Feminism Without Women* than to the nondominant types in Kaja Silverman's *Male Subjectivity at the Margins.*

46. Lizzie's greatest fear is that Fevvers will become the "tableau" of "a woman in bondage to her reproductive system, a woman tied hand and foot to that Nature which your physiology denies" (*NC*, 283). Carter never accedes to a definition of even motherhood as the "natural"; throughout the novel mothers are secondhand representations within fictions, images, and tableaux.

47. Susan Rubin Suleiman, *Subversive Intent: Gender, Politics, and the Avant-Garde* (Cambridge: Harvard University Press, 1990), p. 137.

48. Beryl Markham, *West with the Night* (Boston: Houghton Mifflin, 1942), p. 17.

Index